M000237760

Space Exploration on Film

Space Exploration on Film

PAUL MEEHAN

McFarland & Company, Inc., Publishers

Jefferson, North Carolina

ISBN (print) 978-1-4766-8133-7
ISBN (ebook) 978-1-4766-4437-0

Library of Congress and British Library
Cataloguing data are available

Library of Congress Control Number 2022015310

Front cover: Keir Dullea in *2001: A Space Odyssey*, 1968, directed by
Stanley Kubrick (MGM/Photofest © MGM Photographer: Kevin Bray)

Printed in the United States of America

*McFarland & Company, Inc., Publishers
Box 611, Jefferson, North Carolina 28640
www.mcfarlandpub.com*

Table of Contents

Preface

It is not hyperbole to state that humanity stands on the threshold of a new space age. As of this writing in 2022, a revitalized American space program has enabled astronauts to routinely travel to the International Space Station; the Chinese Yutu-2 rover is exploring the far side of the Moon; and NASA's Osiris-Rex spacecraft has landed on the asteroid 101955 Bennu, located more than 200 million miles from Earth, and gathered samples for its return voyage. The SpaceX consortium is testing its super-heavy Starship reusable launch vehicle that is capable of carrying a 100-ton payload into orbit to transport crew and cargo to the Moon and Mars and into deep space. NASA is planning to return astronauts to the Moon using the newly minted Orion spacecraft in a mission dubbed Project Artemis, and the building of cities on Mars is even being proposed.

Long before humans flew in space, films depicting space flight beguiled audiences. The big screen's first serious interplanetary voyage was launched more than 100 years ago, and over the years, as space flight became a reality, the cinema reflected the shifting paradigms of our understanding of the universe. Early flights of fancy gave way to more scientifically accurate depictions of space exploration that would provide inspiration for those who dreamed of voyages beyond the Earth. The German rocket scientists who built the massive vehicles that launched the Apollo missions cited the silent science fiction classic *Woman in the Moon* as inspiration, while Americans currently working on the U.S. space program were inspired by films such as *2001: A Space Odyssey* and *The Right Stuff.*

In the 21st century, advances in visual effects technology have enabled filmmakers to render vistas of outer space with a new level of verisimilitude. Films such as *Gravity* (2013), *Interstellar* (2014), *The Martian* (2015), *First Man* (2018) and *Ad Astra* (2019) brought the outer space environment onto the silver screen in 3-D and/or IMAX. These films present (more or less) realistic depictions of space travel that embrace hard science instead of the more fantastic notions of flights to other worlds that appear in popular science fiction franchises such as the *Alien, Star Wars* and *Guardians of the Galaxy* action-adventure movies.

The general public possesses a rudimentary knowledge of the scientific concepts involved in astronomy, rocket science and celestial mechanics. Looking up into the night sky, the casual observer regards the Moon, the planets and the stars without a clear realization of the relative distances of these celestial objects from the Earth; that the Moon is close by, the planets much farther away and the stars are so distant that traveling there may be impossible. Hollywood filmmakers tend to ignore these astronomical relationships while depicting nearly instantaneous transits of spaceships over vast distances.

This book, on the other hand, categorizes and analyzes movies about space flight that emphasize science over science fiction. These include, most prominently, fact-based re-enactments of actual American and Russian space missions such as *Apollo 13, First Man, Gagarin: First in Space, The Spacewalker* and *Salyut 7*. It also includes historical accounts of the development of space technology in *I Aim at the Stars, The Right Stuff, October Sky* and *Hidden Figures*, as well as speculative dramatizations made during the formative years of the space age: *Destination Moon, Conquest of Space, Road to the Stars, Countdown* and *Marooned*.

Of course, there's plenty of room for speculative science fiction about the future of space exploration involving voyages to Mars in films like *Robinson Crusoe on Mars, Red Planet* and *The Martian*, trips to the outer planets of the solar system in *2010, Europa Report* and *Ad Astra*, and even journeys to the stars in *Ikarie XB-1, The Andromeda Nebula, Contact* and *Interstellar*. While current technology has not yet reached a level of complexity that would enable such voyages, these films may point the way to humankind's future in space, as all of them are grounded in some level of scientific factuality.

In Homer's *Odyssey*, composed in ancient Greek times, the eponymous hero undertakes a perilous journey over uncharted waters, where he undergoes many trials and visits unknown lands. The almost incomprehensible vastness of outer space, however, makes Homer's wine-dark seas seem like a mere puddle. Yet, as in the *Odyssey*, these similarly uncharted realms are fraught with myriad dangers. Here be monsters and perils uncountable: extraterrestrials, meteors, strange energies, deadly microbes and the unforgiving environment of the cold, airless void itself that imperils humans and machines alike. These space odysseys have been undertaken by some of the cinema's most acclaimed filmmakers, a list that includes Fritz Lang, George Pal, Andrei Tarkovsky, Stanley Kubrick, Robert Wise, Ron Howard, Philip Kaufman, Robert Zemeckis, Ridley Scott and Christopher Nolan. As humankind forges ahead to explore these mysterious realms, we may gain inspiration from the cinema visionaries who went there first and showed us the way.

Introduction:
Space Travel in Science Fiction
and Science Fact

Since time immemorial, humankind has lifted its eyes to the heavens and wondered what mysteries are within the orbits of the Moon, the planets and the stars. Myths, legends and literature imbued these realms with fantasy and magic. It seemed likely that our sister worlds were inhabited by beings like ourselves, existing in exotic landscapes that we would like to visit. In the second century, the Syrian writer Lucian of Samosata penned a story about people who ascend to the Moon by means of a waterspout. The story *Orlando Furioso*, written in 1516, featured a trip to the Moon in a flaming chariot, while in Englishman Francis Godwin's 1638 work *The Man in the Moone,* an explorer is pulled there by magical birds. The 17th-century French writer Cyrano de Bergerac devised a number of fanciful methods of ascending to the lunar surface in his 1649 book *The Voyage to the Moon*, in which the protagonist finally reaches his objective in a craft powered by firecrackers.

Notions of space exploration really took off during the 19th century with the advent of science fiction literature. The seminal SF author Jules Verne posited a lunar journey in his 1861 novel *From the Earth to the Moon* and its 1870 sequel *Around the Moon*, in which the protagonists are launched to the Moon by a gigantic space gun. In H.G. Wells' 1901 novel *The First Men in the Moon,* lunar explorers fly to our satellite by means of a fictional anti-gravity substance called Cavorite, and encounter a race of Moon-dwellers dubbed Selenites.

Besides the Moon, the planet Mars loomed large as a destination for space fantasists. In the early 19th century, British astronomer Sir William Herschel observed that Mars, like the Earth, had north and south polar caps that waxed and waned with the seasons. He posited the existence of water on the Red Planet, although today we know that its polar caps are composed largely of frozen carbon dioxide. Similarly, in 1877 the Italian astronomer Giovanni Schiaparelli, gazing at Mars through his telescope, saw what he believed to be a network of "canals" that conveyed water around the arid world. He was probably looking at the Mariner Valley, an enormous canyon that stretches for many miles across the Martian surface. At the turn of the century, Schiaparelli's ideas were amplified by the American astronomer Percival Lowell, who stated unequivocally that Mars "is inhabited by beings of some sort or other we may consider as certain as it is uncertain what these beings may be."[1]

In the popular imagination, Mars was thought to be a desert world that was home to a decadent, dying race. In Wells' 1898 alien invasion novel *The War of the Worlds*, a force of de-evolved Martians descends upon the Earth to slake their thirst for human blood. The notion of Mars as a desiccated planet inhabited by vanishing Martians persisted in science fiction literature from Edgar Rice Burroughs' *A Princess of Mars* (1917) to Ray Bradbury's *The Martian Chronicles* (1950) and beyond.

Other planetary bodies in our solar system were also pressed into service to provide grist for the SF writer's mill. Venus, a world which orbits closer to the Sun and is shrouded in a perpetual cloud cover, was thought to be a hothouse planet teeming with great jungles and exotic life forms. Other planets such as Mercury and Jupiter were also supposed to harbor alien life. It was not until the late 1960s, however, that planetary probes revealed that these worlds were inhospitable to the evolution of higher life forms.

In 1926, publisher Hugo Gernsback established the first science fiction magazine, *Amazing Stories.* It printed tales set in outer space and popularized the emerging literary genre. A bevy of sci-fi–oriented pulp magazines followed: *Astounding Science Fiction, Marvel Science Stories, Fantastic Adventures* and many other titles. While much of this pulp fiction featured bug-eyed alien monsters, damsels in distress and muscular, swashbuckling space cadets, other stories offered more realistic, science-based depictions of space exploration. A prime example: the works of sci-fi luminary Robert A. Heinlein, who wrote stories of off-world adventure such as *Rocket Ship Galileo* (1947), *Red Planet* (1948) and *Have Spacesuit, Will Travel* (1958).

The period following World War II witnessed an explosion of technology that would fundamentally transform society, including jet planes, computers, atomic weapons, television and rocketry. Also in the mix was the enigmatic phenomenon of flying saucers, or UFOs, mysterious aerial craft that suggested that beings from other worlds were visiting the Earth. These technological advances brought the notion of humans traveling into outer space into the realm of possibility.

During the early 1950s, the iconic spaceship was a sleek silver cylinder that tapered to a sharp point on top, resting on three prominent fins that served as both a takeoff platform and landing gear for the rocket as depicted in George Pal's seminal science film *Destination Moon* (1950). This contraption bore no resemblance to the utilitarian, multi-stage launchers soon deployed by the Soviet Union and America. The Space Age officially began in 1957 when the Soviets shocked the world by launching the first artificial satellite, dubbed Sputnik, into orbit. Sputnik sent shock waves through the American technological establishment as our own fledgling space program scrambled to catch up with the Russians. Four months later, America launched its own satellite, *Explorer I,* signaling the beginning of the "space race" between the U.S. and the U.S.S.R. for dominance of the new high frontier. This competition quickly became a deadly serious technological, political and military struggle between the forces of Soviet communism and American democracy.

Another shock came in 1961 when Russian cosmonaut Yuri Gagarin became the first human to orbit the Earth. His flight heralded a number of firsts in the space race by the Soviets, including the first extravehicular spacewalk, the first woman in space and the first three-man flight. In response, in 1961 President John F, Kennedy committed America to "putting a man on the Moon and returning him safely to Earth" before the end of the decade. As depicted in the 1983 movie *The Right Stuff*, the American Mercury Program launched astronaut Alan Shepard into space on a sub-orbital flight, and soon afterward, future Senator John Glenn became the first American to orbit the Earth.

As America flexed its newfound technological muscles, it began to catch up with the Soviets. The two-man Gemini program performed rendezvous and docking maneuvers in space that would be required for a Moon shot. Future Moonwalker Neil Armstrong performed the first docking in space during the flight of Gemini 8, as shown in the film *First Man* (2018). By the conclusion of the Gemini program, the U.S. had caught up with, and even surpassed the Soviets and was poised to launch the first lunar missions. For their part, the Russians had their own plans to land a cosmonaut on the Moon.

The Soviet program suffered a fatal setback with the premature death of their "chief designer" Sergei Korolev in 1968. Korolev's genius at rocketry was responsible for the launchers and spacecraft that had given the Russians their early lead in space, and are still in use today. Deprived of his enormous talents, the Soviet Moon program languished. Meanwhile, in America, the equally brilliant German émigré engineer Wernher von Braun headed up a team that built the massive Saturn V launch vehicle that would propel astronauts to the Moon during the Apollo program.

In December 1968, astronauts Jim Lovell, Frank Borman and William Anders circumnavigated the Moon on the Apollo 8 mission. This was followed by the ultimate triumph of Apollo 11, which landed Neal Armstrong and Buzz Aldrin on the Moon's surface on July 20, 1969; Michael Collins manned the Command Module in lunar orbit that returned the astronauts to Earth. NASA conducted five more Apollo lunar missions, which all went smoothly except for Apollo 13 in April 1970, during which Jim Lovell, Fred Haise and John Swigert nearly lost their lives when a major component failed and the astronauts had to nurse their crippled spacecraft home, as depicted in Ron Howard's acclaimed film *Apollo 13* (1995). The Apollo program ended in 1975 with the Apollo-Soyuz test project, during which American astronauts and Soviet cosmonauts linked up in orbit for the historic "handshake in space" that heralded the end of the space race and a coming era of cooperation in space exploration.

After the Soviets lost the race to the Moon, their space program shifted its emphasis to the building of space stations in Earth orbit. Beginning in the mid–1970s, the Russians launched a series of seven Salyut space stations, and their cosmonauts set records for long-duration space flights. This was followed by the first modular station, the Mir, which was built in increments to become the most elaborate construction ever attempted in space. The Mir remained in service for nearly a decade, but toward the end of its life it had become decrepit and "an accident waiting to happen"—for example, an onboard fire and a collision with an unmanned cargo ship. The rundown state of the Mir was satirized in the 1998 action film *Armageddon*. The Mir was de-orbited and burned up in the Earth's atmosphere in 2001.

During the 1970s, the United States followed up the Apollo Moon ships with a reusable space plane. The Space Shuttle, which first flew in 1981, consisted of two solid rocket boosters and a large external fuel tank, and the airplane-like orbiter was intended to function as a "space truck" that hauled heavy payloads into orbit. Over its 30-year history, the Shuttle flew 135 missions and, beginning in the 1990s, it was instrumental in the construction of the International Space Station. Unfortunately, the Shuttle's reusability did not live up to its cost-effective expectations. After the catastrophic losses of the crews of the *Challenger* orbiter in 1986 and *Columbia* in 2003, the program was phased out in 2011. On the big screen, however, the photogenic Shuttle, or Shuttle-like craft, became the iconic spaceship for a generation of science fiction films, including *Moonraker* (1979), *Space Camp* (1986), *Space Cowboys* (2000), *Armageddon* (1998), *Deep Impact* (1998) and *Gravity* (2016).

In 1984, NASA began to plan the construction of a permanent space station with other nations. This eventually led to a joint venture between Russia, the U.S., Japan, Canada, Brazil, Italy and the European Space Agency to create the International Space Station. Work on the project did not commence until 1998. The first Russian-American crew manned the station in 2000. Completed in 2011, the ISS has been continually inhabited by various crews from its inception to the present day. It has provided a platform for numerous scientific experiments conducted in its unique microgravity environment. The People's Republic of China has also established a presence in space, sending its "taikonauts" into orbit in their Shenzhou spacecraft in 2003, and to their Tiangong 1 space station in 2011. India has recently become the Earth's newest spacefaring nation.

In the 21st century, concerns about global climate change and the possibility of an asteroid collision (or other extinction-level catastrophe) has inspired a new generation to look to space. Foremost among these are the so-called "rocket billionaires" who have invested their own money in public and private partnerships with the U.S. government that may usher in a new space age by introducing innovations that have reduced the cost of launching payloads into space. In 2004, SpaceShip One, a rocket plane funded by Microsoft co-founder Paul Allen, became the first privately developed spacecraft to soar past the edge of space, roughly 60 miles up. After it made a second sub-orbital flight within a two-week period, the craft was awarded the coveted $10 million Ansari-X prize. The design has provided the basis for the upgraded SpaceShip Two, funded by British billionaire Richard Branson's Virgin Galactic, which is designed to loft tourists into space. Branson is currently building a New Mexico spaceport designed to enable space tourism. Amazon CEO Jeff Bezos has founded Blue Origin, a space corporation that is designing ballistic rockets to take tourists on brief forays into space on reusable boosters.

PayPal entrepreneur Elon Musk has made the largest contribution to the economics of space flight. He founded his space firm, SpaceX, in 2002 to make access to orbit cheaper and more efficient by instituting revolutionary cost-cutting measures. SpaceX's Falcon rockets, including the Falcon 9 and the Falcon Heavy, have become reliable launch vehicles that routinely fly satellites into space. In 2012, SpaceX's Dragon capsule became the first privately designed unmanned spacecraft to dock with the International Space Station; a manned version lofted astronauts to the ISS in 2020. In 2017, the Falcon Heavy launched a Tesla automobile containing a spacesuited astronaut manikin toward Mars, to demonstrate the Heavy's ability to reach deep space. In 2020, SpaceX began testing the engines for its super-heavy launch vehicle dubbed the "Starship." Musk has made no secret of his goal of having humans establish colonies on the Moon and Mars. "Eventually, history suggests, there will be some doomsday event," he has stated. "The alternative is to become a spacefaring civilization and a multi-planet species."[2]

The U.S. has recently announced its commitment to return to the Moon by 2024 in an updated lunar project called "Project Artemis," designed to eventually establish a permanent base there. Artemis will utilize Boeing's newly designed Orion spacecraft to loft astronauts on their journey. So humanity stands on the threshold of a new space age.

At one time, Moon rockets and orbiting space stations were the stuff of science fiction. Now they are in the realm of reality.

* * *

"Space," Elon Musk is fond of saying, "is hard." Rocket launchers are the most powerful, expensive and complex machines ever built, and they must endure enormous stresses. Space is a hostile, unforgiving environment devoid of air and gravity, and subject to extremes of temperature and radioactivity. Distances between celestial bodies are, as celebrity astronomer Carl Sagan used to say, "*extremely* far." Celluloid spacefarers, however, manage to overcome these difficulties in a uniquely cinematic fashion.

Vast distances, even those between star systems, present no problems for spaceships in the movies. They are able to travel halfway across the galaxy in mere minutes of screen time. The starships in the *Star Wars* and the *Guardians of the Galaxy* films can propel themselves through "hyperspace" to various points in the universe, while the U.S.S. *Enterprise* in the *Star Trek* series goes at "warp speeds," velocities that are multiples of the speed of light. Of course, these speeds are not achieved by the use of chemical rockets. In the case of *Star Trek*, interstellar speeds are achieved through matter-antimatter reactions enabled by "dilithium crystals," but the propulsion systems in the *Star Wars* and *Guardians* films are never clearly explicated. Yet while these imaginary spaceships supposedly travel at hyper-velocities, they are sometimes filmed as if they are moving in slow motion, a technique pioneered in *2001* and *Alien*, that serves to accentuate the massiveness of the craft but give the viewer the impression that they are gliding through the ether at a stately, leisurely pace.

In the *Star Wars* movies, interstellar starships are frequently depicted as low-tech affairs that seem like flying hot rods. Han Solo's space buggy, the *Millennium Falcon*, is frequently in need of repairs that can be achieved using simple tools like a screwdriver, a hammer and an Allen wrench. In *Episode One: The Phantom Menace,* a vital part for a starship is found in a junkyard lot. The *Star Wars* and *Guardians* ships are equally at home flying through a planet's atmosphere or traversing the vacuum of space, and are seemingly immune from concerns about the fiery heat of re-entry. In short, the filmic spaceships of the imagination pictured in these space operas bear little resemblance to realistic notions of space flight.

Movies that take place in outer space present unique challenges for filmmakers. A hefty budget is required to visualize the space environment, off-world heavenly bodies and massive ships that must be rendered using detailed model work or expensive computer graphics. One persistent difficulty consists of showing humans floating in zero gravity, which is usually achieved via complicated wire work. Zero-G was first depicted in Fritz Lang's silent classic *Woman in the Moon*, and has since been realistically portrayed in movies like *2001, Apollo 13* and *Mission to Mars*. Moviemakers frequently cheat by resorting to the sci-fi concept of artificial gravity. This might actually be accomplished on the circular outer rim of a spinning space station due to the action of centrifugal force, but the crews of the *Enterprise* and the *Millennium Falcon* never have to contend with the zero gravity of outer space.

An interesting aspect of many science fiction movies is the "hibernaculum" or "sleep chamber," in which spacefarers lie in suspended animation during long-duration voyages in order to preserve life. This was depicted in *2001*, where three astronauts are placed in sleep chambers during their journey to Jupiter space. Hibernacula subsequently became a fixture of sci-fi films such as *Planet of the Apes, Alien, Aliens, Avatar, Interstellar, The Wandering Earth* and *Passengers*. NASA actually studied the idea of placing astronauts in suspended animation, but concluded that this technique was not possible given the current state of our technology.

Scenes involving hibernacula are some of the most memorable in science fiction cinema. In *2001*, the three hibernating astronauts are murdered by the renegade

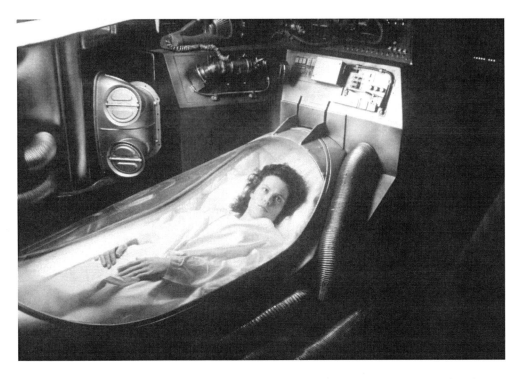

Ripley (Sigourney Weaver) prepares to enter hypersleep inside a hibernation chamber in *Alien* **(1979).**

HAL 9000 computer, which terminates their life support while they lie helpless in their cocoons. *Alien* begins with a dramatic scene in which the crew of the starship *Nostromo* is awakened by the ship's computer, and ends with the last survivor of the alien creature's rampage going back into the sleep chamber. *Avatar* opens with the protagonist dreaming while he is in suspended animation, traveling between worlds. The entire plot of *Passengers* revolves around an interstellar colonist who prematurely awakens from a hibernaculum during a long space voyage.

Space exploration began on the silver screen long before the first rockets blasted off into the void. The first serious film about space travel was the Danish silent feature *Heaven Ship* (1918), in which the crew of the titular vehicle journeys to Mars. The next spaceship to the Red Planet was from the Soviet Union in *Aelita* (1924), while the first lunar landing was pictured in the German silent *Woman in the Moon* (1929). American films did not venture into outer space until sci-fi luminary George Pal's seminal *Destination Moon* (1950), a Technicolor production that realistically depicted an off-world voyage. It spawned the science fiction boom of the 1950s. Pal followed up with *When Worlds Collide* (1951), in which the crew of a rocketship blast off for a new world to save the remnants of humanity, and *Conquest of Space* (1955), which recounts an expedition to Mars. Pal's color space extravaganzas inspired a raft of fanciful interplanetary expeditions such as *Rocketship X-M* (1950), *Flight to Mars* (1951) and *Missile to the Moon* (1959) that would persist for nearly two decades.

Then, in the wake of the burgeoning American and Soviet space programs, cinema began to portray space flight in a more realistic fashion. *I Aim at the Stars* (1960), *X-15* (1961), *Countdown* (1968) and *Marooned* (1969) reflected the realities of NASA's space program. In 1968, director Stanley Kubrick's brilliant *2001: A Space Odyssey*, informed by a screenplay by science fiction visionary Arthur C. Clarke, forever changed the course of the SF film. Subsequently, films such as *The Right Stuff* and *Apollo 13* dramatized non-fiction events in the history of space exploration. More recently, a series of Russian films, including *Gagarin: First in Space* (2013), *Salyut 7* (2017) and *The Spacewalker* (2017), have extolled the virtues of the Soviet-era space program.

Speculating on humanity's future in space, the cinema has contemplated a number of provocative themes. Mars has always held a special fascination for the human psyche, and the U.S. is currently formulating plans to land astronauts on the Red Planet. A number of recent films have depicted the exploration of Mars, including *Red Planet* (2000), *Mission to Mars* (2000) and *The Martian* (2015).

Evidence of planet-killing meteoric impacts in Earth's past has stoked concerns about perils descending upon us from above. A number of films have exploited fears of possible disasters originating in outer space. In *Moonraker*, a mad genius threatens to exterminate the human race from the high ground of an orbiting space station. A desperate mission to the Sun to prevent a solar flare from destroying the Earth forms the basis for the plot of *Solar Crisis* (1992). Four aging astronauts return to space to deactivate a malfunctioning Russian satellite that could unleash nuclear weapons and precipitate World War III in *Space Cowboys* (2000). In both *Armageddon* and *Deep Impact*, asteroids threatening to devastate Earth must be neutralized in space by teams of astronauts. A mega-project is instituted to move our planet to a new habitable zone in *The Wandering Earth* (2019). All of these films posit that the space program is essential for the very survival of humanity.

Some films go beyond depicting the exploration of our solar system and imagine journeys of exploration to faraway stars. The most dramatic version of this remains *2001*'s astounding "star gate" sequence, in which a spacefarer is propelled to the ends of the universe. Similarly, a spaceship crew travels through a black hole in *The Black Hole* (1979). An alien machine propels an intrepid traveler across vistas of time and space in *Contact* (1997), while astronauts on a mission to locate habitable worlds journey through a wormhole to other star systems in *Interstellar* (2014).

While cosmonauts and astronauts seek to explore the mysteries of outer space, and most of these films reflect these endeavors in a manner consistent with current scientific paradigms, some of them go beyond what is known to speculate about the mind-bending question "Are we alone in the universe?" There is no evidence that intelligent life exists or has ever existed in our solar system, and no signals from other civilizations have been detected by the Search for Extraterrestrial Intelligence (SETI) program, but this has not prevented science fiction filmmakers from speculating about the discovery of aliens or alien artifacts in space. Enigmatic monoliths are discovered on the Moon and Jupiter space in *2001*, while cosmonauts on a space station orbiting an alien world are confronted by an alien intelligence in *Solaris* (1972). A signal intercepted from outer space provides the means to connect with an extraterrestrial intelligence in *Contact*, and still-functioning alien machines are discovered inside the "Face on Mars" in *Mission to Mars*. If this scenario ever comes to pass, it will be the most profound event in the history of humankind. Thus, the challenges and possibilities inherent in space flight would provide inspiration for filmmakers stretching back over a hundred years.

ONE

First Flights

The dawn of the 20th century witnessed a cascade of technological wonders. Electricity, the automobile, the telephone, radio and the airplane were among the techno-marvels of the new age. Among these new miracles was the cinema, an art form that could depict the fantastic more realistically than any other medium. The first filmmaker to exploit the possibilities of this novel invention was the French director Georges Méliès. A former stage magician, Méliès set up the world's first movie studio in the Paris suburb of Montreuil and began turning out a series of short films on fantastic subjects. He pioneered the use of cinematic special effects such as slow and accelerated motion, fades and dissolves, and he utilized elaborate sets and mechanical devices to realize his imaginative creations.

In 1902, Méliès produced the world's first science fiction film, *A Trip to the Moon* (*Le Voyage dans la Lune*), a 13-minute space adventure that liberally borrowed elements from both Jules Verne's *From the Earth to the Moon* and H.G. Wells' *The First Men in the Moon*. The film begins at the royal astronomical society with a professor explaining the details of his proposed trans-lunar flight. The next scene shows the construction of the Moon ship, which resembles a giant bullet. At launch time, a crew of five elderly gents enters the ship. Amid much pomp and circumstance, a line of chorus girls load it into a humongous gun. The gun fires the ship into outer space where, in the film's most iconic sequence, it penetrates the eye of the Man in the Moon.

The five explorers exit the spacecraft armed with umbrellas, The Moon's surface is a tortured landscape of twisted crags, craters and pits. In a fantastic forest of gigantic mushrooms, they encounter the first in a long line of alien beings in the history of the cinema: an insectoid Selenite that astonishes the Earthlings with a series of gyrations and contortions. The Selenite disappears in a puff of smoke when struck by one of the explorer's umbrellas. Then a troop of the creatures take the men prisoner and escort them to their leader. Using their umbrella weapons, the men quickly escape, race back to the ship and take off on the return trip to Earth, along with one of the Selenites as a stowaway. The Moon ship makes a water landing and the men are rescued by a steamboat. Afterward the spacefarers are feted in another gala ceremony as the alien is displayed before the cheering crowds as a curiosity.

By modern standards, Méliès' theater-bound production, with its painted backdrops, hokey sets, lines of chorus girls and primitive special effects, hardly seems like science fiction at all, and in truth the film embodies a strong element of fantasy. It must be kept in mind that *A Trip to the Moon* was made over a century ago, during the infancy of the cinema, and at a time when knowledge of outer space was rudimentary. Thus the Moon is depicted as having a breathable atmosphere, normal gravity, forests of giant fungi and humanoid inhabitants. Despite its zaniness, however, the film draws on concepts from contemporaneous science fiction. The "space gun" that propels the explorers to the Moon was derived from Jules Verne's novel, while the Selenites were lifted from the work of H.G. Wells.

The cinema's first alien beings were portrayed by a troupe of theater acrobats who cavort around the screen in a series of comic gyrations. In his book *Science Fiction in the Cinema*, film historian John Baxter notes, "It is easy to laugh at Méliès' music hall depiction of space flight, but *A Trip to the Moon* differs little from the polished products of today's SF film producers. The chorus lines of Folies Bergère *poules* who load the projectile into the space gun serve roughly the same purpose as the sexy heroines of Fifties space opera, and the 'Selenites' with pop-eyes and prickly cardboard carapaces display as much imagination on the part of their designer as more modern bug-eyed monsters."[1]

Inspired by *A Trip to the Moon*, Thomas Edison's film company produced *A Trip to Mars* (1910), another off-world romp in a similar whimsical vein. In this five-minute short, a scientist cooks up an anti-gravity powder in his laboratory. After testing the stuff on a bowl and a chair, which float about the room in zero G, he applies it to his noggin and zips out the window into the sky. Freed from the confines of gravity, he ascends into outer space and lands on Mars. He traverses a forest of animated trees similar to the ones that would later appear in *The Wizard of Oz*, that grab at him with clutching branches. His next encounter is with a Martian overlord, a bald-headed giant with huge, pointed ears. The overlord holds him in the palm of his hand and blows his smoky breath on him, whereupon he is propelled back whence he came.

More in the realm of fantasy than science fiction, *A Trip to Mars* nonetheless depicts the first Martian in screen history who doesn't look too much different from the aliens that would appear in later sci-fi flicks. Director Ashley Miller uses optical superimpositions and other special effects to enliven what some film historians consider the first American science fiction film. Note that no spaceship was involved in the interplanetary journey, and the notion of an anti-gravity material was probably cribbed from H.G. Wells' 1901 novel *The First Men in the Moon*.

The Wells novel itself was adapted for the screen by the British Gaumont studio as *First Men in the Moon* (1919). The screenplay by R. Byron Webber compressed the book's narrative into a 16-minute running time while adding a romantic subplot that does not appear in the novel. In the film, Professor Sampson Cavor (Hector Abbas) discovers an anti-gravity substance that he "humbly" dubs Cavorite. With the aid of industrialist Rupert Bedford (Lionel D'Aragon), he constructs a spherical spaceship that looks something like an onion. Stocking up on Jacob's Biscuits and HP Sauce and donning form-fitting suits for the journey, Cavor and Bedford travel through space and land on the Moon at the end of the 14-day lunar night to witness the rapid blooming of cactus-like plants.

A group of Selenites, the Moon's humanoid inhabitants, take the spacefarers to their leader, the Grand Lunar (Cecil Morton York), a macrocephalic figure seated on a throne. Cavor is well received by the Selenites' ruler. Bedford sneaks back to the ship and returns to Earth, stranding Cavor on the Moon. Bedford's aim is to make a fortune from the professor's invention and woo Cavor's niece Susan (Heather Thatcher), who is in love with Hogben (Bruce Gordon), a young engineer. Susan is told that Cavor died on the Moon but that he first told Bedford that she should marry him (Bedford). Fortunately for the course of true love, Susan manages to contact Cavor via a radio transmission and learns that he is alive and well, and he exposes Bedford's scheme. The film ends on a happy note as Susan and Hogben wed.

First Men in the Moon was the first screen adaptation of a work by H.G. Wells. The author reportedly visited the set to oversee details of the production (as he would do again in 1936 with another adaptation of one of his novels, *Things to Come*). It is a lost film, but a number of surviving stills give an idea of the film's visuals. By today's exalted sci-fi standards, the sets and costumes appear chintzy and unimaginative. The film's lunar landscape is a two-dimensional stage set, while the alien Selenites resemble a line of blackface minstrels and are much less imaginative than the Méliès film's Moon dwellers. Only the Grand Lunar, the first in a long line of big domed extraterrestrials, exhibits any verve. Locating an existing print of the film is high on the British Film Institute's list of priorities. The Wells novel was lensed once more in 1964 in a production that featured special effects by stop-motion animator Ray Harryhausen.

While Méliès' short was a comic fantasy, a much more serious treatment of the space travel theme appears in the feature-length Danish film *Heaven Ship* (1919), which presented the screen's first voyage to Mars. The story revolves around adventurer Avanti Planetaros (Gunnar Tolnaes), who looks to explore new realms after returning from a long sea voyage. His father, Professor Planetaros (Nicolai Neiiendam), suggests that he turn his attention to the heavens. "In space," the professor declares, "there are thousands of mysteries, planets that we long for and long for us." Inspired, Avanti vows to "build a bridge between planets," and organizes an expedition to Mars.

Working with his friend Dr. Krafft (Alf Blütecher), Avanti constructs an unlikely-looking interplanetary vehicle dubbed the *Excelsior*, which resembles a blimp equipped with biplane wings and a pusher propeller in the rear, with the whole affair mounted on four bicycle wheels. Avanti and Krafft lead a crew of nine men into outer space on a mission to the Red Planet. Six months into the voyage, one crew member, the burly David Dane (Svend Kornbeck), begins to suffer from severe claustrophobia and succumbs to alcoholism. Grousing "We cannot bear to live anymore in this flying hell," he attempts to lead a mutiny. The revolt is cut short as they finally reach their destination.

Martians, who look like humans and dress in white robes, watch in wonder as the *Excelsior* appears in the skies. As it lands, their leader (Philip Bech) greets the spacefarers in peace. A clash of cultures arises when the strictly vegetarian Martians learn that the visitors eat meat and one of the crew shoots a bird. A horrified crowd moves to restrain the Earthlings; one of the crew members tosses a grenade, severely injuring a Martian (Nils Asther). Because the visitors have "brought the curse of blood on this planet of peace," they are remanded to the House of Judgment until they realize the error of their belligerent ways. There they are shown movie-like images of violence and war in the Martian past until they renounce their old ways and swear to "never more use weapons," because "sin opens the gates of hell."

After their conversion to pacifism, the Martian leader's daughter (Marya Jacobson) becomes enamored with Avanti. After they reveal their love to each other at the Tree of Longing, the couple plights their troth in the Forest of Love. The Earthlings are loath to leave this paradise, but Avanti insists that they return to their home planet to preach the Martian doctrine of pacifism. They leave for Earth in the *Excelsior*, bringing Marya with them to help spread the message of peace, love and vegetarianism to our troubled world. The ship lands back in Denmark amid the adulation of cheering crowds.

The first serious film about space flight, *Heaven Ship* was an elaborate, imaginative and expensive production for Danish cinema of the silent period. Producer-director Forest Holger-Madsen delivers a smoothly paced space adventure that combines science fiction with elements of fantasy. Adapted from a novel by Sophus Michaelis by scenarist Ole Olsen, it is one of a very few films that attempts to depict a utopian society. Impressive even by today's standards, the monumental Martian sets, dominated by a huge pyramidal structure, were constructed in a rock quarry outside of Copenhagen. Mars is populated by hundreds of extras clothed in white toga-type garments like the ancient Greeks, while their rulers wear tall white hats and carry staffs, outfits that make them resemble Catholic bishops. Made during World War I, the film is a sincere anti-war screed inspired by the myriad horrors of the Great War. It was a lost film for many decades until a print was discovered and restored by the Danish Film Institute in 2006.

Little was known about other planets or space flight when the film was made. Mars is depicted as a temperate, Earth-like world with normal gravity, a breathable atmosphere and human inhabitants, notions that persisted into the early 1960s in science fiction cinema. Interestingly, the trip from Earth to Mars takes six months, a figure that is roughly accurate. The interior of the spacecraft is cramped and narrow and sports industrial-type rivets, gauges and valves that make it resemble the inside of a submarine, and the astronauts eschew spacesuits and other protective gear in favor of uniforms consisting of leather double-breasted tunics and riding boots. Despite its many anachronisms, *Heaven Ship* offers a fascinating vision of interplanetary exploration and first contact with an alien civilization.

The next spaceship to arrive on Mars was launched from the Soviet Union a few years later in *Aelita* (1924). Based on the novel by the acclaimed Russian writer Alexi Tolstoy, the film's complex plot unfolds on two planets. On Earth, a mysterious radio message reading "Anta Odeli Uta" is received from the Red Planet. Its meaning eludes scientists around the world. Moscow engineer Los (Nikolai Tsereteli) becomes obsessed with the message and begins to design an interplanetary spaceship. Meanwhile, on Mars, the Martian queen Aelita (Yuliya Solntseva) views scenes on Earth via a new hi-tech telescope, through which she happens to observe Los smooching with his wife Natasha (Valentina Kuindzhi). Aelita yearns for Earthling-style physical passion, much to the chagrin of the Martian ruler Tuskub (Konstantin Eggert). The Martians live in a city constructed in a strange, angular geometric style, ruled by a king and queen and a group of aristocratic elders. They are served by an underclass of robotic slaves who live beneath the city.

Back on Earth, Los continues "seeking a power source that would overcome the Earth's gravity," and begins to construct a rocketship that will transport him to Mars. Things are not well on the home front, however, as he suspects that Natasha is having an affair and shoots her in a jealous rage. To evade the police, Los uses a clever disguise to assume the identity of senior engineer Spiridonov (also played by Tsereteli). Unbeknownst to him, however, a detective named Kravtsov (Igor Ilyinsky) is investigating Spiridonov for selling sugar on the black market. When the ship is completed, Los prepares to launch into space with his buddy, Red Army soldier Gusev (Nikolay Batalov). Kravtsov, who is trailing Spiridonov, inadvertently stows away in the ship.

The mighty rocket blasts off and is seen for a fleeting moment onscreen as a tapered, bullet-shaped craft speeding through the sky. Los reveals his true identity to the detective, now a passenger on the cosmic journey. The spaceship crash-lands on Mars and the three Earthlings are promptly arrested and brought before King Tuskub, who consigns them to the underground slave pens, along with Aelita, who has fallen in love with Los. While imprisoned with the proletarian androids, Los and Gusev foment a revolt with the aim of establishing a Soviet Socialist Republic on Mars. At first Aelita is part of the revolution, but she betrays Los and orders the Martian army to fire their weapons on the rebelling slaves. Los kills her for her treachery. Then Los awakens back on Earth; an advertisement for a tire company using the mystery words Anta Odeli Uta is in front of him, indicating that his Martian adventure was a dream. In the aftermath, he is reconciled with his wife and abandons his plans to build a space vehicle.

A complex mixture of soap opera and space opera, *Aelita*'s narrative shifts back and forth between the story of its Russian protagonists and Earth and the fantastic events on the Red Planet. (Most of the scenes taking place on Mars occur in the film's third act.) Director Yakov Protazanov alternates between the Russian story, shot in the Soviet style of Socialist Realism, and the fantastic alien cityscape on Mars. Interestingly, Protazanov did not employ the experimental montage techniques pioneered by his contemporaries Eisenstein and Kuleshov, but chose to employ a more conventional editing style. The bizarre sets and costumes, which have been described as being fashioned in a "Constructivist, Egypto-cubist" style, were designed by Isaac Rabinovich, Viktor Simov and Aleksandra Ekster of the Tairov Theater, and are *Aelita*'s most endearing feature. Yuliya Solntseva's performance as the sexually voracious, treacherous Aelita is the most powerful screen presence in the film, while Nikolai Tsereteli, in a dual role as engineers Los and Spiridonov, is stolid but unremarkable. Igor Ilyinsky's detective Kravtsov provides some weak comic relief.

Despite a spate of bad reviews, *Aelita* proved to be very popular with Russian movie audiences. Much of the criticism was leveled at the "it was all a dream" ending, which does not appear in Tolstoy's novel. The film's imaginative production design and novel space exploration theme struck a chord with filmgoers. *Aelita* was the most expensive movie made by the state-run Mezhrabpom-Rus Studio, which employed clever publicity stunts and an extravagant premiere gala to promote the film. The acclaimed composer Dmitri Shostakovich performed a piano score he composed for the film during showings in Leningrad. *Aelita*'s subplot involving the exploitation of an underclass of subterranean workers likely inspired a similar theme in Fritz Lang's dystopian sci-fi classic *Metropolis*, made just two years later.

Unlike the Rube Goldberg spaceship that propels space travelers to Mars in *Heaven Ship*, *Aelita* featured the first depiction of a rocket launch in screen history. The concept of using rocket technology to explore outer space was formulated by the brilliant Russian theoretical mathematician Konstantin Tsiolkovsky (1857–1935), who correctly calculated equations of the physical force needed to escape Earth's gravity. He wrote scientific papers on subjects like "Investigating Space with Rocket Devices," published in 1898, and subsequently constructed models of teardrop-shaped rocketships. *Aelita*'s Mars ship, seen very fleetingly, is obviously modeled after one of Tsiolkovsky's designs. The film depicts the dramatic burning of the rocket engines, followed by a wide shot of the ship streaking through the sky. When the craft reaches Mars, it crash-lands into the soil at great speed. The interior of the spacecraft is entirely prosaic and resembles a factory floor littered with machines of dubious function and other industrial paraphernalia. At one point, Kravtsov peers out a porthole to watch the Earth quickly dwindling in size as they travel at an impossible speed. The spacefarers arrive at their destination with great rapidity without suffering the effects of acceleration or zero gravity.

Once again Mars possesses an Earth-like environment that obviates the need for oxygen tanks, protective gear and spacesuits. *Aelita* exerted an influence on 1950s-era space flight movies such as *Rocketship X-M* (1950), *Flight to Mars* (1951) and *Queen of Outer Space* (1958). A radio message received from the planet was central to the plot of *Red Planet Mars* (1952).

The acclaimed Austrian director Fritz Lang, who was responsible for the sensational science fiction epic *Metropolis* (1926) that was set in a dystopian future city, returned to the genre with *Woman in the Moon* (*Die Frau im Mond*, 1929). The inspiration for the film came from one of Lang's discarded ideas for the ending of *Metropolis*, in which the male and female protagonists blast off from a launch pad in the futuristic city on a journey to outer space. But unlike *Metropolis*, which contained a number of fantasy elements, *Woman in the Moon* evolved into the first "hard" science fiction film that utilized the scientific principles of space travel, and even showed an uncanny prescience in its anticipation of the Apollo Moon landings. The film tapped into Germany's optimistic, pro-technology sentiments, especially in the fields of rocketry and aviation. Lang employed German rocket scientists Hermann Oberth and Willy Ley as technical advisors. Many of the movie's ideas were lifted from Oberth's non-fiction book *By Rocket to Interplanetary Space*, which described a manned voyage to the Moon in strictly scientific terms.

Woman in the Moon begins with industrialist Wolf Helius (Willy Fritsch), head of the Helius Aircraft Works, paying a visit to the elderly Professor Georg Manfeldt (Klaus Pohl), an eccentric scientist whose academic career was ruined 30 years earlier over his theories about trans-lunar travel and finding gold deposits on the Moon. Helius informs the professor that his dreams are about to be realized, as he is in the process of building a gigantic rocket designed to carry a crew to the Moon and back. Manfeldt tells Helius that mysterious men have lately been attempting to steal his notes and scientific papers, and he entrusts them to Helius for safekeeping. Helius is drugged and the notes stolen from his automobile. Later, men break into his home and pilfer papers from his office safe.

Helius is visited by Walter Turner (Fritz Rasp), a sinister individual who represents a group of shadowy financiers called "The Five Brains and Checkbooks." This group, motivated by the possibility of mining gold on the Moon, is responsible for the industrial espionage. Turner makes Helius an offer he can't refuse: The Five will offer financial backing for the Moon shot if Helius will take Turner along on the expedition; if he refuses, they will sabotage his Moon rocket. Helius has no choice but to accept.

We see the Five (four men and a tough-looking lady who chomps on a cigar) examining an intricate model of the rocket and viewing flight data and photographs of the Moon taken by an unmanned probe. The financiers have an interest in the lunar voyage because if gold is found on the Moon, the price of gold on Earth will nosedive; they want to be in a position to control the flow of gold from outer space. Turner's hidden agenda is to verify the existence of gold deposits on the Moon, and to watch out for the interests of the Brains and Checkbooks.

After these expository scenes, the camera glides over an aerial view of the gigantic Cape Canaveral–like space complex from which the Moon rocket will be launched at moonrise for the 36-hour trip. The crew will consist of Helius, his chief engineer Hans Windegger (Gustav von Wangenheim) and his fiancée Friede Velten (Gerda Maurus). Professor Manfeldt is included because of his ability to locate gold, and Turner will go as the agent of the Five. Massive crowds assemble to watch the launch, along with throngs of reporters and photographers. Excitement builds to a fever pitch as the huge doors of the main hangar open and the rocket moves slowly out of the building, supported by an enormous crane. Intense searchlights shine on the spaceship as it is guided to the launch pad and placed in a pool of water to support its great weight. The film depicts the first countdown ever seen or heard anywhere. The ground crew counts backwards 5-4-3-2-1 as the engines ignite and the rocket streaks into the night sky.

Wolf Helius (Willy Fritsch) struggles against acceleration forces to launch the second stage of his lunar rocket in *Woman in the Moon* (1929).

Gravitational forces experienced during the acceleration phase cause the crew to lose consciousness, but Helius manages to fire the rocket's second stage before blacking out. When the crew comes to, they find that the spaceship is on course, but the ordeal of the launch has affected Hans, who is beginning to experience mental problems. Soon they discover that they have a stowaway, an adolescent boy named Gustav (Gustl Stark-Gstettenbauer), an avid reader of sci-fi pulp fiction who has put his life on the line for his hero worship of Helius.

Entries in the ship's log describe highlights of the crew's trip through space. At a distance of 227,000 miles from Earth, they experience the effects of zero gravity, which is ameliorated by foot straps built into the floor and handholds on the ceiling. At one point, globules of fluid float around the ship in a weightless state. As the ship draws closer to its destination, the spacefarers observe the Earth through a porthole with awe and reverence. At last the 36-hour journey is over as the ship approaches the lunar surface, kicking up great clouds of Moon dust as it lands.

The astronauts are greeted by a bleak, desert-like Moonscape under a black sky. In the distance, rolling dunes and craggy mountain peaks can be seen. Professor Manfeldt has become highly energized by realizing his life's ambition of landing on the Moon. Not waiting for the others, he hurriedly dons a spacesuit and becomes the first human being to venture out on the lunar surface. He experimentally strikes a match; it bursts into flame, indicating that there is breathable atmosphere. Dancing a jig in delight, he removes the suit and wanders off to look for water with a divining rod. Turner decides that it's prudent to keep an eye on Manfeldt and sets out in hot pursuit. Meanwhile, the danger and uncertainty of the trip has kindled romantic feelings between Helius and Friede. Hans is suffering a mental breakdown from the rigors of the trip.

When Turner and Manfeldt fail to return, Helius and Gustav go out searching, while Hans and Friede prepare the ship for the return voyage. Seemingly guided by some mystical intuition, the professor finds his way through a tunnel and descends into a cavern pocked with craters filled with bubbling molten stuff, as well as odd-looking stalagmites and stalactites. It soon becomes apparent that he has discovered massive

Left to right: Gerda Maurus, Fritz Rasp, Willy Fritsch, Gustl Stark-Gstettenbaur and Gustav von Wangenheim explore the lunar surface in *Woman in the Moon* (1929).

deposits of pure molten gold, and the realization makes him cavort madly about the cave. He excavates a large columnar spire of gold that he intends to take back to the ship, but gets spooked when he sees Turner approaching and accidentally falls into a chasm. Undeterred by Manfeldt's death, Turner coldly fills his pockets with gold samples and hides himself when Helius and Gustav pass by.

Scheming to go back to Earth with the gold samples and strand the others on the Moon, Turner returns to the ship, knocks Hans unconscious and attempts to board, but is prevented from entering by Friede. When Helius and Gustav return, a shootout ensues, and Hans wounds Turner. A dying Turner informs them that he deliberately shot at the ship in order to damage it so that the crew cannot return to Earth. Upon inspection of the spacecraft, Helius discovers that half of their oxygen supply has escaped from the ship's tanks, meaning that one person will have to remain on the Moon. Hans and Helius draw straws to determine who will stay behind, and Hans loses. But Helius has other plans. Intending to sacrifice himself, he drugs Friede and Hans and tells Gustav how to operate the ship's launch mechanism; Helius will remain on the Moon until the crew of another Moon mission rescues him. He watches as the spacecraft takes off, then turns to find Friede, who saw through the ruse and elected to stay behind with him. She is now the "woman in the Moon" of the title.

Like *Metropolis, Woman in the Moon* originally contained mystical and occult concepts that were excised from the finished film. In the original script, penned by Lang's wife Thea von Harbou, Professor Manfeldt discovered not merely gold deposits, but golden statues created millennia ago by a vanished race from the lost city of Atlantis. Production stills reveal the last-minute alteration of the golden statuary into lumpen geological forms. Another scene was to have shown Manfeldt encountering a hovering crystal sphere artifact representing the Earth. The deletion of these fantastic elements transformed the film into the first-ever "hard" science fiction film. Hard SF of the literary variety, wherein the purely scientific aspects of an invention or idea are at the core of the plot, has rarely translated well to the screen, making Lang's achievement even more impressive. The science of *Woman in the Moon* was so hard that when the Nazis came to power, they confiscated all prints, negatives and even the rocket models used in the film, due to their resemblance to real rocket weapons being developed by the Reich.

At Germany's prestigious UFA studio at Neubabelsberg, workers filled the set with tons of bleached sand meant to simulate pale Moon dust and constructed the backdrop depicting lunar mountains. This alien Moonscape was designed by art directors Otto Hunte, Emil Hasler and Karl Volbrecht. Elaborate miniatures of the industrial complex from which the lunar ship is launched were built for aerial shots of the spaceport.

Despite its production values and scientific novelty, *Woman in the Moon* is not without its flaws. For starters, with a running time of 167 minutes it's way too long and the pace lags throughout its excessive length. The early scenes portraying industrial espionage perpetrated by a cabal of shadowy figures hark back to Lang's earlier films about criminal conspiracies such as *Dr. Mabuse the Gambler* (1922) and *Spies* (1928), and seem as if they belong in another movie. The most dramatic scene in the film, the rocket launch, comes in the middle of the narrative, making the rest of the movie seem anti-climactic. Principals Willy Fritsch as Helius and Gerda Maurus as Friede are played as Teutonic archetypal heroes and come off as being a trifle dull. Gustav von Wangenheim has a juicy part as the Moon-mad Hans, while Klaus Pohl's Professor Manfeldt adds a zany touch of comedy. The most powerful performance is turned in by Fritz Rasp as the maleficent Turner, a dark character who sports an ominous-looking Hitleresque hairdo. Rasp played a similar role as a villainous private detective in Lang's *Metropolis*.

The film's most serious failing is its lack of sound. It was made during a period of transition from silent movies to talkies; UFA wanted it to be a sound production but Lang insisted otherwise, not even permitting sound effects. This is especially puzzling considering Lang's innovative use of sound in his later films *M* (1931) and *The Testament of Dr. Mabuse* (1933). *Woman in the Moon* could doubtless have benefited from sound during several key scenes. Audiences should have been thrilled by the excited murmurs of the crowd watching the launch, the strident voices of radio announcers and the ground crew in anticipation of the flight, the dramatic countdown and the roar of the giant rocket during ignition. *Woman in the Moon* would go down in history as the last great silent film of the German cinema. The film did lukewarm box-office business and this led to the end of Lang's association with UFA.

On another level, the film exhibits an uncanny prediction of the Apollo 11 Moon shot. The procession of the rocket from the hangar-like structure on an enormous moving crane foreshadows the movement of the Saturn V rocket from the cavernous Vehicle Assembly Building to launch pad 39A at Cape Canaveral. *Woman in the Moon* also featured the introduction of the countdown, the first multi-stage rocket ever shown on film, and the first depiction of weightlessness, including globules of liquid free-floating in zero-G, a scene that became a reality when performed as a stunt by astronauts in space for the entertainment of millions of TV viewers. The foot straps employed in the movie to keep the astronaut's feet anchored to the floor were similar in function to the Velcro restraints used in the Apollo spacecraft.

Woman in the Moon was wrong about a number of things, including the rocket being suspended in water to support its weight during launch (although smaller amounts of water are placed underneath rockets to dampen the noise and force of the launch), the discovery of air on the Moon (although gold has been found in minuscule amounts), and the onset of weightlessness over 200,000 miles from the Earth (in reality, it occurs in low Earth orbit at 100 miles altitude). Lang's Moon ship has a spacious interior with plenty of atmosphere and multiple levels connected by ladders. The spacefarers cavort on the lunar surface in street clothes.

Despite its faults, *Woman in the Moon* far surpasses the concepts of space flight found in the works of the eminent European science fiction writers Jules Verne and H.G. Wells. In 1968, Lang was an honored guest at a space science seminar held at the U.S. government research center in Huntsville, Alabama, where he was warmly acknowledged as one of the fathers of rocket science. Shortly before the Apollo 11 flight, he discussed the first Moon landing with the eminent German rocket scientist Willy Ley, a technical advisor for the film. Looking up at the Moon, Lang jokingly referred to it as "my location set." *Woman in the Moon* exerted an enormous influence on space odysseys to come. A linear descendent was George Pal's 1950 classic *Destination Moon*, a film that "launched" a Hollywood sci-fi cycle.

The advent of sound spawned a novel genre, the Hollywood musical, which became very popular during the late 1920s and '30s. Science fiction was melded with the musical in the futuristic fantasy *Just Imagine* (1930), which is set half a century in the future, in 1980 New York. In this brave new world, mega-structures tower 250 stories into the sky, automobiles have been replaced by vertical takeoff and landing aircraft, numbers have replaced personal names, pills substitute for food and drink, and marriages are arranged by a government tribunal.

J-21 (John Garrick), pilot of the airliner *Pegasus*, and LN-18 (Maureen O'Sullivan) are sweethearts, but the pair cannot wed because he lacks the requisite social status; the marriage tribunal has decreed that she marry MT-3 (Kenneth Thomson). J-21's buddy RT-42 (Frank Albertson) tries to distract his friend from his woes by taking him to the laboratory of scientist Z-4 (Hobart Bosworth) to witness the revival of a man who was struck by lightning back in 1930. Amid sparking electric machines, the man (comedian El Brendel) is resuscitated and assigned the moniker Single-O. J-21 and RT-42 decide to adopt the hapless Single-O until he can adjust to his new environment.

Soon afterward, Z-4 contacts J-21 about piloting a rocket plane on the first trip to Mars, and he accepts because the excursion will boost his status and enable him to marry LN-18. Surrounded by news reporters in a dramatic scene that recalls Lindbergh's historic trans–Atlantic flight, the spaceship takes off in a burst of flame and a cloud of dust with J-21 and RT-42 aboard. Once they are in space, they discover that Single-O has stowed away. The trip to the Red Planet takes three months, and the astronauts can spend only five days on Mars before they have to return to Earth.

After making a soft landing on Mars, the men disembark. Single-O regards a Martian forest of strange-looking trees and comments, "So dis is Mars!" The crew soon encounters their first alien, a young woman in a scanty costume, who leads them to the palace of the Martian queen Loo Loo (Joyzelle Joyner) where they get a warm reception from Loo Loo and her husband, King Loko (Ivan Linow). The astronauts are offered food, drink and entertainment, which consists of a performance by dancers dressed in white ape suits. While they watch the dance number, a second group of Martians attacks and takes the Earthlings prisoner.

It seems that every Martian consists of a pair of good and evil twins, and the astronauts learn that have been abducted by Loo Loo's evil twin sister Boo Boo and King Loko's doppelgänger Boko. J-21 is particularly depressed because they have been imprisoned for several days as he fears that he won't return to Earth in time to prevent LN-18's marriage. Not to worry, though, because Loko helps them to escape. They rush back to the ship and prepare to take off, but Boko arrives to stop them and wrestles with Single-O, who overcomes him. The rocketship blasts off and swiftly returns to Earth, landing in New York's Roosevelt Field in time for J-21 to marry LN-18. Boko is led into the courtroom as proof that they have been to Mars.

Arguably the goofiest movie ever made on the subject of space travel, *Just Imagine*'s misguided meld of musical comedy and science fiction crash-landed at the box office. The early scenes of a futuristic, Art Deco New York of 1980 recalls Fritz Lang's *Metropolis*, while the latter part of the film set on Mars may have been inspired by *Aelita*. The film's megalopolis cityscape was constructed in a former Army Air Corps dirigible hangar at a cost of $168,000 and remains the movie's most notable feature. Director David Butler struggles valiantly with this crackpot material and manages to turn out a silly but oddly entertaining product. Principals John Garrick, Frank Albertson and Maureen O'Sullivan seem like mere window dressing, while the film is dominated by the zany antics of El Brendel, Joyzelle Joyner and Ivan Linow. Vaudeville comedian Brendel's schtick as a Swedish immigrant is particularly unfunny as he postures in a dopey hat while delivering lines like, "Is there no yustice?" in his irritating ethnic vocal inflection. The bizarre Martian costumes designed by Alice O'Neil and Dolly Tree add another eccentric touch to the proceedings.

Comedian El Brendel and a woman riding a futuristic rocket plane are featured in this poster for the science fiction comedy *Just Imagine* (1930).

The film's interplanetary "rocket plane" is a modest vehicle that has the dimensions of a medium-sized aircraft. Although it is referred to as a "plane," it lacks wings but nonetheless launches horizontally by rocket power. Controls are minimal, just a lever, a wheel and some gauges comparable to the simple control system of an automobile. Additional power is provided by a "gravity neutralizer," while the ship is flawlessly guided through space by a built-in automatic control system. Interestingly, the crew notes that the Earthmen have augmented strength in the lower gravity of Mars (roughly two-fifths the surface gravity of the Earth). Once again Mars has an Earth-like environment with breathable air, moderate temperatures and humanoid inhabitants, but little of the planet's landscape is shown. The Martians can speak, but they can only communicate with the Earthlings via sign language and are overwhelmingly female in gender. Universal's serial department re-used *Just Imagine*'s rocketship and various futuristic props in *Flash Gordon* (1936) and *Buck Rogers* (1939) space operas.

A much more serious approach to science fiction was brewing across the pond in England. SF pioneer and literary luminary H.G. Wells, who had penned *The First Men in the Moon* among his other works, was developing a screenplay adaptation of his 1933 novel *The Shape of Things to Come* for producer Alexander Korda. The result was *Things to Come* (1936), a big-budget extravaganza directed by William Cameron Menzies, best known as the production designer on films such as *Gone with the Wind* (1939) and *The Thief of Bagdad* (1940).

The film chronicles events in and around the mythical metropolis of Everytown (think London) from 1940 to 2036. John Cabal (Raymond Massey) and his friend Passworthy (Edward Chapman) discuss the impending threat of war between England and an unnamed foreign power. Their fears are realized as Everytown is subjected to bombardment by a fleet of enemy bombers. Cabal, a pilot, joins the war effort. The war is waged on a global scale until civilization collapses.

By 1970, war and plague have reduced Everytown to an almost pre-industrial ruin ruled over by a warlord called "The Chief" (Ralph Richardson). His main weapon of war is a fleet of World War I–era biplanes tended by engineer Richard Gordon (Derrick De Marney). An advanced aircraft piloted by John Cabal lands in Everytown and Cabal is taken to see the Chief. Cabal has come as an emissary of a group of aviator technocrats who call themselves Wings Over the World, who hope to bring law, sanity and advanced science to Everytown. Right after his meeting with the Chief, Cabal is promptly arrested and forced to work on the Chief's decrepit airplanes, but he convinces Gordon to steal one of the aircraft and fly to his (Cabal's) base in Malta.

Gordon does so and convinces Wings Over the World to mount an aerial assault on Everytown with their fleet of giant futuristic aircraft. During the ensuing battle, the Chief's antiquated airplanes are shot out of the sky. The population is subdued by "peace gas" bombs that kill the Chief and end his reign of terror and herald a new age of peace and prosperity.

The marvels of the future world of 2036, including a Moon-bound spaceship, are depicted in this poster for William Cameron Menzies' *Things to Come* (1936).

Cut to the year 2036, where high technology has rebuilt Everytown into a gleaming underground megalopolis. John Cabal's great-grandson Oswald (Massey) administers this utopia along with Passworthy's descendant Raymond (Chapman). Cabal has supervised the construction of a gigantic Space Gun designed to launch a projectile with two crew members to circumnavigate the Moon. Thousands have volunteered to make the journey, but the task falls to Cabal's daughter Catherine (Pearl Argyle) and Passworthy's son Maurice (Kenneth Villiers). Opposing the Moon flight is the charismatic sculptor Theotocopulos (Cedric Hardwicke), who rails against progress in general and the space mission in particular, stating, "People don't like it, shooting humans away into hard, frozen darkness."

As preparations for the launch are completed, Theotocopulos riles the citizens of Everytown into open revolt, causing a mob to march on the launch site to prevent the firing of the gun. Alarmed, Cabal flies Maurice and Catherine to the site in a helicopter, and the crew members are installed inside a rocket-like projectile that is inserted into the barrel of the gun by means of a crane. As the gun prepares to fire, the crowd is warned to retreat from its concussion force of the gun. The rioters pay no heed and continue to swarm over the huge device like ants. The gun fires and launches the spacefarers on their way to the Moon.

In the film's final scene, Cabal and Passworthy stand in front of a giant telescope, observing the spaceship's journey through the heavens. When Passworthy asks if there will ever be any rest for humankind, Cabal eloquently replies, "But for man, no rest and

Raymond Passworthy (Edward Chapman, left) and Oswald Cabal (Raymond Massey) track the progress of a lunar spacecraft on a giant telescope in *Things to Come* (1936).

no ending. He must go on—conquest beyond conquest. This little planet and its winds and its ways, and all the laws of mind and matter that restrain him. Then the planets about him, and at last out across the immensity to the stars. And when he has conquered all the depths of space and all the mysteries of time, still he will be beginning." This stirring speech perfectly expresses the pioneering ethos of space exploration.

Film historians consider *Things to Come* the first science fiction classic of the sound era. With a sizable budget, lavish production design by Vincent Korda, special effects by Ned Mann, a musical score by Sir Arthur Bliss and a prestigious cast, nothing like it had been seen on the screen before. Its major flaw is Wells' screenplay, which was overly complex and contained a good deal of awkward, stilted dialogue. Wells was 68 at the time, and despite his literary reputation was unused to writing for the medium of cinema. The characters are unengaging and are reduced to the level of ciphers and symbols within the fabric of the episodic multigenerational plot. Director Menzies, who did a workmanlike but uninspired job, returned to production design after completing this project, although he would go on to direct the sci-fi classic *Invaders from Mars* (1953).

The film's most interesting aspect is the way that aviation technology is used to symbolize the evolution of the future. In the opening episodes, 1930s-era aircraft devastate England and disrupt the world order in a war that serves to destroy 20th-century civilization. Wells had correctly predicted the potentialities of aerial warfare in his 1904 novel *The War in the Air*, and the destruction of London in the film would prove to be a grim prophecy of the Nazi blitzkrieg attacks just four years later. The enormous flying wing airplanes of the Wings Over the World technocrats are responsible for restoring sanity and reason to Everytown. A helicopter, which was a science fiction flying machine circa 1936, is used to circumvent the anachronistic rage of the angry mob. Perhaps the film should have been titled *Wings to Come*.

Finally, the massive Space Gun, surrounded by an enormous crane and a system of loading ramps, is the ultimate symbol of the future. Wells, who had castigated Jules Verne for his use of a giant cannon to propel astronauts to the Moon in *From the Earth to the Moon* as being unrealistic, fell back on using Verne's idea in *Things to Come*. Wells' Space Gun utilizes electricity rather than gunpowder as its motive force, but the movie provides no explanation of how it functions. An anonymous scientist wrote in a *Journal of the British Interplanetary Society* article that, given the gun's dimensions, the crew would suffer a force of 435 tons on their bodies as the projectile reached escape velocity. The Moon ship itself resembles a conventional rocket, but no hint is given as to how the spacecraft will be able to return to Earth.

The year 1936 saw another big-budget vision of space exploration, this one originating in the Soviet Union. *Cosmic Voyage* (*Kosmicheskiy Reys: Fantasticheskaya Novella*) was suppressed by Soviet censors shortly after its release and was practically unknown in the West until it resurfaced in the 1980s. While it borrowed elements from *Woman in the Moon*, the film offered the most realistic depiction of space travel up to that point.

Cosmic Voyage takes place in 1946, ten years in the future. At the sprawling Tsiolkovsky Institute of Interplanetary Communication, two massive "rocket planes," CCCP1 and CCCP2 (CCCP is Russian for U.S.S.R.), stand ready to be launched on the first voyage to the Moon. In an early scene, the camera glides past the two spaceships, which dwarf the workers and machines surrounding them. The elderly Professor Pavel Ivanovich Sedikh (Sergey Komarov) is set to make the flight, but his rival, Professor Karin (Vasili Kovrigin), and senior officer Captain Viktor Orlov (Nikolay

Feoktistov) oppose the idea, citing his advanced age. But on the launch date, Sedikh out-wits his opponents and commandeers CCCP1, taking Karin's assistant Marina (Kse-nia Moskalenko) with him, while young pioneer Andryusha (Vassili Gaponenko) stows away.

As the launch progresses, the rocket plane is brought out of the hangar and moved into position on the launching ramp with heavy, complex machinery, while the astro-nauts place themselves inside fluid-filled chambers that will allow them to survive the force of the ship's acceleration. Then the rocket engine ignites, and CCCP1 flies up the launching ramp at a 45-degree angle and sails into the stratosphere. A second stage is fired, and five minutes into the flight the crew members emerge from their chambers to experience the weightlessness of outer space. "What a world without weight," they exult as they float around the ship in zero gravity.

In a few moments of screen time, the rocket has reached its destination and comes in for a hard landing on the far side of the Moon. The ship's oxygen supply is damaged in the landing. To provide proof that they have reached the Moon, Sedikh, Marina and Vassili travel over the lunar surface to the near side and signal the Earth using reflec-tive mirrors. They don cumbersome spacesuits and set off on their journey, leaping like grasshoppers over giant boulders in the Moon's reduced gravity. Sedikh gets trapped under a boulder. Marina and Andryusha use the mirrors to spell out the letters "CCCP," which Professor Karin observes through a telescope. When Sedikh is freed from under the boulder, he discovers a white powdery substance: the remains of the Moon's depleted atmosphere. Using the powder, they are able to replenish their oxygen supply and return to Earth and a triumphal celebration.

Consigned to an undeserved obscurity by Soviet censors who objected to the film's perceived departure from the tenets of socialist realism, *Cosmic Voyage* has been redis-covered and is now revealed as one of the early classics of Russian science fiction cin-ema. Made during the era of sound, the film was nonetheless produced as a silent feature by the state-run Mosfilm Studio in order to play in cinemas in the far-flung provinces of the Soviet Union, most of which were not equipped for sound. Director Vasily Zhu-ravlyov made use of lavish sets, elaborate miniatures and stop-motion animation to con-struct a space exploration adventure as grand as anything achieved in Lang's *Woman in the Moon*. Clocking in at a mere 65 minutes, it is much more focused and dynamic than *Woman in the Moon*.

The film's genesis began in 1932 when the Komsomol, or Communist Union of Youth, requested the production of a film that extolled the wonders of space flight. Accordingly, the film has a juvenile quality designed to appeal to youngsters and inspire them to explore space, and exhibits the naïve, simplistic approach of Stalin-era Soviet propaganda. The three principal characters are a grandfatherly old man, a sweet maiden and a young lad and they function in the manner of characters in a child's adventure story and the film sparkles with a youthful exuberance. Sergey Komarov, sporting a bushy white beard and a mop of white hair, is the spitting image of Father Christmas.

While the plot has the ambience of a fantasy story, the science fiction elements were inspired by the work of pioneering space scientist Konstantin Tsiolkovsky, who acted as a technical consultant on the production and conceived many of its realistic touches. The Tsiolkovsky-inspired Moon vehicle employs multi-stage rockets, the astronauts experience weightlessness, spacesuits with oxygen supplies are needed in the airless environment of the lunar surface, the Moon explorers enjoy the advantages of reduced gravity, and the spacecraft lands on Earth via parachute, the method employed by the early Russian and American space flights. The use of a ramp to launch the rocket had been proposed by space engineers; a similar ramp appears in the George Pal production *When Worlds Collide* (1951).

The film also contains a number of elements that originated in the imagination of the filmmakers. In real life, it has never been proposed that astronauts immerse themselves in liquid to protect them from the effects of acceleration during liftoff. The Moon's gravitation is too feeble to have retained an atmosphere, and oxygen is not found in powdered form there or anywhere else. The CCCP1 ship is incredibly massive in comparison to the cramped dimensions of the real-world Apollo 11 spacecraft.

The 20th century began with flights of fancy such as *A Trip to the Moon*, *Heaven Ship* and *Aelita*, but fantasy would soon yield to scientific reality as filmmakers became influenced by the ideas of early rocket visionaries such as Herman Oberth, Willy Ley and Konstantin Tsiolkovsky. Advancements in special effects technology also helped to create the cinematic reality of space flight on the big screen. Yet after this early start, the rocket's red glare would be dimmed for nearly a decade and a half until the advent of the science fiction movie wave of the 1950s, when spaceships would take off for the Moon, Mars, Venus and other destinations in the universe.

Two

The '50s and '60s: From George Pal to Stanley Kubrick

Serious films about space travel and rocketry were absent from movie screens between the years 1937 and 1950. Their absence was part of a period of stagnation in the science fiction genre, which had been subsumed by the horror film in programmers such as *Son of Frankenstein* (1939), *The Man They Could Not Hang* (1939), *Dr. Cyclops* (1940), *Man Made Monster* (1941) and *The Lady and the Monster* (1944). When the bottom fell out of the horror market at the end of World War II, science fiction features practically ceased to be produced in Hollywood, and space adventures were relegated to the realm of kiddie matinee serials. In *The Purple Monster Strikes* (1945), for instance, a Martian invader arrived from the Red Planet in a cheesy-looking rocketship. A miniature spacecraft from the planet Krypton ferried an alien infant to Earth in *Superman* (1948).

During this same period, however, giant strides in space technology had taken place. Beginning in the late 1930s, German scientists under the leadership of engineer Wernher von Braun had worked on perfecting rockets that would eventually reach the edge of outer space. But during the war, von Braun's team of rocketeers was pressed into service constructing the world's first ballistic missiles, which rained supersonic death on London and other European cities. The weapon they concocted, known to the Allies as the V-2 and to the Germans as the A-4, was the first vehicle to reach the so-called Karman line at 62 miles altitude, which is considered the boundary between the Earth's atmosphere and outer space.

Although von Braun was a member of the Nazi party, and produced terror weapons for the regime, his true aim was to create rockets for space exploration. In March 1944, he was arrested and briefly imprisoned by the Gestapo for making "loose talk" about his desire to explore space. As Allied armies advanced into a defeated Germany in 1945, von Braun and his rocket scientists surrendered to the Allies and were allowed to emigrate to the U.S., where they were put to work on developing rocketry for the Army. Von Braun became an integral figure in the American space program and was instrumental in the creation of the mighty Saturn rockets that took the Apollo astronauts to the Moon. A vocal proponent of space exploration, he was the subject of the biopic *I Aim at the Stars* (1960) and appears as a minor character in *The Right Stuff* (1983).

Another factor that put space travel front and center in the public mind was the phenomenon of unidentified flying objects, or UFOs. Beginning with the sighting of "flying saucers" by pilot Kenneth Arnold in July 1947, these mysterious UFOs captured the American imagination and inspired decades of flying saucer movies. Although the true nature of the UFO phenomenon has yet to be determined, the prevailing hypothesis was that they were alien spaceships that were transporting visitors from other planets to Earth. And if they could come *here*, then humans might one day travel *there*.

In 1935, German science writer and rocket enthusiast Willy Ley, who had worked as a *Woman in the Moon* technical advisor, emigrated to the U.S. and became a key proponent of space travel. His 1949 book *The Conquest of Space*, subtitled *A Preview of the Greatest Adventure Awaiting Mankind,* proposed a realistic approach to the space exploration extending 50 years into the future. It contained exquisite illustrations by landscape artist Chesley Bonestell, whose eye-popping vistas of alien worlds perfectly complimented the text. The book's cover featured a winged, silver rocketship standing on its fins with craggy lunar mountains in the background and the Earth hanging in the black sky while spacesuited astronauts set up scientific instruments. Ley and Bonestell's imaginative work was later incorporated into producer George Pal's influential *Destination Moon* (1950).

The Hungarian-born Pal was best known for "Puppetoons," the series of animated shorts he made for Paramount during the 1940s. Pal was looking to move into feature film production and hit on a screenplay entitled *Journey to the Moon,* penned by SF luminary Robert A. Heinlein. Working with scenarist Rip Van Ronkel, Heinlein adapted his own juvenile novel *Rocketship Galileo,* along with elements of his short story "The Man Who Sold the Moon," into an adventure story about the first lunar landing. Pal bought the script, changed the title, and hired Heinlein to be a technical consultant on the film. Another recruit was Chesley Bonestell, whose incredibly detailed paintings for the film added immensely to its visual power. Veteran Irving Pichel was brought on board to direct.

Destination Moon opens at a U.S. Army missile base, where the commanding officer, General Thayer (Tom Powers), and rocket scientist Charles Cargraves (Warner Anderson) test Cargraves' design for an atom-powered rocket designed to launch a satellite into orbit. They watch the rocket take off (actually stock footage of a captured V-2 missile launch), only to crash and burn a few moments later. Thayer suspects sabotage, but he and Cargraves know that whatever the cause of the rocket's failure, the government will close down the atomic rocket project due to heavy cost overruns.

Two years later, Thayer (now a civilian) arrives at Barnes Aircraft for an appointment with its founder and CEO, Jim Barnes (John Archer), a Howard Hughes–like aviator-entrepreneur. Thayer explains that his research group has produced a new atomic-powered rocket engine with enough raw thrust to propel a spaceship to the Moon and back. "Well, Jim," he asks at the conclusion of his spiel, "do we go to lunch, or do we go to the Moon?" Barnes answers by lighting Thayer's cigar.

Thayer and Barnes organize a presentation given to a group of industrialists in hopes of convincing them to collaborate on the Moon project. A charming animated cartoon, with Woody Woodpecker demonstrating the principles of rocketry, is shown to the assemblage. When the lights come up, Barnes and Thayer explain to the group that they are not the only ones contemplating a trip to the Moon, and that an unnamed foreign government may have sabotaged Thayer's early missile experiments. Thayer points out that whoever controls the high ground of outer space will hold an important military advantage. "The race is on," he warns, "and we'd better win it." The industrialists are convinced.

A montage of scenes showing the construction of the rocket follows. The graceful silver spaceship, christened *Luna*, begins to take form in the middle of the desert at

Barnes' launch facility at Drywell Base. Everything is progressing smoothly until Barnes gets a letter from the Atomic Energy Commission denying him permission to launch the ship. Rather than close down the project, Barnes opts to launch in 17 hours. Now the crew members (Barnes, Thayer, Cargraves and a fourth man) scramble to prepare for the voyage. The fourth man comes down with appendicitis and is replaced by Brooklynite Joe Sweeney (Dick Wesson), who goes along to provide electronics expertise (and comic relief).

At zero hour, there are mass demonstrations protesting the launch, and a court order to stop it. Police cars race to the launch pad with sirens blaring as the countdown commences. The atomic rocket works as advertised as the astronauts blast off on humankind's first journey into space. Multiple G-forces distort the crew members' faces as they escape the Earth's gravity, and after much grimacing they find themselves in a state of weightlessness as the engines cut off. Barnes hands out boots with magnetic soles that enable the men to walk around the spaceship normally. Peering out of a porthole, they are the first people to observe the Earth from space, an awe-inspiring sight.

A radar antenna malfunctions and Barnes, Cargraves and Sweeney space-walk outside the ship to repair it. During the procedure, Cargraves starts to drift away into space, and Barnes uses an oxygen tank as a miniature rocket to bring him back to the ship. With the antenna repaired, the voyage continues until it is time to land on the Moon. As the ship approaches the designated landing site, Barnes overshoots, wasting precious fuel. At last the ship makes a perfect landing on the Moon surface.

The astronauts don their spacesuits and step through the airlock. The camera slowly pans across the bleak, yet strangely beautiful Moonscape as spooky music plays on the soundtrack. Stepping out on the surface of the Moon, Barnes claims the satellite "in the name of the United States, for the benefit of all mankind." He also reflects on the "utter barrenness and desolation" of the lunarscape before him, describing the absence of sound and the velvety black sky. The surface of the Moon is covered by a complex webwork of cracks and craters, and jagged mountain peaks tower in the distance.

They begin exploring, leaping around like children in the one-sixth gravity. A large telescopic camera is set up to observe the Earth, and uranium is discovered in lunar rocks, causing Sweeney to quip, "Then you could blow up the Moon, too." Cargraves takes a trick shot of Sweeney as if holding up the Earth like a modern-day Atlas. These light-hearted antics are interrupted by some serious news from Drywell Base: According to their calculations, the extra fuel expended during the landing has left them with insufficient power to take off again. Asked if there could be a mistake, Drywell replies, "I could be wrong, but I don't think the computer could."

The men frantically starts removing all excess equipment from the *Luna*, but despite their efforts they still come up about 110 pounds short, causing them to contemplate the necessity for one of the men to remain behind. As they deliberate, Sweeney quietly slips out of the ship, intending to sacrifice himself for the others. At the last minute, Barnes comes up with a clever plan to blow yet more excess baggage out through the airlock. The plan works, and with the loss of weight accomplished, the ship blasts off for the trip back to Earth. The movie finishes with the superimposed words "This is the end … of the beginning."

Destination Moon was made during the early years of the Cold War era, and there is a feeling of great haste and urgency about it, exemplified in the scenes where the rocket builders race to launch the spaceship before the authorities can stop them, and in the astronauts' frantic scramble to lighten the ship for its takeoff from the Moon. The movie accurately predicted the coming U.S.-Soviet race to the Moon while warning about the necessity for America to control the "high ground of space." Just seven years later, the Russians launched the world's first artificial satellite into orbit, initiating the space race that would culminate in the American Apollo 11 Moon landing.

Irving Pichel's direction is steadfast, sober and well-paced, while Heinlein's screen-play is tightly constructed and does not compromise scientific veracity. The cast members turn in solid, believable performances, although Dick Wesson's portrayal of the Brooklyn-ese Sweeney gets irritating. Using overblown dialect, words like "Earth" and "work" come out sounding like "oith" and "woik" in his cartoonish jargon. Perhaps the film's real stars are Chesley Bonestell's superb paintings that captivate the eye and make the imagination soar. His multicolored vistas and craggy peaks were in fact more visually arresting than the TV images of rounded lunar hills and colorless terrain that American astronauts broadcast from the Moon during the Apollo missions. The imagery of sharp pointed mountains was due to an illusion caused by sunlight falling on the Moon's surface at an extremely oblique angle that, in photographs taken from Earth, exaggerated their shape. Pal's special effects team won an Academy Award for the film's visual artistry, although scenes such as the crew repairing the *Luna* in space are very dated by today's effects standards.

Destination Moon contains what is probably the first reference to computers in screen history. Circa 1950, computers were room-sized monstrosities utilizing vacuum tube technology and punch card input, and had science fiction names like ENIAC and UNIVAC. *Destination Moon* correctly predicted the future role of computers in space flight; today they are essential. Other details about outer space were also correct, such as the black sky, lack of air and sound and the one-sixth gravity on the Moon. In the film, the astronauts discover uranium on the Moon; in real life, the decades-later Apollo missions brought home to Earth Moon rocks containing radioactive uranium 236.

On the other hand, some of the film's technology was far off the mark, such as the *Luna* being powered by a nuclear rocket, a technique that has never proven to be practical. Unlike the multi-stage rockets featured in *Woman in the Moon* and *Cosmic Voyage*, *Luna* is a single-stage spacecraft, a concept called "direct ascent" that was quickly discarded by rocket designers. Pal's Moon rocket was 151 feet tall and its rocket engine generated three million pounds of thrust, while Apollo's three-stage Saturn V launch vehicle was 364 feet high and generated seven and a half million pounds of thrust. In the film, the astronauts monitor the ship's takeoffs and landings on TV monitors, a technology that was never employed by NASA or the Soviets. The movie featured a cracked-looking lunar surface that resembled a dry lake bed, an impossibility given the absence of water. Art director Ernst Fegté created this fissured surface so that forced perspective could be used to make the set seem larger by making the cracks smaller as they receded into the distance.

Pal and his crew had to use their ingenuity to compensate for the film's modest budget of $586,000. To create the illusion of zero gravity, the spaceship set was mounted inside a huge drum that was three stories high. The drum, built at a cost of $35,000, could be rotated in any direction, making the actors appear to float or walk up walls. In 1968, a similar device was later used in Stanley Kubrick's *2001*. Some scenes involved the actors being strung in harnesses and wires, sometimes for hours at a time, in order to simulate zero-G. Other similarities with *2001* include a sequence in which astronauts perform a dangerous spacewalk to repair the antenna, a scene where an astronaut enters a spaceship via the airlock in an unorthodox manner, and the use of color-coded space-suits for the individual astronauts. The scene in which excess equipment is stripped from the rocket to reduce its weight for takeoff was later replicated in *The Martian* (2015).

Destination Moon was a modest financial success and provided the impetus not only for Pal's future sci-fi projects, but also for the raft of science fiction movies that followed. Its popularity established the commercial viability of the SF genre for the first time, and for that reason alone, it must be considered one of the most influential SF films of all time.

The most egregious of the *Destination Moon* rip-offs was Kurt Neumann's *Rocketship X-M* (1950), a black-and-white low-budgeter rushed into production to take advantage of the advance publicity for Pal's film. Released a few weeks before *Destination Moon*, the film featured Lloyd Bridges leading a group of five astronauts on a spaceship bound for the Moon that gets detoured to Mars instead. Landing on the alien world, they find the ruins of a post-apocalyptic civilization populated by a race of degenerate mutant troglodytes who promptly attack the Earthlings. Three of the five escape from the creatures and blast off in their rocketship for the return trip. But the spacecraft lacks sufficient fuel for a landing and crashes, killing all aboard.

Thought by many critics to be superior to Pal's film, *Rocketship X-M* is composed primarily of static, talky scenes during the space voyage and contains numerous scientific inconsistencies. The astronauts do not experience weightlessness in outer space, and wear street clothes and oxygen masks instead of spacesuits on Mars. Worst of all, the filmmakers display their ignorance of astronomy by diverting their Moon expedition to Mars. The Moon is roughly a quarter of a million miles from Earth and was reached by Apollo astronauts in three days, while Mars, at its closest distance, is 34 million miles away and would takes months to reach. The first trip to the Red Planet in color took place in *Flight to Mars* (1951), an interplanetary journey led by Arthur Franz. The space-farers contend with an underground civilization of human-looking Martians. The ladies wear miniskirts and the planet's leaders scheme to steal the astronauts' ship and invade the Earth.

Pal's next project was based on a literary property purchased by Paramount in 1934, the novel *When Worlds Collide* by Philip Wylie and Edwin Balmer, which would emerge as the first color spectacular end-of-the-world flick in the apocalypse-obsessed era of the 1950s. As the film opens, the eminent astronomer Dr. Hendron (Larry Keating) observes through his telescope a couple of runaway worlds on a collision course with Earth. He christens the twin planets Bellus and Zyra, and calculates that Zyra will pass close to the Earth, causing earthquakes, volcanic eruptions and other geologic cataclysms. Nineteen days later, Bellus will actually hit Earth and smash it to smithereens. Pilot Dave Randell (Richard Derr), assigned to fly a set of photographic plates from an observatory in South Africa to the U.S. gets the story from Dr. Hendron. An emergency meeting of the United Nations is convened to discuss the situation, and the world's foremost scientific authorities scoff at Hendron's theories.

The astronomer's findings do not fall on deaf ears, however. Wheelchair-bound billionaire Sydney Stanton (John Hoyt), convinced of the coming apocalypse, hires Hendron to construct a "space ark," a gigantic rocketship that will ferry 40 human passengers from the Earth to Zyra in order to preserve the human species. Stanton stipulates that he will be one of the passengers, while the rest of the crew will be chosen from among the project's workforce. Randell joins the project and becomes romantically involved with Hendron's daughter Joyce (Barbara Rush). Project member Tony Drake (Peter Hanson) competes with Randell for Joyce's attentions.

As Bellus and Zyra approach, the people of Earth are finally forced to confront the grim truth, and society begins to disintegrate. In the meantime, Stanton's team has assembled the rocket, a winged, silver ship that resembles *Destination Moon*'s *Luna*, except that it will take off horizontally on rocket-sled tracks. With the hour of doom approaching, Zyra passes into the Earth's gravitational field, causing major geologic upheavals. Spectacular special effects scenes of destruction follow as New York City is engulfed by a tidal wave. The launch complex workers who have lost the lottery to be taken aboard the spaceship begin to riot. As the mob approaches, the spacefarers hurry to ready the ark for takeoff, and at the last moment Dr. Hendron prevents Stanton from boarding the ship so that a young couple can go in their place. Then Randell fires the big rocket engine, propelling the ship into space just as Earth is being destroyed. The ark makes a safe landing on Zyra where the passengers—all that is left of humanity—find breathable air. They exit the ship to find a new world glowing in pastel tones.

Deftly directed by European filmmaker Rudolph Maté, best known for helming the film noir thrillers *The Dark Past* (1948) and *D.O.A.* (1949), *When Worlds Collide* packed a knockout punch at the box office. As he had done with *Destination Moon*, Pal relied on a cast of little-known actors and a plausible, intelligent screenplay to craft one of the

The "space ark" rocket that will carry survivors of a worldwide cataclysm to a new world is pictured in this lobby card for George Pal's *When Worlds Collide* (1951).

most spectacular of the '50s sci-fi movies. Perhaps the film's main weakness is in the relative lack of emotional connection with the characters, who seem to exist just to put a human face on all the spectacle. The scenes showing the flooding of Times Square are much more memorable than anything the characters do. The film's team of special effects technicians, headed by Gordon Jennings and Harry Barndollar, won an Academy Award for visual effects, the second in a row for a George Pal production. Paintings by Chesley Bonestell were used to depict the vistas of the planet Zyra.

Like *Destination Moon, When Worlds Collide* is suffused with the paranoid obsessions of the early nuclear age. Sydney Boehm's screenplay contains strong religious overtones, and the film is essentially a space age retelling of the Biblical story of Noah's Ark. Ironically, the film seems even more relevant today, as perils from space are thought to present existential threats to the survival of the human race, as evidenced in the 1998 sci-fi thrillers *Armageddon* and *Deep Impact*. A more direct descendant is the disaster epic *2012* (2011), which also featured a survival ark. As for the film's main premise, present-day astronomers theorize that there are so-called "rogue planets," worlds that are not part of a solar system but rove around the universe like the fictional Bellus and Zyra. Note that, as in *Destination Moon*, the space venture is funded by private enterprise instead of the U.S. government, a detail that seems prescient in light of Elon Musk's crusade to build colonies on Mars to preserve humanity in the event of a planetary catastrophe.

Pal's science fiction productions opened the floodgates to a host of off-world adventures to the Moon, Mars, Venus and points beyond. Unfortunately, most of these were poorly scripted, low-budget programmers with minimal special effects. In many of these films, astronauts discovered that the heavenly bodies were peopled with heavenly bodies. A team of space explorers encountered a race of feline female aliens living beneath the lunar surface in the classic cheapie *Cat-Women of the Moon* (1953). Its cockamamie remake was *Missile to the Moon* (1958). In *Abbott and Costello Go to Mars* (1953), Bud and Lou went "out of this world on a misguided missile," to the planet Venus, where they contended with a race of gorgeous Amazons. In a British entry, the *Fire Maidens from Outer Space* (1956), resembling showgirls, resided on the 12th moon of Jupiter, discovered by an expedition from Earth. Zsa Zsa Gabor headed the cast of another movie about a world (this time Venus, the planet of love) populated by alien glamor girls, the Technicolor-CinemaScope *Queen of Outer Space*. All of these films represented juvenile erotic fantasies in which male astronauts were thrust into all-female societies where they were surrounded by throngs of adoring women.

Not all space ventures of the period were so empty-headed, however. Robert Heinlein scripted *Project Moonbase* (1953), in which a spaceship with a crew of three crash-lands on the Moon, killing one of the astronauts. The other two, a man and a woman, are married via television by the female American president. In *Spaceways* (1953), a space program technician is accused of murdering his wife in a meld of detective story and science fiction. *Satellite in the Sky* (1956) featured a space station imperiled by a malfunctioning rocket carrying a "tritonium bomb."

George Pal returned to the realm of the hard science space exploration film with *Conquest of Space* (1955), a realistic account of a journey to Mars. It was based on the book by Willy Ley and Chesley Bonestell and material from Wernher von Braun's non-fiction book *The Mars Project*. In Pal's original conception, it was to feature a grand tour of the solar system, including trips to Mars and Venus, but Paramount execs soon

THEY'RE OUT OF THIS WORLD ON A MISGUIDED MISSILE!

ALL NEW! ...and too wild for one world!

MARS THATAWAY

BUD ABBOTT and LOU COSTELLO GO TO MARS

MARI BLANCHARD · ROBERT PAIGE · HORACE McMAHON AND THE MISS UNIVERSE CONTEST BEAUTIES

Bud Abbott and Lou Costello aim for Mars but wind up on Venus where they encounter the Miss Universe contest beauties in *Abbott and Costello Go to Mars* (1953).

scaled back his ambitious plans and ordered up a more conventional space adventure about the first manned expedition to Mars.

"This is a story of tomorrow," the film's narration begins, "or the day after tomorrow," when humankind has constructed a wheel-shaped space station in orbit around the Earth. "The Wheel" is operated by a multi-national, quasi-military agency, the Supreme International Space Authority. A powerful new multi-stage spacecraft, being assembled in orbit, will be flown to the Moon by General Samuel T. Merritt (Walter Brooke) and his son Barney (Eric Fleming). They soon learn that the Moon is to be bypassed in favor of a trip to Mars. Earth's ecosystem is on the verge of collapse, and the Space Authority is anxious to begin colonizing other worlds. The rest of the Merritts' crew consists of Japanese geologist Imoto (Benson Fong), Austrian medical researcher Andre Fodor (Ross Martin) and Brooklynite Jackie Siegel (Phil Foster). Like *Destination Moon*'s Sweeney, he's there to provide electronics expertise and comic relief.

The ship is a winged craft designed to operate in the Martian atmosphere. The forward viewing screen malfunctions, and Fodor and Siegel must perform a spacewalk to fix it. As they are completing the repairs, a meteor narrowly misses the spacecraft, but Fodor is killed when a small meteoroid penetrates his space helmet. His body hangs limply in space, tethered to the ship. Released into the void, Fodor's corpse drifts away into the depths of the universe in the very first space funeral scene depicted on film.

As the ship approaches Mars, the general, a deeply religious man, begins to have second thoughts about the mission. Showing signs of a mental breakdown, he rants about the spiritual "abomination" of humans landing on the Red Planet. During the final approach, he suddenly pulls back on the throttle, a maneuver that almost destroys the ship. Barney wrests the controls away and manages to land safely.

Mars presents a bleak planetscape of Technicolor red sand punctuated by jagged mountain peaks. The sky, however, is bright blue, giving Mars a decidedly terrestrial appearance. The absence of a breathable atmosphere means that the astronauts must wear spacesuits on the planet's surface as they begin setting up a base camp and performing various experiments. Imoto plants Earth seeds to see if they will grow in the Martian soil. In the meantime, General Merritt, not content with having attempted to sabotage the landing, tries to further compromise the mission by expelling rocket fuel from the ship's tanks. Barney discovers the plot and struggles with Merritt, who holds off the crew with a pistol. The gun goes off, killing the general.

The astronauts must wait for months while the Earth and Mars re-align for the return trip. They stay alive by obtaining water from Martian snow. At last the day to return to Earth arrives, but as they are preparing for launch, Imoto notices that one of the experimental seeds planted in the alien soil has sprouted, indicating that humankind has brought life to a barren world. Some well-timed Martian earthquakes create suspense during the takeoff scene, but the spaceship manages to reach escape velocity to take the weary space explorers home.

Competently directed by Byron Haskin, who had helmed Pal's *The War of the Worlds* (1953) and *The Naked Jungle* (1954), *Conquest of Space* was a reasonably well-made SF adventure. Special effects were provided by Hollywood veteran John P. Fulton, who had worked on visual effects for scores of films going back to *The Invisible Man* (1933), and Chesley Bonestell's astronomical art once more splendidly depicted the grandeur of the universe. On the downside, the acting by its little-known actors is wooden, and the script is replete with outer spatial dangers that promptly materialize on cue.

The film's biggest flaw is that it seems like an interplanetary rehash of *Destination Moon,* in which scenes and situations from the earlier film are replayed. These include the grotesque stretching of the astronaut's faces during multi–G rocket accelerations, a perilous spacewalk due to an equipment malfunction, an endangered blast-off on the voyage home and a wisecracking astronaut from Brooklyn. Comedian Phil Foster, best known for his role as Laverne's dad on the TV sitcom *Laverne & Shirley,* practically steals the movie playing the goofy Brooklynite Sgt. Siegel. The characters are so two-dimensional that even General Merritt's descent into space madness has little emotional valence.

Regardless of the film's shortcomings, it left its mark on future science fiction movies. The space funeral sequence became a staple of later sci-fi flicks, including *The Black Hole* (1979), *Alien* (1979), *Star Trek II: The Wrath of Khan* (1982) and *Starship Troopers* (1997). The film's wheel-shaped space station spinning in orbit around the Earth was later featured in *2001* (1968). Pal and Haskin revisited the exploration of the Red Planet in their 1964 effort *Robinson Crusoe on Mars* (to be discussed in Chapter Seven).

The film's conceptions of space travel were drawn from Wernher von Braun's 1952 book *The Mars Project.* Von Braun envisioned a Mars-bound spacecraft being launched from a massive orbiting space station on a nine-month interplanetary journey. The winged spaceship employed aerodynamic lift to make a soft landing on Mars' south polar region, where the spacefarers extract water from the ice cap. While a Mars voyage would likely be made by a spacecraft assembled in Earth orbit, what we now know about the planet's environment makes von Braun's scenario untenable. The atmosphere of Mars is much too thin to provide lift for a heavy winged vehicle, and while the planet's polar caps are thought to contain some water ice, it is mixed with frozen carbon dioxide, so extracting water would likely prove problematical. The film is correct, however, in having the astronauts need to wait for months until Earth and Mars are in their proper positions for the return trip.

After *Conquest of Space,* Pal eschewed realistic space exploration movies for nearly a decade, and in the interim the sci-fi genre embraced thrillers featuring monsters. In *King Dinosaur* (1955), a spacecraft crash-lands on the planet Nova, where the astronauts are menaced by a gaggle of vicious dinosaurs (actually a bunch of photographically magnified lizards). A rocketship returns from an expedition to Venus with a gelatinous egg that hatches a creature that grows to monstrous size in *20 Million Miles to Earth* (1957). In *It—The Terror from Beyond Space* (1958), a monster stows away on a spaceship returning from Mars and proceeds to slay members of the crew.

Sparked by UFO reports, movies featuring flying saucers were also very popular during the 1950s. In the popular imagination, the saucers were believed to be spacecraft flown from other planets, operated by alien beings. A couple of big-budget film from this period depicted humans traveling to other worlds in saucer-shaped craft. In Universal's *This Island Earth* (1955), two Earth scientists are abducted by aliens and transported across the gulf of interstellar space to the planet Metaluna, where they are expected to use their nuclear expertise to aid the Metalunans in their war against their enemies, the Zaghons. The film was shot in color and sported production values on a par with George Pal's space epics. Its flying saucer was an elaborate model that weighed 18 pounds. Its palatial interior was a set built on a large Universal stage. An exercise in pulp fiction space opera, the film nevertheless depicted the first journey through interstellar space by human beings in screen history.

While the humans transported to the stars in *This Island Earth* were mere passengers, the flying saucer in MGM's *Forbidden Planet* (1956) was flown by a cadre of space cadets from Earth. As the film opens a narration informs the audience, "In the final decades of the 21st century, men and women in rocketships landed on the Moon. By 2200 A.D., they had reached the other planets of our solar system. Almost at once there followed the discovery of hyperdrive, through which the speed of light was first attained, and later greatly surpassed. And so at last mankind began the conquest and colonization of deep space."

The crew of the saucer shaped United Planets cruiser C-57D has traveled to the planet Altair IV to investigate the mysterious disappearance of a group of colonists. Landing on the bleak world, they confront a mad scientist, his beautiful daughter, a sophisticated robot and the still-functioning great machine built by a vanished alien race that materializes homicidal "monsters from the Id" from the depths of the human mind. The film does not reveal the ship's power source, but it is steered by an "astrogator" who orients the craft using a transparent globe engraved with a schematic of the stars. MGM effects technicians constructed an elaborate model of a flying saucer that was 88 inches in diameter, and the film's production design featured a full-sized mock-up of the spacecraft resting on its massive landing gear on the planet's surface.

Alas, both *This Island Earth* and *Forbidden Planet* were expensive to produce and underperformed at the box office. Although they are considered two of the most

United Planets cruiser C-57D lands on planet Altair IV in a distant star system in *Forbidden Planet* **(1956).**

memorable genre films of the decade, their financial failure signaled the death knell for George Pal–style science fiction epics for the remainder of the 1950s. These flights of fancy would soon be superseded by the real world of rockets, astronauts and exploratory probes to other worlds as the American and Russian space programs lifted off into the cosmos on journeys of scientific discovery.

Before people had actually flown in space, there was much uncertainty as to how the human body would function in the weightless environment. Medicos theorized that eyeballs would explode, or that the heart or brain of a space traveler would cease to function in the hostile, zero gravity vacuum, and a number of films of the period fancifully addressed these uncertainties. In the British film *The Quatermass Xperiment* (1955), the first rocket probe into space returns to Earth with an astronaut who has been infected with an alien organism that slowly transforms him into a giant amoeba-like creature. Another British entry, *First Man into Space* (1959) featured a spaceship pilot whose body gets coated with extraterrestrial gunk that turns him into a vampire. Most embarrassing of all, an astronaut returns from the first space flight through the Van Allen radiation belt having been impregnated with several alien embryos in *Night of the Blood Beast* (1958). In all of these films,. pioneering spacefarers on their initial journey into the void were infected with horrific life forms. (Outer space would eventually turn out to be biologically sterile.)

The critical and popular success of the Disney 1954 adaptation of Jules Verne's *20,000 Leagues Under the Sea* led to a number of films based on the pioneering SF author's work, including *Around the World in 80 Days* (1956), *The Fabulous World of Jules Verne* (1958), *Journey to the Center of the Earth* (1959), *Master of the World* (1961) and *Mysterious Island* (1961). In modern parlance, these films would be considered examples of "steampunk," that is, retro science fiction set in the 19th century. A screen adaptation of Verne's novel *From the Earth to the Moon* was lensed in 1958 by Byron Haskin, who had directed the interplanetary saga *Conquest of Space*.

The narrative begins in 1865, after the end of the Civil War, during a dinner meeting of the International Armaments Club, an organization of war profiteers. Maverick weapons manufacturer Victor Barbicane (Joseph Cotten) makes a startling announcement. He has invented a new explosive called Power X and is seeking financial support to develop the material, which he believes will eventually bring an end to war between nations. His rival, former Confederate armorer Stuyvesant Nicholl (George Sanders), has also developed a technological breakthrough in the form of a super-hard metal, and wagers $100,000 that it can withstand Power X. A demonstration is arranged in which Barbicane fires a projectile containing his explosive at a sheet of Nicholl's wonder metal—which is instantly obliterated. At the conclusion of the experiment, Barbicane discovers that fragments of the metal have fused into a lightweight, heat-resistant ceramic substance.

Barbicane builds a small town in an uninhabited area to work on developing his explosive, but during the process he is called to Washington for a clandestine meeting with President Ulysses S. Grant (Morris Ankrum). The president is dismayed by Barbicane's experiments because foreign nations believe that America is developing Power X as a weapon of war, and he entreats the inventor to shut down the project. Barbicane decides to redirect his efforts into constructing a spacecraft capable of reaching the Moon. Toward this goal he collaborates with his rival Nicholl in building the Moon ship out of the ceramic material derived from his metal. The spacecraft will be propelled by Power X.

The scientists toil mightily on their spaceship until it is ready for launch. Amid much pomp and circumstance, the *Columbiad* blasts off for the Moon in a thunderous explosion amid cheering crowds. On board are Barbicane, Nicholl and Barbicane's assistant Ben Sharpe (Don Dubbins). What no one knows is that Nicholl has secretly sabotaged the ship's gyrocompass because he believes that Barbicane has violated God's laws and wishes to kill him.

As they leave the Earth behind, Sharpe discovers that Nicholl's daughter Virginia (Debra Paget) has stowed away. Nicholl must now cooperate with Barbicane to repair the spacecraft as a close encounter with a meteor swarm complicates their task. They do not succeed, and Sharpe and Virginia are sent back toward Earth in a modular section that detaches from the main part of the ship. The *Columbiad* lands on the lunar surface with Barbicane and Nicholl aboard.

Attempting to cash in on the popular and critically acclaimed *20,000 Leagues Under the Sea* and *Around the World in 80 Days*, the production began life at RKO, but was abandoned when the studio went bankrupt. The project was subsequently picked up and completed by Warners. The Moon landing, which should have been one of the film's high points, takes place off screen, possibly as a result of a budget cut. In addition, the fates of Barbicane and Nicholl, who will presumably perish from lack of life support on the Moon, and the fate of Sharpe and Virginia on their trip back to Earth, is similarly unclear as scenarists Robert Blees and James Leicester play fast and loose with the plot of Verne's novel. Screen veterans Joseph Cotten and George Sanders turn in workmanlike but uninspired performances.

The *Columbiad* resembles a modern rocket much more than a ballistic projectile; it has plush, Victorian-style interiors. Note that the plot elements consisting of a crew member sabotaging the space mission and the peril of a meteor collision had previously appeared in Haskin's *Conquest of Space*. Critics have pointed to the film's antiwar theme of mutually assured destruction, with the fictional Power X substituting for the Cold War era's nuclear weapons. For some reason, the filmmakers resorted to using the electronic music score composed by Louis and Bebe Barron for MGM's 1956 space opera *Forbidden Planet* during the space scenes, their avant-garde "tonalities" providing a jarring futuristic soundscape that is at odds with the film's 19th-century setting. Director Haskin went on to helm the acclaimed *Robinson Crusoe on Mars* in 1964.

Verne's novel received a comic treatment in *Jules Verne's Rocket to the Moon* (1967). In this iteration, "inspired by the writings of Jules Verne" and set in Victorian England, German scientist Von Bulow (*Goldfinger*'s Gert Frobe) conducts a public demonstration of his novel explosive and so impresses American impresario P.T. Barnum (Burl Ives) that Barnum decides to bankroll Von Bulow's experiments. Famed aviator Gaylord Sullivan (Troy Donahue) is assigned to construct a Moon rocket powered by the savant's explosive substance, but the spaceship's design only allows for a one-way trip. Two bunglers, Dillworthy (Lionel Jeffries) and Washington-Smythe (Terry-Thomas), who have embezzled funds from the project, attempt to sabotage the spaceship with the aid of Russian spy Bulgeroff (Joachim Teege). Traveling to the launch site in Wales, the trio accidentally activates Gaylord's rocket, which sends them on a one-way ride to the Moon. A group of Russians is already there. This forgettable British satire of Verne's work, directed by Don Sharo and written by Dave Freeman, was released under the alternative titles *Blast Off* and *Those Fantastic Flying Fools*.

The other seminal steampunk lunar exploration novel, H.G. Wells' *The First Men in the Moon*, got the big screen treatment in 1964. Filmed in Panavision, Technicolor and Dynamation as *First Men in the Moon*, it begins with a startling discovery made by a team of United Nations astronauts who have made the first Moon landing in 1964. A tattered Union Jack flag is found on the lunar surface, along with a note from one Katherine Callender that claims the Moon for Queen Victoria. Katherine has been dead for some time, but a pair of UN investigators (Hugh McDermott and Margaret Hoy) manage to trace her husband, Arthur Bedford (Edward Judd), to a nursing home, where he relates the story of his lunar voyage in flashback.

In 1899, in the small English village of Dymchurch, Bedford makes the acquaintance of eccentric Professor Joseph Cavor (Lionel Jeffries). Cavor purchases a cottage from Bedford where he conducts experiments with his invention, a paste-like anti-gravity substance he calls Cavorite. The professor proposes to use a Cavorite-infused spaceship to travel to the Moon, where he expects to find extensive gold deposits. Bedford and his fiancée Katherine (Martha Hyer) accompany Cavor to the Moon in a spherical spaceship.

The explorers have nothing to eat but canned sardines on their journey and must cope with the novelty of weightlessness. After a rough landing on the lunar surface, Bedford and Cavor don deep-sea diving suits equipped with scuba-like oxygen tanks and set out to explore the Moon. After bouncing around in the reduced gravity, they fall into an cavern where they encounter a diminutive race of insectoids that Cavor dubs Selenites. Even worse, they find that the Cavorite sphere, with Kate inside, has been transported into the Selenite's underground realm.

The Earthlings are attacked by a "Moon Cow," an alien beast that resembles a humongous caterpillar. It is neutralized by the Moon men's laser weapons. Taken into custody by the Selenites, they witness the marvels of their subterranean city, including a machine that uses solar energy to produce power and oxygen via perpetual motion. Bedford and Cavor are brought before the Selenites' ruler, the Grand Lunar, who strikes up a long conversation with Cavor about human society and technology. After learning about the Earthling's propensity for war, the Grand Lunar comes to the conclusion that there should be no contact between the civilizations, leading Bedford to conclude that the humans will not be allowed to return home. Cavor elects to remain with the Selenites, but Bedford shoots his way back to the ship and he and Kate manage to take off.

Back in 1964, the now aged Bedford relates how the Cavorite sphere splashed down in the Indian Ocean off the island of Zanzibar and sank beneath the waves as he and Kate swam ashore. On television, he and the UN investigators watch the live feed from the Moon as the astronauts reach the underground Selenite city, and find it decrepit and uninhabited. They come to the conclusion that the entire civilization was destroyed by a cold virus (spread among them by Cavor), to which they had no natural immunity.

The film was conceived by producer Charles H. Schneer as a showcase for stop-motion animator Ray Harryhausen, whose work had enlivened the financially successful fantasy classics *The 7th Voyage of Sinbad* (1958) and *Jason and the Argonauts* (1963). As such, the treatment of Wells' work is much closer to fantasy than science fiction. The real star of the movie is Harryhausen's effects, but the Disney-esque comic antics in the early scenes detract from the seriousness of the Moon sequences. *First Men* was scripted by acclaimed British scenarist Nigel Kneale, who had written the entries in the classic *Quatermass* sci-fi series, and directed by science fiction veteran Nathan Juran, but these luminaries crafted a mediocre adventure programmer. It has imaginative production design and fine special effects, but it failed to score at the box office. One of the reasons for this failure is a dearth of the fantastic Harryhausen creations that graced *Sinbad* and *Jason*, both of which were replete with dragons, giants, harpies, skeleton men and the like. *First Men*'s only animated creatures are the giant caterpillar and the Selenites, who for budgetary reasons were portrayed by children wearing costumes in most scenes.

The filmmakers reportedly consulted then-current NASA blueprints in imagining their landing vehicle, *UN-1*, which bears only a passing resemblance to Apollo 11's lunar landing module *Eagle*. It's unclear how Cavor's spaceship is steered through outer space to the Moon and back; the spacefarers enmesh themselves in hanging net harnesses during takeoff and landing. Cavor and Bedford cavort about the lunar surface in diving suits that have oxygen tanks mounted on their backs, but their improvised spacesuits lack gloves, temperature control and radiation protection equipment. The filmmakers reportedly chose to depart from Wells' novel by making the Selenites extinct to comport with a more modern paradigm of a lifeless Moon. This plot device echoes the demise of the Martian invaders from the virulence of terrestrial germs in Wells' novel *The War of the Worlds*.

The science fiction film boom that began with *Destination Moon* had waned by the early 1960s. One of the main reasons was the revelations about the nature of the solar system recorded by Soviet and American unmanned spacecraft. In October 1959, the Russian Luna 3 probe took the first pictures of the far side of the Moon, and subsequent photographic missions showed no traces of Selenites or Cat-Women. In July 1965, the American Mariner 4 spacecraft returned images of Mars' surface that measured the planet's meager atmosphere and revealed no evidence of canals or other artificial structures. These data prompted the news magazine *U.S. News & World Report* to proclaim "Mars is dead" in their August 9, 1965, edition. Likewise, the Mariner 2 flyby of Venus in December 1962 indicated that the planet had an extremely hot surface temperature. When the Soviet Venera 4 probe landed on Venus in 1967, it recorded a superheated atmosphere with a pressure 90 times that of Earth. These realities demolished the long-standing science fiction myths about life and civilizations existing on our sister worlds. The advent of U.S. and Russian manned space flights in 1961 caused SF cinema to refocus its emphasis as films began to explore the implications of these new realities.

During much of this period, SF films largely shifted their emphasis away from outer space adventures to other themes, including time travel in *The Time Machine* (1960) and *The Time Travelers* (1964), the threat of nuclear apocalypse in *Panic in Year Zero!* (1962), *Dr. Strangelove* (1964), *Fail-Safe* (1964) and *The War Game* (1965), submersible adventures in *Voyage to the Bottom of the Sea* (1961), *Around the World Under the Sea* (1966) and *Captain Nemo and the Underwater City* (1969), as well as prehistoric melodramas such as *The Lost World* (1960) and *One Million Years B.C.* (1966). But the space exploration film was set to make a huge comeback in 1968 with Stanley Kubrick's brilliant sci-fi epic *2001: A Space Odyssey*.

Kubrick and acclaimed science fiction writer Arthur C. Clarke collaborated on the screenplay. It was inspired in part by Clarke's short story "The Sentinel," in which an alien artifact is discovered by space explorers on the Moon. The movie begins with the "Dawn of Man" sequence, set on the African veldt four million years in the past, where a tribe of Australopithecines (ape men) struggle to survive in the hostile environment. Their fortunes improve dramatically after they encounter a featureless black monolith that boosts their intelligence and transforms them into tool-using meat eaters. The tribe's leader, Moonwatcher (Daniel Richter), using a bone as a weapon, leads the group to dominance over a rival tribe and, ultimately, to survive and evolve into modern humans.

Four million years later, American scientist Heywood Floyd (William Sylvester) is en route to an orbiting, wheel-shaped space station in a Pan-Am *Orion* shuttlecraft. After docking, he is questioned by Russian scientists about rumors concerning an outbreak of disease at the U.S. base at Clavius crater on the Moon. Dr. Floyd deflects their queries and continues on to Clavius Base in a globular *Aries* spacecraft, and upon landing delivers an address about maintaining a cover story concerning a quarantine at the base. Dr. Floyd next boards a "Moon Bus" craft that conveys him and two other scientists across the lunar surface to the crater Tycho. On the way, he is briefed on the discovery of an anomalous object radiating a strong magnetic field that was deliberately buried millions of years ago. At the Tycho site, the men don spacesuits and approach the alien artifact, an identical black monolith that unexpectedly emits an ear-splitting radio burst aimed in the direction of the planet Jupiter.

The narrative then shifts to the *Discovery*, a 700-foot-long deep space probe traveling to Jupiter. Aboard are astronauts Dave Bowman (Keir Dullea) and Frank Poole (Gary Lockwood), along with three crew members placed in suspended animation in sarcophagus-like hibernacula. The sixth crew member is HAL, a supercomputer that runs life support and all other vital functions on the ship, and which communicates with the astronauts in a pleasant speaking voice. As the *Discovery* approaches Jupiter, HAL

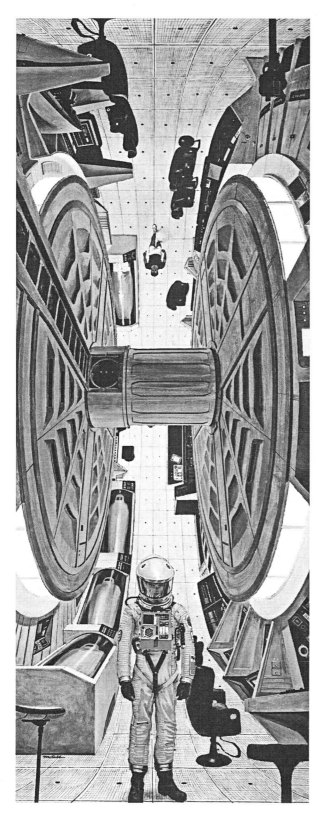

begins to act squirrelly, making mistakes that cause Bowman and Poole to contemplate shutting him down. HAL gets wind of their plans and manages to kill Poole by taking command of an EVA pod while the astronaut is repairing the ship's antenna. The computer then terminates the life functions of the three hibernating crew members. When Bowman leaves the ship to retrieve Poole's body, HAL refuses to allow him back aboard. He manages to re-enter through the emergency airlock.

Bowman shuts down the errant HAL and continues his journey to Jupiter space alone. When he reaches his destination, he locates another monolith in orbit around the giant planet and approaches it in an EVA pod to investigate. The alien artifact propels Bowman through a portal where he views distant worlds and witnesses the birth and death of stars and entire galaxies. He winds up in a plush hotel suite, where he lives out the remainder of his natural life and is reborn as a fetal "star child," the next step in the evolution of humankind. The film ends with the godlike star child suspended in space above the Earth, watching in silent contemplation.

Like the film's star child, *2001* represented the next step in the evolution of science fiction

Opposite: **Astronaut Frank Poole (Gary Lockwood) is pictured in the command module of the *Discovery* spacecraft in concept art for Stanley Kubrick's *2001: A Space Odyssey* (1968).**

cinema. Working with a budget of $10.5 million, Kubrick meticulously paid attention to detail, resulting in a space epic with a vivid realism the likes of which had never been seen. The director's vision was realized in Super Panavision by a special effects team (led by Douglas Trumbull and Con Pederson) that devised novel techniques such as sophisticated front screen projection (used to create the African veldt scenes) and the "split scan" photographic process (utilized in the "star gate" sequence). Shooting on the massive MGM stages at Boreham Wood in England, the director was able to conjure his exquisite vision of the spaceships that traversed the infinite vistas of space.

The screenplay embraces several central science fiction themes, including first contact with an alien intelligence, the exploration of space, the revolt of a self-aware artificial intelligence (called the "singularity" in SF parlance) and "post-humanism" (speculation about existence after the demise of humankind). The film's human characters are

David Bowman (Keir Dullea) prepares to enter the multi-dimensional stargate in his EVA pod in *2001: A Space Odyssey* (1968).

deliberately depicted as bland and colorless, like manikins or ghosts who are a mere transitional form between ape and star child in an evolutionary game being played by enigmatic extraterrestrials. These concepts bring a detached, anti-human quality to the film.

The film's strong suit is its depiction of a futuristic spacefaring civilization via a kind of cinematic space tourism. It takes place in Earth orbit, on the Moon, in Jupiter space, in distant galaxies and on a prehistoric Earth that resembles an alien world. The film's eye candy visuals provide a lively space travelogue to the viewer. Space travel is shown to be so commonplace and routine that it's practically boring. Dispensing with the silver rocketships of the 1950s, *2001*'s spacecraft are sophisticated and scientifically accurate. The *Orion* shuttlecraft is a winged space plane launched into orbit by a reusable first stage that returns to Earth as a conventional airplane. This concept anticipates the design of the Space Shuttle vehicle, which employed a pair of recyclable solid rocket boosters to propel it into space, from which it returned as a winged glider. The *Aries* Moon transport is basically a greatly scaled-up version of the Lunar Module used to land Apollo astronauts on the Moon.

Some of the other space hardware is a bit problematical. The enormous wheel-shaped space station had a diameter of 1000 feet and rotated to produce an artificial gravity effect generated by centrifugal force around its perimeter. This was a concept that dated back to the 1950s (a similar space wheel was featured in Pal's *Conquest of Space* [1955]), but it has never been put into practice because scientists believe that the constant rotation might induce motion sickness in spacefarers. Clavius base, an imposing facility constructed underneath the Moon surface, would constitute an enormous engineering undertaking. The *Discovery* Jupiter spaceship was 700 feet long with a spherical command module in which the astronauts were housed in front. The command module rotated to create artificial gravity so that the astronauts' bodies would not degenerate after exposure to zero G for long periods during long-duration space flight.

Conspicuously absent from *2001*'s space hardware are the launch vehicles used to send all this material up the gravity well into Earth orbit and beyond, which would need to be truly massive. In the real world, the contemporaneous Saturn V rocket needed 7.6 million pounds of thrust to send the Apollo spacecraft, which weighed a little over 10,000 pounds, into orbit. The enormous rocketry that would be needed to loft the components of a 1000-foot space station, the elements of an underground Moon base and a huge interplanetary spaceship are still beyond the imagination of engineers or the economics of space planners 50-plus years after the film.

Kubrick's visual mastery and technical acuity enabled him to create space environments that had a stunning verisimilitude. He received input from NASA individuals such as scientist Frederick Ordway, administrator Dr. George Mueller and astronaut Deke Slayton in designing the spaceships of the future, which were elaborately detailed models. The *Orion* Pan Am shuttle was a three-foot model; the globular *Aries* Moon lander measured two feet in diameter. The Space Station model was eight feet across and was lit with tiny air-cooled lights inside. Most impressive of all, the *Discovery* ship was 54 feet long with a six-foot-diameter circular command module at his head.

The interior sets of these spacecraft were even more impressive, such as the curved Space Station corridor that was nearly 300 feet long and 30 feet high. *Discovery*'s curvilinear command module was mounted on a $750,000 centrifuge that rotated behind the actors to create the illusion that the astronauts were walking along its rim in artificial gravity. Elaborate wirework was employed to simulate weightlessness in a more realistic fashion than anything that had previously been achieved. In April 1969, the film received an Academy Award for its special effects, and the British Film Academy Awards for cinematography, art direction and sound. Mercilessly panned by media critics, *2001* went on to become an enormous financial success. All in all, it set a new standard for special effects and production design that would not be equaled for decades, while its mystical and mysterioso thematics remain unique in SF annals.

Pal's *Destination Moon* and Kubrick's *2001* neatly bookend the nearly two decades between 1950 and 1968 during which the exploration of space transitioned from fantasy to reality. Both films embraced hard science fiction concepts inspired by major SF luminaries (Robert A. Heinlein and Arthur C. Clarke), and both were visionary, seminal works. Nine months after the release of *2001*, in December 1968, the Apollo 8 mission took astronauts into orbit around the Moon, and in July 1969, Apollo 11 landed Neil Armstrong and Buzz Aldrin on the lunar surface. Cinema was poised to focus on more realistic depictions of the exploration of space, starting with the beginnings of the space program.

THREE

Getting into Space

After the end of World War II, the Americans and the Soviets scrambled to acquire rocket technology that had been developed by German scientists during the war. Head rocketeer Wernher von Braun and his team surrendered to the Allies and were allowed to immigrate to America, where they were tasked with developing rocketry for the U.S. In 1950, Von Braun and his rocket scientists were installed in a testing facility in Huntsville, Alabama, where they began by working on improvements to their wartime V-2 missiles. During this period, the Air Force was also developing rocket-powered aircraft designed to fly faster than the speed of sound. On October 14, 1947, Chuck Yaeger broke the so-called "sound barrier" piloting the Bell X-1 rocket plane, which resulted in further experimentation with rocket-propelled aircraft that would fly to the edge of space. The 1957 launch of the Soviet Sputnik satellite led to the inception of the American Mercury program to launch astronauts into space in 1958. These early days of space exploration were chronicled in a number of films released both before and many years after this seminal period of space flight.

Set against the backdrop of 1950s-era flying saucer invasion flicks and flights of fantasy to alien worlds were the works of Hungarian-born producer Ivan Tors. Like George Pal, Tors preferred to produce "hard" science fiction films that embraced speculative scientific concepts. *Riders to the Stars* (1954) was a modest exploration of a fictional program to launch the first humans into space. Dr. Donald Stanton (Herbert Marshall) heads the Office of Scientific Investigation, which is experiencing difficulty with the metals used in their rockets. They are unable to withstand the effects of cosmic rays in the environment of space. He believes that the answer lies in materials found in meteors and assembles a cadre of men who will fly into space to capture meteors before they are incinerated in Earth's atmosphere. Twelve potential space jockeys are selected and brought to a launch facility at Snake Mountain Proving Grounds. All of them are unmarried, and all have military or scientific backgrounds.

The candidates are subjected to a battery of psychological and physiological tests, including exposure to extremes in temperature and high-G turns in a centrifuge. Ultimately, three men are selected to be astronauts: Dr. Jerry Lockwood (Richard Carlson), Walter Gordon (Robert Karnes) and Dr. Stanton's son Dr. Richard Stanton (William Lundigan). The plan is to launch all three in separate rocketships to capture meteors in scoop-like attachments in the rocket's nose. The spaceships are equipped with wings that will enable them to glide through the Earth's atmosphere and land like an airplane.

When their training is completed, the trio is launched a few hundred miles into space on a ballistic arc that will take them through a meteor swarm. Gordon's ship makes first contact with a meteor, but it is larger than the scoop, and his rocket is destroyed. When Lockwood spies Gordon's corpse, which has somehow been reduced to a desiccated, spacesuited skeleton, floating past his spaceship, he panics and flies off to his death in deep space. Only Stanton succeeds in snaring a meteor, but he uses up too much fuel in the attempt and crash-lands. He survives, and the meteor is found to be composed of a crystallized carbon compound, which will be used to deflect cosmic rays for future journeys into outer space.

Riders to the Stars was directed by actor Carlson, who appeared in a number of '50s sci-fi classics, including *It Came from Outer Space* (1953) and *Creature from the Black Lagoon* (1954). It features a serious-minded cast of earnest '50s-era space cadets. In addition to the hotshot astronauts, actress Martha Hyer has an interesting role playing one of the period's obligatory female savants, Dr. Jane Flynn, who yearns to experience space flight but, because of her gender, is not considered fit for such an undertaking. The film was scripted by the venerable Curt Siodmak, who had authored a number of classic horror films in addition to science fiction movies *and* novels.

The film is very much in the space exploration vein first mined by *Destination Moon*, but unlike Pal's film, it takes a more documentarian approach. We are shown stock footage showing the launch of a WAC Corporal rocket (basically a souped-up version of von Braun's V-2), along with an experimental film showing white mice coping with weightlessness. The centrifuge seen in the film was a real machine operated by the University of Southern California. The film's central premise of finding spaceworthy material in meteors is pseudo-scientific nonsense, but carbon composite materials are utilized in modern aerospace applications. The effect of cosmic rays and other forms of radiation constitutes a serious hazard during long-duration space flights, but are nowhere near as dire as they are depicted in the film, and the skeleton inside the spacesuit adds a touch of horror to the proceedings. It was the first film to depict men undergoing arduous training and preparation for space flight, something that would become a reality a few years later with the inception of the American Mercury program (as depicted in 1983's *The Right Stuff*).

The second Tors production that revolved around space research was *Gog* (1954), an atypical '50s–era programmer released in color and 3-D. The entire narrative takes place in a top secret space research facility concealed deep under the New Mexico desert. As the film opens, two scientists (Michael Fox and Aline Towne) conducting space survival experiments inexplicably find themselves locked inside a chamber that produces extreme cold and they freeze to death. Soon afterward, Dr. David Sheppard (Richard Egan), an investigator from the Office of Scientific Investigation in Washington, D.C., arrives at the base by helicopter to look into incidents of sabotage and meets with head scientist Dr. Van Ness (Herbert Marshall) and his assistant, Joanna Merritt (Constance Dowling). Van Ness fills him in on the U.S. program to launch a manned space station into orbit that will act as a spy platform able to deploy a weapon (using hi-tech mirrors) to focus solar power into a directed energy beam. Sheppard also learns that all automated functions on the base are controlled by NOVAC, an acronym for the facility's Nuclear Variable Automatic Computer. Several miniaturized radar beacons have been discovered in the facility that were somehow planted by saboteurs.

Joanna escorts Sheppard on a tour of the base, which extends five levels underground and houses 150 of the nation's top scientists. He is issued a radiation badge that will change color if levels become dangerously high. They visit the laboratory of scientists Dr. Pierre Elzevir (Philip Van Zandt) and his wife (Valerie Vernon), who are developing the solar mirror technology that will power the space station and arm it with a beam weapon. In the human factors lab, they observe Dr. Carter (Byron Kane) putting human subjects through their paces in a chamber that can produce reduced levels of gravity. Their next stop is the facility where NOVAC is being tended to by cyberneticist Dr. Zeitman (John Wengraf), who explains the workings of the electronic brain and displays the lab's twin utility robots, Gog and Magog, 600-pound automata that sport four manipulator arms and ride on tank treads. Zeitman must run a program on NOVAC to control the robots. The base's security officer, Major Howard (Stephen Roberts), feels that overflights by an unknown supersonic aircraft may be linked to sabotage events at the facility.

Mysterious deaths continue to plague the base as Sheppard and Van Ness search for answers. One scientist is killed by a radiation overdose and two human subjects die when a centrifuge goes out of control. Mrs. Elzevir narrowly avoids being fried by beams from the solar mirror when the device comes under the control of outside forces. Then Major Howard succumbs to severe acoustic vibrations from a sound detector as the mystery aircraft flies over the base once more. Sheppard and Joanna learn that the robot Magog has gone missing while NOVAC was deactivated, which is seemingly impossible because it is directly controlled by the brain machine. They theorize that the Gog and Magog are controlled by the outside forces.

Gog comes alive and attacks Zeitman, who dies after telling Sheppard how to disable the robots with a flamethrower. Magog has gone down to the level where the base's atomic reactor is housed, with the intent of severing a safety rod that will result in a nuclear explosion. As Sheppard races to stop Magog, he phones Van Ness to tell him that the unknown aircraft is controlling the robots; Van Ness orders jet fighters to scramble and chase after the plane. In the reactor control room, Sheppard and Joanna attack Magog, and Sheppard takes it out with a flamethrower and repairs the control rod. Gog arrives to finish the job. Sheppard's flamethrower is out of fuel, but high over the base the fighter planes intercept the mystery plane and shoot it down. With the controlling signal cut off, the robot stops dead in its tracks.

Joanna's badge shows that she has sustained a dangerous dose of radiation. As she recovers in the base hospital, Van Ness explains that a foreign power had implanted devices inside NOVAC and the robots while they were being built, that allowed them to be remotely controlled by commands from the aircraft flying over the facility. The craft turns out to have been a rocket plane constructed out of fiberglass (rendering it invisible to radar), sent by a hostile foreign power (presumably the Soviet Union) to compromise our space program. The film concludes with stock footage of a V-2 rocket taking off to launch the space station that will herald the beginning of an American space age.

Like *Riders to the Stars*, *Gog* anticipates America's entry into the space race. Unlike the earlier film, however, *Gog* also deals with the stock science fiction themes of errant electronic brains and homicidal robots. Director Herbert L. Strock packs the film with loads of 1950s-era fantastic technology and futuristic thrills, and although it's overly talky at times, it does build to an intriguing and satisfying climax. The robots are highly original in concept, and unlike many other cinematic automata do not resemble human beings. The out-of-control computer NOVAC anticipates later murderous cybernetic brains in *2001* (1968) and *Colossus: The Forbin Project* (1970). The five-level, super-secret underground facility located in the middle of a desert was later replicated in *The Andromeda Strain* (1971). While it has fallen into an undeserved obscurity today, *Gog* has the distinction of being the first science fiction film in color and 3-D, a combination that would not occur again until *Avatar* (2009).

Screenwriters Tom Taggart and Richard G. Taylor, working from a story by producer Tors, trot out an array of futuristic technologies, most of which are pure pseudo-science. Before humans had actually been launched into space, many exotic notions about what might be required abounded in movies. In the film, a monkey is frozen solid and later revived during an experiment that suggests that such a procedure would be useful to ensure survival by astronauts in the extreme cold of space. Solar power is routinely used to provide power to spacecraft, but not in the manner depicted in the film. The chamber in which various modes of gravity are simulated is pure fantasy, but the badges that change colors to indicate heightened levels of radioactivity are real and are used to ensure safety in the closed environment of nuclear submarines. Interestingly, the radar-evading plane anticipates modern-day stealth aircraft, although they are not made out of fiberglass and rocket-powered airplanes have a short flight duration because they consume fuel rapidly and would not be suitable for long-range flights.

The names Gog and Magog are derived from the Bible, where they refer to a pair of godless, pagan tribes. Unlike most SF films of the era, which usually featured a single female scientist inserted into the plot merely to provide some cheesecake and be menaced by the monster, *Gog* depicted several women researchers working alongside their male colleagues, and at one point Joanna Merritt quips, "In space, there is no such thing as the weaker sex." Tors went on to produce the hard science fiction TV series *Science Fiction Theatre*, which ran on syndication from 1955 to 1957 and featured the work of directors such as Jack Arnold and William Castle.

By 1960, the American-Soviet space race was in full swing, and films portraying space travel began to shift from science fiction to science fact as fantasy was overtaken by reality. The Wernher von Braun biopic *I Aim at the Stars* (1960) moved away from sci-fi entirely into the realm of drama, biography and technological history. It chronicles von Braun's controversial career, beginning with a young Wernher (Gunther Mruwka) experimenting with a rocket that burns down a neighbor's greenhouse. The adult von Braun (Curt Jurgens) continues his rocket experiments as technical director of the Peenemunde Rocket Center, developing missiles for the German Army during the 1930s, while he secretly yearns to engineer rocketry for the exploration of space. During World War II, von Braun is pressed into service developing the V-2, the world's first guided ballistic missile for the Nazi regime. The weapon wreaks havoc on London and other European cities. He is assisted in his efforts by fellow rocketeers Anton Reger (Herbert Lom), Captain Dornberger (Karel Stepanek) and Herman Oberth (Gerard Heinz).

After months of testing, the V-2 is perfected and emerges as a potent weapon of war. The film depicts the devastating Allied air attacks on the Peenemunde facility, with von Braun narrowly escaping with his life. As the war progresses, von Braun expresses anti–Nazi sentiments, and is arrested and jailed by the Gestapo for opining that rocketry should be used for space travel rather than warfare. Dornberger convinces them to release him because his talents are sorely needed for the war effort. In 1945, as Allied armies close in from the east and west, von Braun and his team choose to surrender to the Americans rather than the Soviets, and are brought to the U.S. under the auspices of Operation Paperclip to continue their rocketry experiments at Fort Bliss, Texas, and then at the Marshall Space Flight Center in Alabama.

In America, von Braun becomes a vocal proponent of space exploration, but he is taken to task by former Army Major William Taggert (James Daly), whose wife and child were killed during a V-2 attack on London. Taggert utters the film's most memorable line of dialogue, "He aims at the stars but sometimes hits London," as he brands von Braun a war criminal. Despite the public's misgivings, however, the nation turns to him when the Soviets launch the first artificial satellite (Sputnik) into space in October 1957. The film ends with von Braun's triumphal launch of the first American satellite, Explorer One, during the following year as the U.S. enters the space race.

Competently directed by J. Lee Thompson, best known for the World War II actioner *The Guns of Navarone, I Aim at the Stars* is a tightly paced, stylish production that caroms from Nazi Germany to 1950s America. Jay Dratler's screenplay touches on all the major controversies surrounding von Braun, although some critics felt that it whitewashed him by painting a portrait of a starry-eyed, apolitical dreamer who later proved himself indispensable to the American space program. Inserted into the story is a fictional American spy (Gia Scala) who infiltrates von Braun's Peenemunde operation and photographs rocket schematics with a James Bond–style miniature camera which was done to add more melodrama to the plot. One of the film's major flaws was German actor Curt Jurgens' portrayal of von Braun, who comes off as an earnest but dour individual, where the real von Braun was reportedly more witty and charming.

The film was produced by Columbia at the Bavaria Studios production facility in Geiselgasteig, Germany. Director Thompson and producer Charles H. Schneer conferred with historical advisor Walt Weisman, a wartime associate of von Braun, and received technical input from Major General John Medaris, commander of the Army Ballistic Missile Agency at Huntsville, Alabama, and Randy Morris, chief of technical liaison at the U.S. Army Ordnance Mission at White Sands Proving Ground in New Mexico. The film contains rare stock footage of V-2 launches culled from wartime German archives that will be of interest to aerospace enthusiasts.

I Aim at the Stars was not a popular success due to its controversial subject matter. There were protests in London during the film's premiere, while theaters in Antwerp, Belgium, which had been the victim of more V-2 attacks than London, refused to permit the showing of the movie.

During the nascent days of the space race, the U.S. Air Force was attempting to engineer its own space program to augment NASA's. Instead of launching astronauts inside a tiny capsule mounted atop a ballistic rocket (derisively referred to as the "Spam in a can" approach), the Air Force was committed to developing rocket-powered aircraft designed to send men into space under a pilot's control. In 1947, Air Force test pilot Chuck Yaeger broke the sound barrier flying the Bell X-1 rocket plane, and in the years that followed, other experimental aircraft were developed and tested at Edwards Air Force Base in California. The culmination of these efforts was the North American X-15, a rocket-powered aircraft designed to fly at hypersonic speeds that would propel pilots to the edge of space; journalists dubbed it "America's first space ship." The X-15 was mated to a B-52 bomber and flown to an altitude of 40,000 feet, where it separated from the mother ship, ignited its rocket engine and took off like the proverbial bat out of Hell. When its rocket fuel was exhausted, the plane glided to a landing on the dry lake bed at Edwards. In 1958, producer-screenwriter Tony Lazzarino began developing a film project that would dramatize the Air Force's space efforts, and received support from the Pentagon for his semi-documentary *X-15* (1961).

The film relates the exploits of three test pilots, Lt. Colonel Lee Brandon (Charles Bronson), Major Ernest Wilde (Ralph Taeger) and NASA civilian Matt Powell (David McLean), along with the travails of project administrator Tom Deparma (James Gregory). From its inception, the X-15 program is plagued with technical problems. A launch must be scrubbed due to a glitch, and the static test of a new rocket engine leads to an explosion, much to the chagrin of Deparma, who must explain these failures to a skeptical press corps. The pilot's wives Margaret (Patricia Owens), Diane (Lisabeth Hush) and Pamela (Mary Tyler Moore) must endure the uncertainties posed by their spouses' dangerous and potentially fatal undertaking.

Once the bugs have been worked out, the X-15 program begins to bear fruit. Brandon breaks the world speed record when he pushes the rocket plane to Mach 5, five times the speed of sound. On the next flight, Wilde is set to take the X-15 into outer space, but an engine flameout causes him to return to Earth prematurely. The rocketship manages to land safety, but Brandon, who is flying a chase plane, is killed when his jet malfunctions at low altitude and explodes in a massive fireball. Pushing ahead, Powell makes the next flight, during which the X-15 reaches the edge of space. The rocket plane returns safely to Edwards at the conclusion of its first successful voyage into the new frontier.

The best thing about *X-15* is the documentary footage of the aircraft in action provided by the Air Force, although the visuals are marred by being converted from 1:37 aspect ratio in which they were originally filmed into Panavision anamorphic widescreen format. This makes the aircraft appear stretched as the images are noticeably distorted in the horizontal dimension. Even so, it's a thrill for aerospace enthusiasts to watch the X-15 fire its rocket engine and streak away over the horizon from the chase plane, leaving nothing but a contrail behind. Ad copy for the film proclaimed breathlessly that the movie was "actually filmed in space," but in reality only a few seconds of footage show the transition from the blue sky of the stratosphere to the blackness of outer space. External shots of the rocketship in space were made using a model and special effects.

This was the first directorial effort by Richard Donner, who went on to helm the popular *The Omen, Superman* and *Lethal Weapon*. The bare bones of the documentary footage are knitted together with dramatic scenes of the pilot's wives and the project director's verbal jousts with the press, to form a coherent narrative. Donner handles these scenes reasonably well, and the film is graced by the gruff screen presence of Charles Bronson and the charms of a youthful Mary Tyler Moore. Made during a period of patriotic filmmaking cooperation between Hollywood and the Pentagon, the film was produced by Frank Sinatra's Essex Productions, and narrated by veteran actor and World War II aviator James Stewart.

The X-15 program went on to break speed and altitude records, flying in excess of Mach 6, and several of its pilots who crossed the boundary of the Karman Line into space were awarded astronaut's wings. Two of its most illustrious test pilots were Scott Crossfield and future Apollo 11 commander Neil Armstrong. The X-15 was expected to evolve into the X-20 Dyna-Soar, a true space plane that would be launched into space on a ballistic booster and flown back to Earth like a conventional aircraft *à la* the Space Shuttle, but as NASA's Mercury and Gemini programs progressed, Congress decided that it could not fund two competing space programs, and the Air Force space effort was scrubbed.

NASA was established in July 1958, during the Eisenhower administration. Its primary development and test facility was the Langley Research Center in Langley,

Virginia. In December 1958, America's manned space program, Project Mercury, was announced to the public. By April 1959, seven aviators had been chosen from the ranks of the Air Force, Navy and Marines to be the first Americans in space. Dubbed the Mercury 7 by the press, the astronauts had been subjected to a rigorous selection and testing process to ensure their ability to withstand the rigors of space flight. America's first spacefarers won worldwide acclaim and were a source of national pride during those years.

While the missions of the Mercury 7 were lauded by the media at the time, it was not until several decades later that their stories were brought to the big screen. In 1979, journalist Tom Wolfe published *The Right Stuff*, a work of narrative non-fiction that followed two basic storylines. It contrasted the exploits of test pilot Chuck Yaeger, who made the first supersonic flight in the X-1 rocket plane in 1947 and labored in relative obscurity, with the fame and fortune accorded to the Mercury astronauts by an adoring public. Wolfe's satiric and often sardonic account of military aviation culture was adapted for the screen in Philip Kaufman's epic production *The Right Stuff* (1983).

The film opens with the sound of wind and images of something hurtling through the clouds as a narrator intones, "There was a demon who lived in the air," namely the sound barrier. As airplanes approach the speed of sound at 750 miles per hour, they experience severe buffeting and loss of control due to what is called "compressibility." A group of elite aviators dedicated to breaking through the barrier has assembled at Muroc Air Force Base in California. "They were called test pilots," the narrator relates, "and no one knew their names." The Bell X-1 rocket-powered aircraft is being tested at Muroc. Previous attempts to go supersonic have led to a series of catastrophic failures.

The test pilots congregate at the Happy Bottom Riding Club, a desert saloon operated by retired aviator Pancho Barnes (Kim Stanley). Air Force project managers have gathered at Pancho's, where they are attempting to recruit a test pilot to fly the X-1. Civilian pilot Scott Crossfield (Scott Wilson) offers to make the attempt for a mere $150,000 and is turned down. When Air Force pilot Chuck Yaeger (Sam Shepard) is approached, he agrees to make the flight for nothing more than his modest officer's salary. That night, while he is out horseback-riding through the desert with his wife Glennis (Barbara Hershey), he falls off his horse and breaks two ribs. Fearing that he may not be permitted to make the flight, he secretly visits a civilian doctor and has the ribs taped. He will have limited use of his left hand until the ribs heal.

Arriving on the flight line the next day, Yaeger confides to his buddy, B-29 pilot Jack Ridley (Levon Helm), that he will be unable to use his left hand to secure the hatch on the X-1. Ridley saws off the end of a broom handle for Yaeger to use as a lever to close the hatch. The X-1 is carried aloft, mated to a four-engine B-29 bomber, and at the appointed time Yaeger crawls into the rocket plane and closes the hatch with the broom handle. When he is dropped from the mother ship, Yaeger fires the X-1's rocket engine and streaks away. He fights to maintain control of the aircraft, experiencing severe instability as the plane pushes the envelope toward supersonic speed. Ground observers hear an explosive sound and think that the X-1 has crashed, but it is the sound of a sonic boom, indicating that Yaeger has broken the sound barrier. In the aftermath, news of Yaeger's achievement is kept secret from the public by the military for security reasons.

Flash forward to 1953: Military pilot Gordon "Gordo" Cooper (Dennis Quaid) is reporting for duty at the former Muroc, now renamed Edwards Air Force Base, as a test pilot. At Pancho's, he meets with his former flying buddies Virgil "Gus" Grissom

(Fred Ward) and Deke Slayton (Scott Paulin), who are also assigned to test flight duties at Edwards. They are soon apprised of their status as lowly "pudknockers" compared to Yaeger, Crossfield *et al.* As the newbies settle their families into the military housing, Yaeger undertakes another risky flight in the upgraded X-1A experimental rocket plane, where he exceeds Mach 2 but nearly loses control of the aircraft.

Later in the decade, the launch of Sputnik makes an American manned space program an imperative. Test pilots from all over America are recruited for the daunting task, and Grissom, Cooper and Slayton answer the call. At the Lovelace Clinic in New Mexico, they are subjected to a battery of psychological and physiological tests to determine who is best able to endure a space flight. The "lab rats" are forced to endure extreme procedures that resemble medieval tortures at the hands of the sadistic Nurse Murch (Jane Dornacker). When all the testing is completed, America's newly minted astronauts, dubbed the Mercury 7, are introduced to the public at a press conference. Cooper, Grissom and Slayton have all made the cut, along with John Glenn (Ed Harris), Alan Shepard (Scott Glenn), Wally Schirra (Lance Henriksen) and Scott Carpenter (Charles Frank).

The seven astronauts undergo a rigorous training regimen to prepare them for space flight, but are dismayed when the rockets themselves suffer a series of catastrophic failures. Yaeger and the old guard decry the Mercury approach to flight as being "Spam in a can," in which the astronauts passively ride inside a tiny "capsule" instead of a spacecraft controlled by a pilot. Their objections become moot when Soviet cosmonaut Yuri Gagarin becomes the first person to orbit the Earth. Stung by NASA's failure, the Mercury 7 astronauts redouble their efforts to reach the high frontier. A few weeks after Gagarin's flight, Alan Shepard becomes the first American in space when he is launched on a short, sub-orbital arc during which he is weightless for 15 minutes. Shepard is feted in a New York ticker tape parade and invited to meet President Kennedy, to the delight of his wife Louise (Kathy Baker).

Next, it is Gus Grissom's turn to ride the rocket in a repeat of Shepard's flight. Things go well until the capsule splashes down. Grissom panics while waiting for the rescue helicopter to arrive and blows the escape hatch. He tumbles out of the spacecraft into the ocean, bobbing in the water while the rescue crew seems more intent on saving the capsule and ignores him. Weighted down by some rolls of dimes and tiny Mercury models he has taken into space inside his suit as souvenirs, Grissom struggles to stay afloat while the capsule takes on water and sinks. Finally pulled out of the drink, the astronaut claims that the hatch "just blew" by itself, but NASA engineers dispute his account and it is agreed that he "screwed the pooch." In the aftermath, Grissom is not accorded the accolades showered on his predecessor, much to the chagrin of his wife Betty (Veronica Cartwright).

Preparations get underway for John Glenn's flight on the more powerful Atlas rocket. He blasts off on his mission to complete seven orbits around the Earth in February 1962. The astronaut marvels at the beauty of the planet from his perch in space. On the second orbit, an indicator light in Mission Control shows that the heat shield on the underside of the Mercury capsule has become loose. If it is not in place, the spacecraft will be incinerated in the 3000-degree heat of atmosphere re-entry. For safety's sake, Mission Control decides to cut the mission short and de-orbit the capsule after only three orbits. It turns out that the indicator light was in error, and Glenn returns safely to become America's newest hero: He is honored, along with the Mercury 7 astronauts, in another massive New York ticker tape parade.

The Mercury Seven astronauts pose in front of the Mercury spacecraft in *The Right Stuff* (1983). Front, left to right, Alan Shepard (Scott Glenn), Gus Grissom (Fred Ward), Wally Schirra (Lance Henriksen) and Scott Carpenter (Charles Frank). Back, left to right, Deke Slayton (Scott Paulin), Gordon Cooper (Dennis Quaid) and John Glenn (Ed Harris).

By this time, Yaeger and the rocket jockeys at Edwards have realized that the astronauts have gone higher and faster than they ever will and are the exemplars of the "right stuff" in the public mind. Despite this, Yaeger decides to attempt to set a world altitude record in a specially modified F-104 Starfighter jet. As he soars into the wild blue yonder, the Mercury 7 are being celebrated in connection with the establishment of the new Manned Space Center in Houston. Lyndon Johnson presides over this mammoth and somewhat vulgar event being held at the cavernous Sam Houston Coliseum, complete with whole sides of barbecued beef, copious booze and an exotic dancer.

While the astronauts enjoy the entertainment from their place of honor, Yaeger struggles to gain altitude, and as he approaches the Karman boundary he catches a glimpse of the stars in the black sky of the upper atmosphere, which is as close to space as he will ever come, before he suddenly loses control of the aircraft. As the F-104 plunges earthward, Yaeger bails out, and is burned by chemicals in the helmet of his pressure suit on his way down. Jack Ridley races to the crash site with the rescue crew, where they encounter Yaeger, his face burned, marching forward heroically and presenting the very image of a man with "the right stuff." The film ends with Gordon Cooper blasting off on the last Mercury flight as the narrator intones, "For a brief moment, Gordo Cooper became the greatest pilot anyone had ever seen."

The first, and still one of the best historical docudramas about the American space program, *The Right Stuff* sparkles with wit, humor, satire and tension as test pilots and astronauts take to the skies on their quest to win the space race and become "the greatest pilot anyone had ever seen." Director Kaufman captures the spirit of the brave men who cheated death as they dared to push the envelope for patriotism and personal glory.

Gordon "Gordo" Cooper (Dennis Quaid) is ready for his first space flight in *The Right Stuff* (1983).

Kaufman lovingly recreates the American zeitgeist at the dawn of the space age with a keen satiric insight inspired by Wolfe's best-seller. The film's epic sweep never falters over its three hour–plus length. A number of comic scenes serve to lighten the tone, including Alan Shepard having to urinate inside his spacesuit during a launch delay, LBJ fuming in his limo after being snubbed by Mrs. Glenn, and Gordon Cooper falling asleep inside his capsule while waiting to be launched. Most of the satiric scenes involve the press coverage of the Mercury 7, such as the "Hallelujah Chorus" playing in the background as the astronauts are introduced to the public during a press conference, and hordes of journalists who swarm after them, accompanied by the irritating clicking of their camera shutters. None of this comedy or satire detracts from the heroic feats of America's first spacefarers.

Kaufman's production and special effects team did a marvelous job recreating historic rocket planes such as the X-1 and X-1A, and utilizing vintage aircraft like the B-29 Superfortress. Elaborate airplane models were enhanced by special effects to simulate the aircraft in flight, and documentary footage of Mercury rocket launches are seamlessly edited into the narrative. A stellar cast turns in riveting performances. The film was nominated for nine Academy Awards, including Best Picture and Best Supporting Actor for Sam Shepard, but only won for Original Score, Film Editing, Sound and Sound Editing. Critics showered acclaim upon the movie, with the influential Roger Ebert naming it the best film of 1983.

All of this having been said, Kaufman's screenplay is severely flawed as an historical account, and contains several narrative oddities. There are a number of characters who are nameless and can be described as "emblematic" or "symbolic" in nature. Chief among these are the characters played by Harry Shearer and Jeff Goldblum, who are not historical personages and are listed in the cast roster simply as "The Recruiters." Royal Dano plays a character called "The Minister," an undertaker-like personage who symbolizes the mortality of the test pilots and is tasked with delivering the bad news to their widows, a function traditionally performed in real life by the pilot's colleagues. Even head rocket designer Wernher von Braun remains nameless, being referred to only as "Chief Scientist" in the script. Other non-characters include the Head of Program and the Liaison Man.

The first draft of the screenplay was written by veteran scenarist William Goldman, who restricted the narrative to the stories of the Mercury 7 and cut out the material relating to Chuck Yeager. Kaufman rewrote it, emphasizing Yeager's contribution while denigrating that of the astronauts. Yeager is contrasted with Gordon Cooper, who is depicted as an amiable goofball to leave little doubt as to which one really had the right stuff. At the film's conclusion, Yeager is shown heroically striding forward after his near-fatal crash, while Gordo snoozes inside his Mercury capsule. Of the seven astronauts, only Cooper, Glenn, Grissom and Shepard are highlighted, while Slayton, Carpenter and Schirra are practically non-entities despite their significant contributions to the program.

The film's most egregious failure is in its treatment of Gus Grissom, who is depicted as a bit of a dim bulb and a coward. Although there was some controversy about the premature blowing of the hatch of his Mercury capsule, NASA investigated the incident thoroughly and concluded that this was due to an equipment malfunction and not human error. In the movie, Grissom is seen to have blown the hatch in a panic, but this scenario is not factually accurate. Grissom was later assigned to the first flight of the

Gemini spacecraft, something that never would have happened if NASA had lost faith in his abilities. All this was known when Kaufman was writing his script, but he apparently chose to employ creative license to denigrate the astronaut for dramatic effect. Grissom wasn't around to defend himself, as he was burned to death during the ground test of the Apollo 1 spacecraft on January 20, 1966. As to Grissom's intellect, he had a degree in aeromechanics from the U.S. Air Force Institute of Technology, and was instrumental in designing the Gemini spacecraft, which was referred to as the "Gusmobile" by the astronaut corps in his honor.

Despite the awards and critical acclaim, *The Right Stuff* proved to be a box office failure. One possible reason was that some people thought the movie had some connection with the political campaign of John Glenn, who was a U.S. Senator running for president at the time, although the film sometimes shows Glenn in a less than favorable light in the same way as he is depicted in Tom Wolfe's book.

A space docudrama of a very different kind was presented in *October Sky* (1999), the fact-based story of Homer Hickam (Jake Gyllenhaal), a coal miner's son in Coalwood, West Virginia. As the film opens in 1957, he becomes fascinated by the launch of the world's first satellite, Sputnik. Where most other townsfolk experience anxiety at the sight of the Soviet craft traveling through the October sky, Homer develops a sudden obsession with rocketry. His interest is looked down upon by his stern father John (Chris Cooper), the town's mine superintendent, who wants the boy to follow in his footsteps and work in the mine.

Homer forms an amateur rocketry club with his friends Roy Lee Cooke (William Lee Scott), Sherman O'Dell (Chad Lindberg) and math whiz Quentin Wilson (Chris Wilson). Experimenting with homemade rockets, they are encouraged by their Big Creek High School science teacher, Miss Riley (Laura Dern). The four classmates become known, somewhat derisively, as the Rocket Boys. They establish their own launch facility, Cape Coalwood, in a slag heap outside of town. They experience many failures in the process of perfecting their craft (after all, it *is* rocket science), but Ike Bykovsky (Elya Baskin), a machinist at the mining office, helps them fashion more and more successful designs. Their exploits attract the attention of the local newspaper and draw crowds of their students who watch their rockets soar into the sky. Homer even receives encouragement from Wernher von Braun, who has become his pen pal.

The Rocket Boys suffer a major setback when one of their rockets is blamed for starting a forest fire and they are arrested. As a result, they close down their operation and abandon their experiments. Then John Cooper is injured in a mining accident in which Mr. Bykovsky is killed, and Homer elects to quit school to support the family while his father recovers. As he labors in the mine, however, he continues to study rocketry from a book given to him by Miss Riley, and computes the trajectory of the errant rocket. Realizing that it could not have come down in the area where the fire started, he and Quentin conduct a search and locate their rocket in a wooded area far from the site of the fire. Armed with the mathematical proof of their innocence, John is readmitted to high school. He tells his father, who has recovered from his injuries, that he will not continue working in the mine, but intends to follow his own path in life.

Homer and the Rocket Boys enter the school science fair with a device called a de Laval nozzle, an hourglass-shaped metal tube that converts a rocket's hot gasses into kinetic energy to maximize its thrust. The boys win first prize and Homer is selected to travel to Indianapolis to participate in the National Science Fair. The de Laval nozzle is stolen from his presentation overnight, but he calls his father, who quickly arranges to have a replacement nozzle machined and rushed to the Science Fair. Homer wins first prize and is congratulated by his idol von Braun (Joe Digaetano), who is attending the event, and all four Rocket Boys are awarded college scholarships. A sad note is struck when Homer visits Miss Riley in the hospital where she is dying of Hodgkin's lymphoma, and the next launch vehicle is christened the *Miss Riley* in her honor. The rocket is launched from Cape Coalwood and reaches an altitude of 30,000 feet as Homer and his father are reconciled during the ceremony. An epilogue shows footage of the real Rocket Boys and notes that John went on to become a NASA engineer who worked on the Space Shuttle program.

Based on Homer Hickam's 1998 autobiographical memoir *Rocket Boys*, this sensitive coming-of-age story is beautifully directed by Joe Johnston. Its dreary visuals realistically capture the stifling environment of the West Virginia coal town (it was actually filmed in several rural East Tennessee locations). A fine cast brings this inspiring story of unlikely success to vivid life. Jake Gyllenhaal's portrait of the aspiring rocket scientist Homer carries the film, with an able assist from Chris Cooper as his staid father and Laura Dern as the sensitive teacher who inspires him to dream big. Screenwriter Lewis Colick does a mostly accurate job of adapting Hickam's autobiography for the big screen, although some of the events depicted either did not happen or were embellished for dramatic reasons. The film reportedly inspired Amazon billionaire Jeff Bezos to start up his aerospace company Blue Origin.

After the events depicted in the film, Homer Hickam attended Virginia Tech and graduated in 1964 with a Bachelor of Science degree in industrial engineering. He served in the U.S. Army as a second lieutenant in the Vietnam War and was awarded the Army Commendation Medal and a Bronze Star. He served six years of active duty and was separated from the military in 1970 with the rank of captain; he then worked as an engineer for the U.S. Army Aviation and Missile Command in Huntsville, Alabama. Hired as an engineer by NASA in 1981, he was employed by the Marshall Space Flight Center in Huntsville, where he worked on spacecraft design and astronaut training projects, including the training of the first Japanese astronauts for the Spacelab-J Space Shuttle mission. He eventually became the payload training manager for the International Space Station Program. After his retirement from NASA in 1998, Hickam authored his memoir *Rocket Boys* and followed up with his first work of fiction, *Back to the Moon* (1999), a science fiction thriller about a private lunar mission to obtain nuclear fuel from the Moon. He has also written novels set during World War II as well as several non-fiction books.

The film's title *October Sky* was derived from an anagram of "Rocket Boys" when the movie's producers thought that female filmgoers might be averse to going to see a movie with the original title. *October Sky* references the October 4, 1957, launch of Sputnik that inspired Hickam's interest in space exploration. Sputnik's launch was a seminal event in American history, and is described as both "a grim new chapter in the Cold War" and "a milestone in history" in the film. Americans believed that the tiny satellite was taking photographs of the country as it passed overhead, or would descend from space as a nuclear bomb. At any rate, it was a severe shock to the American public when the notion of Uncle Sam's technological superiority over the Soviets was shattered.

Famed writer Stephen King begins his non-fiction book on the horror genre *Danse Macabre* with his remembrance of that fateful day: "For me, the terror—the real terror—began on an afternoon in October of 1957. I had just turned ten. And, as was only fitting, I was in a movie theater: the Stratford Theater in Downtown Stratford, Connecticut."[1] King relates how the showing of the movie, which happened to be the alien invasion flick *Earth vs. the Flying Saucers,* was interrupted by the theater manager. "I want to tell you," the nervous man announced to the audience, "that the Russians have put a satellite into orbit around the Earth. They call it…. Spootnik."[2] The kids in attendance sat in stunned silence while they absorbed the news. The manager then left the stage and the flying saucers resumed their attack on humanity, but science fact had overwhelmed science fiction in King's young mind. "The Russians had beaten us into space," he lamented. "Somewhere over our heads, beeping triumphantly, was an electronic ball which had been launched and constructed behind the Iron Curtain."[3] King's account of that day perfectly captures the angst of that moment, which he compares with the shock experienced by the nation on the day President Kennedy was assassinated.

A different take on the Mercury Program was offered in *Hidden Figures* (2016), an account of African-American women working at NASA's Langley Research Center in Hampton, Virginia, during the early 1960s. Based on Margot Lee Shetterly's best-selling non-fiction book, the film follows the struggles of three of these women against the racism and sexism endemic to the organization during the era of segregation in the South. Katherine Johnson (Taraji P. Henson) is a mathematician who works as a "human computer" calculating flight data for the space program. Mary Jackson (Janelle Monáe) is an aspiring engineer assigned to work on the Mercury capsule's design, while Dorothy Vaughn (Octavia Spencer) is the supervisor of the mathematicians in the segregated West Computing Group.

Katherine works for Al Harrison (Kevin Costner), the exacting head of NASA's Space Task Group, solving problems in analytical geometry and orbital mechanics prior to the launch of the first American astronauts. She is the only African-American and the only woman on the team, but her work is routinely disparaged by Paul Stafford (Jim Parsons), the group's prejudiced chief engineer. Even more humiliating, she is forced to use the "colored only" ladies room located in another building a quarter mile away. In the meantime, Mary identifies design flaws in the Mercury capsule but is frustrated because she cannot advance in her profession due to a lack of education. She is prevented from taking technical courses at a local segregated high school. Taking her case to court, she argues eloquently before a local judge and is granted an exemption. When an IBM mainframe computer is installed at Langley, Dorothy decides to teach herself FORTRAN programming language and becomes an indispensable member of the computing team.

The segregation dilemma at Langley is dramatically resolved when Harrison learns of Katherine's rest room plight and demolishes the "colored only" ladies room sign with a crowbar, indicating the end of this practice at NASA. While some things may have changed, Stafford and the other mathematicians continue to deny Katherine's contributions and her co-authorship of official reports because of her race and gender. Harrison comes to her defense and ensures that her input will be recognized.

The Mercury astronauts, including John Glenn (Glen Powell), pay a morale-boosting visit to Langley, but the Space Task Group is badly shaken on April 12, 1961, when Russian cosmonaut Yuri Gagarin becomes the first human to orbit the Earth. Harrison's team must redouble their efforts to put an American in space, and during this crisis, Katherine's mathematical expertise begins to be appreciated. She is finally allowed to attend NASA planning sessions, where her analytical skills come to Glenn's attention. Tensions mount as the time for Glenn's flight approaches, and at the last minute, possible errors in the computerized flight data are detected. The launch is delayed as Glenn insists that Katherine double-check the IBM computer's figures, which she does with dispatch. All the computations check out, and Glenn becomes the first U.S. astronaut in orbit, an event that lifts the morale of all Americans. A postscript to the film states that Katherine went on to work on the Apollo and Space Shuttle programs, and was awarded the Presidential Medal of Freedom in 2015.

Set during the turbulent era of the civil rights movement in the early 1960s, *Hidden Figures* presents a searing indictment of segregation. It also shows how the Mercury program served to unite the nation and instill pride in our technological progress. The principals turn in remarkable portrayals; Spencer won a Golden Globe for her performance. The women also won a special Screen Actors Guild Award for Outstanding Performance by a Cast in a Motion Picture. Kevin Costner also shines in a supporting role as NASA's maverick champion of racial equality. Director Theodore Melfi captures the tension and anxiety of NASA's geopolitical struggle with the Soviets during the early days of the space race. The film climaxes with a recreation of John Glenn's risky orbital flight.

While the film powerfully dramatizes the myriad perditions of segregation, as in *The Right Stuff* characters and situations have been exaggerated or invented using creative license to advance the narrative. Al Harrison and Paul Stafford are fictitious people, although the Harrison character is probably meant to stand in for Robert Gilruth, who was head administrator of the Space Task Group. The Langley facility was desegregated in 1958 upon the formation of NASA, and this was accomplished via a simple memo rather than a man wielding a crowbar. While it's true that John Glenn requested Katherine Johnson review the IBM computer's data, this happened prior to the flight and not on the launch pad as depicted in the movie.

A quirky postscript to the Mercury program was provided in the dramatic *The Astronaut Farmer* (2006). Billy Bob Thornton stars as Charles Farmer, a former Mercury astronaut who was forced to resign from NASA during the early 1960s in order to save his family's failing Texas ranch from foreclosure in the wake of his father's suicide. Having missed his chance to be an astronaut, he still yearns to fly in space, and after spending decades taking care of his family, he becomes obsessed with building working replicas of the Mercury capsule and the Atlas launch vehicle in his barn. He's so obsessed that he wears his silver spacesuit while performing chores on the ranch and visiting the local elementary school for show-and-tell sessions.

Farmer's quest to fly in space is supported by his family, including his wife Audrey (Virginia Madsen), his teenage son Shepard (Max Thieriot) and Audrey's father Hal (Bruce Dern). Funding for his flight becomes problematical when he runs out of money and the bank threatens foreclosure on his farm in 30 days. To make matters worse, NASA, the FAA and the FBI become aware of his plans when he attempts to purchase a large quantity of rocket fuel. They hold a hearing during which they voice their opposition to a private citizen launching a space rocket, and conclude that Farmer should not be allowed to do so. The would-be astronaut comes to the attention of the press, and his unusual situation goes viral as he is the subject of worldwide TV coverage

Farmer decides to defy the government's edict as well as misgivings expressed by his close friend, USAF Colonel Doug Masterson (Bruce Willis), and attempts to launch using an inferior grade of rocket fuel. He is nearly killed when the Atlas misfires, falls over and speeds along the ground and the Mercury capsule is ejected from the rocket. In light of this catastrophic failure and the impending foreclosure, Farmer abandons his quest. Hal dies unexpectedly and leaves Audrey enough of an inheritance to make back payments on their mortgage—with enough left over to fund a revival of Farmer's space program.

A second Mercury-Atlas spacecraft, christened *The Dreamer*, is constructed and fueled as Farmer prepares for takeoff. This time, the rocket functions perfectly and launches the last Mercury astronaut into Earth orbit as Shepard monitors the flight from his one-man Mission Control facility located inside an Airstream trailer on the ranch. The capsule disengages from the booster while Farmer finally enjoys the glories of space flight as he observes the Earth from space and experiences the thrill of zero gravity. A sudden power failure plunges the spacecraft into darkness and radio contact with Shepard is lost. After several harrowing hours, Farmer regains control of the ship and successfully lands in the vicinity of his ranch after having completed nine orbits. In the aftermath, the maverick spacefarer becomes a celebrity folk hero and is seen appearing on *The Tonight Show* with Jay Leno.

The Astronaut Farmer is primarily a family-oriented drama about a man and his dream facing long odds against its realization. It has affinities with *Field of Dreams*, a similarly themed story about a farmer pursuing an unusual goal. The film's dramatic core is sound, and principal actors Thornton, Madsen, Dern and Willis (in an uncredited role) all turn in sincere, convincing performances under the able direction of Michael Polish. Thornton carries the film with his quirky portrayal of wannabe spaceman Charlie Farmer. *The Astronaut Farmer*'s basic theme can be summed up in a line of Farmer's dialogue: "If we don't have a dream, we have nothing." The film offers a fond view of small town life, but sometimes descends into predictability and maudlin sentimentality.

Of course, its basic premise is absurd and perhaps even dangerous. It's hardly conceivable that a husband and father would subject his family to such risky undertakings as tinkering with volatile fuels and launching rockets from his barn. In the real world, engineer Jack Parsons, who cooked up exotic propellants in his home for NASA's Jet Propulsion Laboratory, blew himself up while brewing a batch of rocket fuel. The notion of do-it-yourself space flight likewise strains credulity, as Farmer and Shepard scavenge used rocket parts from junkyards and manage Mission Control in a single location manned by only one person. While Farmer's single-minded obsession makes him a hero within the narrative, there is a self-centered aspect to his character. He is willing to bankrupt his family and expose them to physical danger and legal jeopardy in order to pursue his dream. Farmer's personality has affinities with *Lucy in the Sky* (2019) protagonist Lucy Cola, who was also obsessed with getting into space.

The road to space was fraught with difficulty and danger that was reflected through the medium of cinema in a process that took decades to bring to the big screen. Although much of the history of the early space program has been dramatized or distorted by the narrative demands of Hollywood filmmakers, some of the tenor of those tumultuous early days of the space race, conducted against the backdrop of the Cold War, manage to shine through. In the 1960s, America stood on the threshold of a new frontier as the nation set its sights on the Moon.

FOUR

The Chariots of Apollo

Before the Mercury program ended, President John F. Kennedy launched a bold new initiative for the space program. On May 25, 1961, he committed NASA to the goal of sending a man to the Moon and returning him to Earth before the end of the decade. What was unspoken was that America should accomplish this before the Soviets did.

NASA had its work cut out for it, as the Soviet program was still way ahead of ours. The Russians had followed Gagarin's historic flight with a series of space spectaculars. Taking full advantage of chief designer Sergei Korolev's expertise in building powerful rockets, the Soviets had sent a number of cosmonauts on long-duration orbital missions. On June 16, 1963, Russian cosmonaut Valentina Tereshkova became the first woman to travel in space. On her five-day mission, she logged more time in orbit than all of the Mercury astronauts combined. The Soviets followed up with the launch of Voskhod 1 on October 3, 1964, with a crew of three. Voskhod 2, launched on March 18, 1965, featured the first extravehicular spacewalk by cosmonaut Alexi Leonov. The Russians were known to be working on a giant launch vehicle called the N1, designed to take cosmonauts on a voyage to the Moon.

America responded with the development of the Gemini program utilizing a two-passenger spacecraft designed to develop techniques of rendezvous and docking in Earth orbit that would be essential for a mission to the Moon. A new group of men, including Neil Armstrong and Jim Lovell, was recruited and trained by NASA. But Gemini was only a stopgap measure to keep America in space while the hardware for the Apollo program was being developed to fulfill President Kennedy's promise.

Opinions were mixed on just how to achieve a Moon landing ahead of the Russians. In 1962, Lockheed and Bell Aerospace engineers proposed a drastic plan to send a habitat module to the Moon ahead of a single astronaut, who would land on the lunar surface, seal himself inside the pressurized structure and subsist on its oxygen, food and life support—and wait there until NASA figured out a way to bring him back. Additional supplies would be sent to the Moon periodically to keep him alive. While this desperate scheme was never seriously considered by NASA planners, it formed the basis for Hank Searis' novel *The Pilgrim Project*, which was adapted for the screen as *Countdown* (1968).

Countdown takes place at the height of the space race in the late 1960s. The Soviet Union sends a civilian geologist into orbit around the Moon before Apollo can get off the ground. NASA has been secretly working on a Plan B called the Pilgrim Project for the past three years: It involves landing a lone astronaut on the Moon in a modified Gemini spacecraft, and having him traverse the lunar surface to a shelter previously placed there. He will be guided to the shelter by a rotating red beacon light, and once inside, he will hunker down and wait for an Apollo moonship to rescue him in a year or so.

When the cosmonaut successfully circumnavigates the Moon, the Russians prepare a three-man mission for a landing in three weeks, while NASA scrambles to implement the Pilgrim Project. Only two astronauts are qualified to make the trip, Air Force Major Chiz (Robert Duvall) and civilian pilot Lee Stegler (James Caan). Chiz is the more qualified of the two, but NASA brass insists that the first American on the Moon be a civilian and choose Lee instead. After Chiz loudly protests to NASA administrator Ross Duellan (Steve Ihnat) to no avail, he must swallow his pride and work to prepare Lee for the mission in only three weeks.

Driven by animosity and envy, Chiz relentlessly puts Lee through a grueling training process, including hours in the Gemini spacecraft simulator and an elaborate vacuum chamber in which Lee is strapped into a "Peter Pan" harness that simulates the one-sixth gravity and airless environment of the Moon. Lee acquits himself well under Chiz's demanding training regimen and is eventually deemed fit to make the flight. Six days before his flight, the shelter is put in position on the lunar surface. The Soviets announce that their three-man mission has launched and is on its way to its destination. Shortly afterward, Lee takes off, hoping somehow to beat the Russians and become the first man to land on the Moon.

En route to the Moon, the Gemini spacecraft experiences a severe power loss and Lee must shut down all non-essential systems to save energy. Temperature drops sharply inside the Gemini and radio communications are partially disrupted, causing Lee to undergo intense psychological strain. In the meantime, word reaches NASA that the Russians have lost contact with their cosmonauts. Once in orbit around the Moon, Lee desperately searches for the shelter's beacon on the lunar surface and makes the decision to set down even though he cannot see it.

Lee lands and exits the spacecraft to look for the shelter, walking slowly over the bleak Moonscape to preserve his precious life support, which will only last for one hour. He has lost all radio contact with NASA, who will only know if he has succeeded when he activates the shelter. While on his moonwalk, he unexpectedly comes upon a grim tableau: the remains of the crashed Russian lander and the bodies of the three cosmonauts. Despite his limited oxygen supply, Lee takes the time to honor the dead by draping the American and Soviet flags over rocks at the crash site. Walking away in a random direction, he eventually sights the rotating beacon atop the shelter with only minutes of oxygen left. He moves toward it, the implication being that he will survive.

Directed by Robert Altman, who would later become well-known for his films *MASH* (1970) and *Nashville* (1975), *Countdown* is considered one of the director's lesser works by critics. He was reportedly fired by Warner Bros. execs who objected to his use of overlapping dialogue, which would soon become one of the director's signature techniques. The film's chief dramatic tension is the contretemps between Chiz and Lee, and it's interesting to watch the chemistry between James Caan and Robert Duvall, who would later appear together in *The Godfather* (1972). The scenes in which these actors do not appear are dull and pointless. Joanna Moore as Lee's wife and Ted Knight as a NASA p.r. man are wasted in throwaway roles. Once the action moves to space, however, the film seems to come alive as it builds to a climax on the surface of an alien world.

Altman received permission from NASA to shoot documentary-style footage at the Houston Space Center and the Cape Canaveral launch facilities. The massive Vehicle Assembly building and a launch tower at the Cape, as well as the Gemini spacecraft simulator and the lunar surface simulator in Houston, provide a dramatic backdrop for the action. *Countdown* accurately depicts the sense of desperation felt by NASA staff during the height of the space race. In the film, the Soviets send a cosmonaut around the Moon, but this feat was actually accomplished by the American Apollo 8 mission, which was launched about nine months after the film's release.

While the movie's NASA hardware adds a certain verisimilitude to the proceedings, its basic premise strains credulity. The Gemini spacecraft was never designed to travel into deep space, and the film is vague about how it is mated to the lunar lander. Stock footage of the launch shows the takeoff of a Titan II rocket, a vehicle that could never have propelled a spacecraft to the Moon. Landing on the Moon was the most demanding task faced by the Apollo astronauts, but the actual landing is never depicted in the film. Instead, the lander is shown comfortably resting on the lunar surface with the Gemini capsule perched on top. The scene in which the spacecraft experiences a power drain that causes the astronaut to shut down all but the basic life support systems, was a scenario that actually occurred during the Apollo 13 mission a few years later. The rivalry between Lee and Chiz over who should be the first person to set foot on the Moon paralleled a real-life competition between Buzz Aldrin and Neil Armstrong as to which one of them should be the first to step out onto the lunar surface.

The Apollo–era space thrillers continued the next year with *Marooned* (1969), based on a novel by aerospace writer Martin Caidin. Three astronauts, mission commander Jim Pruett (Richard Crenna), "Buzz" Lloyd (Gene Hackman) and Clayton "Stoney" Stone (James Franciscus), prepare to return to Earth after an extended stay at a space station in an Apollo command-service module configured spacecraft, *Ironman One*. Their mission was supposed to last seven months, but is being terminated two months early due to Lloyd's declining performance. The astronauts activate the automatic retrofire control that will initiate their re-entry into Earth's atmosphere, but the big engine in the service module fails to fire. After thousands of NASA workers on the ground scramble fruitlessly to come up with a fix, the crew find themselves stranded in orbit 285 miles above the Earth, with a 42-hour supply of oxygen.

NASA administrator Charles Keith (Gregory Peck) is dubious about mounting a rescue mission, but head astronaut Ted Dougherty (David Janssen) comes up with a plan to send an experimental Air Force "lifting body" spacecraft, the X-RV, into orbit on a Titan IIIC rocket. The X-RV prototype has never flown, and the Titan is not man-rated, so Keith rejects Dougherty's plan until the president himself intervenes and authorizes funding for the rescue. As O_2 levels in *Ironman One* drop to dangerous levels, the NASA team races to assemble the spacecraft and succeed, only to have the launch delayed at the last minute by a hurricane. Precious time is lost before the rescue vehicle reaches its next launch window as Cape Canaveral passes through the eye of the hurricane. In Mission Control, the astronauts' wives Betty Lloyd (Mariette Hartley), Celia Pruett (Lee Grant) and Teresa Stone (Nancy Kovack) agonize over the fate of their husbands.

Up in *Ironman One*, the astronauts realize that the rescue ship will not arrive in time—and that while there might not be enough air to sustain all three of them, there might be enough for two. After a brief discussion, Pruett orders the men to don their spacesuits as he opens the Apollo's hatch and exits the ship, ostensibly to repair the service module; it is unclear whether he intends to sacrifice himself to ensure the survival of the others. In any event, Pruett's suit sustains a rupture that quickly drains the air away into the vacuum of space. Buzz and Stone watch in horror as his corpse drifts away into the void. The remaining crewmen return to the command module to await

Spacewalking astronauts and the Apollo Command and Service modules are featured in this *Marooned* (1969) poster.

the inevitable, but unbeknownst to them the Russians have sent their own rescue ship, which arrives before the X-RV. Although the Soviet Vostok spacecraft cannot accommodate all three spacefarers, the cosmonaut is able to furnish enough oxygen to keep Buzz and Stone alive until Dougherty arrives. The American astronaut and the Russian cosmonaut team up to transport Buzz and Stone into the American rescue ship, whereupon the Vostok and the X-RV return to Earth, their mission accomplished, leaving the empty Apollo spaceship in orbit.

Despite an A-list cast, state-of-the-art production values and scientific verisimilitude, the film displays a lack of dramatic effect, especially in comparison with the similarly themed *Apollo 13*. The main problem is that director John Sturges fails to elicit effective performances from his actors. The stolid Gregory Peck delivers a particularly stodgy portrayal of a NASA bureaucrat, while David Janssen, James Franciscus and Richard Crenna fare little better as astronauts caught in a grim life-and-death situation. Only Gene Hackman displays any strong emotion as the mentally unstable astronaut Buzz Lloyd in scenes in which he breaks down into hysterics. While it performed poorly at the box office, the film was nominated for several Academy Awards. It won only in the category of special effects.

On the plus side, the screenplay by Mayo Simon deftly adapts Caidin's novel for the screen, even lifting passages of dialogue verbatim from the book. Caidin served as technical advisor, and pains were taken by the filmmakers to simulate actual space hardware. NASA and contractors such as North American Aviation and Philco-Ford were involved in designing the film's space equipment, and elaborate replicas of the Mission Control Room in Houston and the Air Force launch facility at Cape Canaveral were constructed. The movie's space station, constructed from the S-IVB stage of the massive Saturn V rocket, would be realized in 1973 as Skylab, the first American space station. Also featured in one scene was an astronaut tooling through space using a Manned Maneuvering Unit (MMU), a self-propelled backpack which would come into its own during the Space Shuttle program, when it was used in the construction of the International Space Station. The X-RV rescue vehicle was based on the experimental Martin Marietta SV-5, a wingless, "lifting body" craft employed by the Air Force to test the viability of generating aerodynamic lift without the use of wings. The Martin Marietta corporation proposed that the SV-5 be adapted for a role as a National Orbital Rescue Service (NORS) vehicle, but this was never realized.

The strangest thing about *Marooned* was how it anticipated the Apollo 13 space disaster, during which three American astronauts nearly lost their lives when their spacecraft malfunctioned en route to the Moon. In both the film and the real-life event, the source of the malfunction was in the service module. A few months before the Apollo 13 flight, mission commander Jim Lovell attended a premiere of *Marooned* in Houston with his wife Marilyn. In the film, mission commander Richard Crenna, who was also named Jim in the film, dies and gets sucked out into space, a plot element that gave Marilyn nightmares. Fortunately, all three Apollo 13 astronauts returned to Earth safely. *Marooned* is also credited with being the impetus behind the 1974 Apollo-Soyuz mission, as the Russians and Americans realized that there should be a provision for both spacefaring nations to have the capability for rescuing each other's crews in space.

In 1969, the year *Marooned* was released, the Apollo 11 astronauts landed on the Moon, a momentous event that was watched on television by an estimated 600 million people, a fifth of the world's population. By the late 1970s, however, the Apollo program was in the rear view mirror and NASA's budget had been severely slashed. The glories of space exploration had been replaced in the public mind by concerns about the Vietnam War, civil rights struggles and the Watergate scandal. Faith in our governmental institutions had been eroded, and a paranoid mindset had engulfed the American psyche. This cultural paranoia provided the backdrop for the first post–Apollo space movie, *Capricorn One* (1978).

The film begins with stock footage of a Saturn V rocket (dubbed *Capricorn One*) on the launch pad being prepared for the first manned mission to Mars. Astronauts Peter Willis (Sam Waterson), John Walker (O.J. Simpson) and mission commander Charles Brubaker (James Brolin) are installed inside the command module and are awaiting the final countdown when they are unexpectedly removed from the ship by NASA officials and secretly flown to an abandoned air base. The Mars rocket takes off without the crew on board, and the public is none the wiser, believing that the men are safely on their way to the Red Planet.

The three bewildered astronauts are kept in seclusion at the air base until the arrival of NASA bigwig Dr. James Kelloway (Hal Holbrook), who informs them that their spacecraft's life support was faulty and would have failed three weeks into the mission. When NASA discovered the flaw, it was too late to scrub the launch; fearing that this failure would mean the end of the space program, Kelloway and a secret cabal decided to fake

The crew of the first Mars mission: Left to right, Peter Willis (Sam Waterson), Charles Brubaker (James Brolin) and John Walker (O.J. Simpson) pose in *Capricorn One* (1978).

the mission instead. He leads the astros into a large hangar area where mock-ups of the command module and landing craft have been installed, along with a panoramic simulacrum of the Martian surface and a sophisticated television studio. The men are told that unless they participate in the hoax, their families will be killed by government agents.

Back at Mission Control in Houston, technician Elliot Whitter (Robert Walden) notices a transmission time discrepancy between the telemetry data and the TV broadcasts received from the *Capricorn One* spacecraft. He reports this anomaly to Kelloway and later confides the info to his friend, journalist Robert Caulfield (Elliott Gould). After their conversation, Whitter mysteriously disappears. Mystified, Caulfield finds that another tenant has been moved into Whitter's apartment overnight, and that there is no record of his friend ever having worked for NASA. Smelling a story, Caulfield decides to investigate what appears to be a sinister conspiracy tied to the Capricorn One mission, but as his investigation progresses, secret government forces tamper with his car and he is almost killed, the police frame him for possession of cocaine.

In the meantime, the phony Mars landing is staged and broadcast to the world, and after 259 days the crewmen have supposedly entered Earth orbit. The men converse with their wives from the bogus Command Module. While speaking to his wife Kay (Brenda Vaccaro), Brubaker makes a puzzling remark about their family vacation the previous year. Kelloway's plan goes off the rails when the spacecraft's heat shield comes loose and the command module is incinerated during re-entry, supposedly killing the astronauts. Realizing that the cabal will be forced to do away with them, Brubaker, Willis and Walker break out of confinement and escape.

UNTERNEHMEN CAPRICORN

The stage is set for a hoaxed Mars landing in this German lobby card for *Capricorn One* (1978).

Caulfield continues his investigation and notices Kay's bewildered reaction to her husband's remarks in tape replays of the TV broadcast from *Capricorn One* and decides to pay her a visit. She tells him that the family had visited a theme park where a western movie was being shot and that her husband said of the filmmaking process, "With that type of technology, you could convince people of almost anything." This remark gives Caulfield a clue about what's really going on, and he sets out for the desert air base hoping to unravel the truth.

The astronauts, fleeing their NASA captors in a stolen plane, run out of fuel and land in the desert. Realizing that the government forces will pursue them, they split up in three different directions. Two armed helicopters hunt them through the desert while they use all their survival skills to avoid capture. Despite their best efforts, Walker and Willis are located and killed.

Caulfield makes his way to the abandoned base and finds evidence that Brubaker had been there. Reasoning that the astronauts are probably still in the area, he hires a crop-dusting plane from garrulous local pilot Albain (Telly Savalas) and the two fly out into the desert. Albain spies the choppers and follows them to an abandoned gas station where Brubaker is holed up. They swoop down to pick up the astronaut and a thrilling air chase follows as the biplane is pursued through the desert hills and valleys by the helos until Albain's flying skills and his airplane's superior maneuverability cause their pursuers to crash. The movie ends with Caulfield leading Brubaker to his own memorial service as the nefarious NASA plot is thwarted.

Writer-director Peter Hyams crafts an intriguing science fiction thriller that gradually builds suspense until reaching the rousing action climax. The helicopters that stalk the astronauts through the wasteland are particularly sinister, appearing as a pair of deadly flying insects. Elliott Gould's quirky performance as a maverick journalist taking on the power structure drives the film, and he is ably supported by the square-jawed James Brolin as an intrepid astronaut, Brenda Vaccaro as his grieving "widow," Hal Holbrook as a sleazy bureaucrat and Telly Savalas as an ill-tempered crop duster. O.J. Simpson's presence strikes a discordant note in light of his subsequent biography. NASA permitted the use of its facilities and stock film footage despite the movie's negative portrayal of the agency.

The film's main problem is a plot front-loaded with too many oddball situations that tend to strain credulity. NASA is depicted as a sinister, murderous outfit involved in kidnapping and murder with seemingly godlike powers to make people disappear and erase their very existence. A civilian organization, they are nonetheless able to commandeer a military base and attack helicopters to accomplish their villainous goals. The film has much in common with contemporaneous post–Watergate exercises in political paranoia like *The Parallax View* (1974) and *Close Encounters of the Third Kind* (1977) in its portrayal of clandestine governmental conspiracies.

Capricorn One's most enduring legacy is its role in popularizing the conspiracy theory that the Apollo Moon landings were a hoax, and that visuals of Neil Armstrong and Buzz Aldrin walking on the lunar surface were concocted in a studio. While it's ostensibly about a Mars mission, Apollo hardware such as the Saturn V and the lunar module are used in the movie. The hoax scenario did not originate with the film, however. As early as 1969, author Norman Mailer questioned the reality of the low-quality Apollo video footage and speculated that it could have been produced in a studio. In the James Bond film *Diamonds Are Forever* (1971), Bond (Sean Connery) discovers a facility in which spacesuited astronauts are being trained on a simulation of the Moon's surface.

The main proponent of the hoax theory, however, was writer Bill Kaysing, author of the 1974 book *We Never Went to the Moon: America's Thirty Billion Dollar Swindle*. Kaysing, a former Navy officer, claimed to have inside knowledge that NASA was unable to land on the Moon and merely sent the Apollo 11 astronauts into Earth orbit. No hard evidence of this scenario was ever offered, but Kaysing sued *Capricorn One* writer-director Hyams for plagiarism. The lawsuit never went very far. Subsequent rumors fingered director Stanley Kubrick as the filmmaker responsible for the faked footage because of the Moon sequences in his 1968 film *2001: A Space Odyssey*. Some conspiracy theorists speculate that Kubrick even placed clues to his involvement in the hoax in his 1980 film *The Shining*. Recent polls have shown that five to ten percent of Americans believe that the Apollo 11 Moon landing was bogus.

Hyams claims that the idea for *Capricorn One* originated in the early 1970s while he was working for CBS-TV in Boston, where he became aware that NASA video feeds provided to the network included a lot of simulated material, and wondered if an entire mission could be fabricated. Inspired by this idea, he began writing the film in 1974, around the time that Kaysing's book was published, but could not get into production until the end of the decade. Hyams returned to outer space-themed movies with *Outland* (1981) and the *2001* sequel *2010: The Year We Make Contact* (1984), to be discussed in later chapters.

Decades later, the Moon landing hoax was the basis for the Canadian-American independent feature *Operation Avalanche* (2016). The film purports to be found footage produced by two CIA agents (Matt Johnson, Owen Williams), attached to the agency's Audio-Visual Department and assigned to ferret out a mole at NASA. Purporting to be documentarians making a film about the space program, they infiltrate the outfit and bug the phone of head NASA administrator Jim Webb. From an intercepted phone call, they learn that the Apollo 11 lunar module is unable to land on the Moon and that the astronauts will merely orbit the satellite. Johnson and Williams come up with an idea to concoct fake footage of the lunar landing and sell the idea to the CIA as Operation Avalanche.

Traveling to England, they visit Kubrick's *2001* set, where they learn about sophisticated front projection techniques employed by the director to create realistic backdrops. The agents rent studio space and use front projection to create a phony lunar environment and film their version of Neil Armstrong's "giant leap for mankind." This bogus footage is supposed to be substituted for the real thing when the astronauts are incommunicado as they pass behind the far side of the Moon. From this point on, the narrative becomes increasingly confusing as Johnson and Williams are hunted by CIA agents and their film is buried in a field.

This amateurish mockumentary frequently comes off as a juvenile and often confusing take on the serious issue of governmental conspiracy and the manipulation of history. Principals Matt Johnson and Owen Williams (the actors use their real names) appear as smarmy film school nerds posing as a couple of naïve intelligence agents. The filmmakers used 1960s-era film equipment such as Moviola editing machines and 16mm Arriflex cameras, as well as employing techniques to give the film a vintage look. Documentary conventions such as hand-held camerawork, choppy editing and echo-laden sound are very much in evidence. The screenplay by Josh Boles and Matt Johnson is larded with gratuitous violence, political paranoia and a plethora of opaque subplots. In addition to the Operation Avalanche Moon hoax, the film posits that our government was supposedly also involved in Operation Deep Red, an intelligence investigation of Kubrick and Operation North Woods, a CIA plan to shoot down Apollo 11 and blame it on the Soviets. There is no historical basis for any of these outlandish conspiracy theories.

As to the film's central premise, it relies heavily on the notion that Kubrick was central to the perpetration of the Moon landing hoax, although in this case he is not the one doing the hoaxing. "Kubrick is getting NASA to make sure his space movie looks like real space," Johnson observes, "and so we're going to make sure the 'real' space movie looks like space" by using the director's sophisticated front projection techniques. For *2001*, Kubrick created a series of realistic lunar panoramas, state-of-the-art in cinematic illusion circa 1968, but his imagined Moonscape resembled the Chesley Bonestell imagery of jagged Moon mountains that was prevalent before the Apollo missions revealed the softly rounded slopes of the alien terrain; so *2001*'s Moon actually didn't "look like space." Taking its cue from *Capricorn One*, the film exploits the same political paranoia as the JFK and Roswell UFO conspiracies with its tag line "It's not a lie if you believe it."

Hollywood space program fantasies gave way to reality with Ron Howard's factual account of the most harrowing mission in NASA history, *Apollo 13* (1995). Tom Hanks stars as Jim Lovell, who is commanding the third lunar landing mission in 1970. Lovell, who had circumnavigated the Moon on the Apollo 8 in 1968, has been driven by the idea of walking on the Moon throughout his astronaut career, but his wife Marilyn (Kathleen Quinlan) has vague misgivings about the upcoming launch. He and his crewmates,

Ken Mattingly (Gary Sinise) and Fred Haise (Bill Paxton), have been training hard, but two days before the launch, Mattingly is exposed to German measles and is bumped. He is replaced by his backup, Command Module pilot Jack Swigert (Kevin Bacon). Lovell is forced to accept the change although it breaks down the cohesion of his team.

Two days later, Apollo 13 lifts off on its way to the Moon, but the third proposed lunar landing is hardly covered by the media. On the second day of the mission, Swigert is instructed to stir the spacecraft's oxygen tanks, a routine procedure. But an electrical short sparks a fire that causes an explosion in the Service Module, depriving the ship of its electrical power and rocket propulsion. Lovell informs Mission Control, "Houston, we've had a problem."

It has become impossible for them to land on the moon under these circumstances and the crew's lives are now in jeopardy. Without the Service Module's rocket engine, they are unable to turn around directly, but must continue to go around the Moon in order to use its gravity to fling them on a return trajectory back to Earth.

In Houston, flight director Gene Kranz (Ed Harris) organizes teams of NASA specialists to work the problem while insisting, "Failure is not an option." The first order of business is to shut down the Command Module *Odyssey* to preserve its battery power, which will be needed for re-entry, and power up the Lunar Module *Aquarius* so it can be used as a lifeboat. The first order of business is to stabilize the spacecraft, which is spinning wildly out of control due to gasses venting from the damaged Service Module. Using the Lunar Module's attitude control thrusters, the astronauts manage to get the ship on a free return trajectory that will take them around the Moon and return them to Earth.

As they travel around the far side of the Moon, the astronauts burn the Lunar Module's rocket engine in a maneuver that successfully puts them on a return path,

Mission commander Jim Lovell (Tom Hanks) leads his crew up the launch gantry to their spacecraft in *Apollo 13* (1995).

but afterwards they have to shut down all non-essential systems to conserve power. The extreme cold of outer space begins to seep into the spacecraft and Haise comes down with a fever caused by a urinary infection. Back home, Marilyn and the Lovell family endure the torments of uncertainty as media "science advisors" like ABC-TV's Jules Bergman broadcast unrelentingly negative assessments of the crew's chances for survival, while Ken Mattingly struggles in Houston's simulator to solve the problem of acquiring enough power to restart the Command Module during re-entry. Another crisis emerges when the spacecraft's carbon dioxide levels rise to dangerous levels. A method must be devised to mate dissimilar types of CO_2 scrubbers using duct tape, plastic bags, tubing and other materials found on the ship. The improvised device works, but as they get nearer to Earth the crew must perform a critical course correction burn with their computer shut down, employing only a stopwatch for timing, and aligning their trajectory using visual orientation alone.

As the astronauts prepare for re-entry, they must power up the Command Module, which has never been restarted in space before. A solution is finally found and transmitted to the astronauts. Their final worry concerns the possibility that the Module's heat shield might have been damaged. Lovell's family, along with millions around the world, anxiously await Apollo 13's return to Earth. Lovell, Haise and Swigert ride the Command Module on their fiery re-entry through the atmosphere to a

"Houston, we've had a problem." Left to right, astronauts Fred Haise (Bill Paxton), Jack Swigert (Kevin Bacon) and Jim Lovell (Tom Hanks) attempt to fly their crippled spacecraft back to Earth in *Apollo 13* (1995).

successful splashdown in the Pacific and are safely transported to a waiting aircraft carrier.

Numerous Hollywood productions have been advertised as being "based on a true story" or "inspired by true events," but *Apollo 13* is one of a very few instances in which this is literally true. Director Ron Howard, working from a screenplay by William Broyles Jr., Al Reinert and John Sayles, went to great lengths to reconstruct the events of the mission while not straying far from the orbit of the facts. Based on Jim Lovell's book *Lost Moon,* the film is an accurate and stirring recreation of the Apollo program's only "successful failure," and a brilliant evocation of this bygone era. Howard's pacing is superb, and relentlessly engages the viewer from launch to splashdown while explicating the myriad technical details of the flight with realism and clarity.

A large part of its success is due to sterling performances by a cast of A-list actors. Tom Hanks carries the film in the main role of veteran space traveler Lovell, ably supported by Bill Paxton, Kevin Bacon and Gary Sinise as fellow members of the astronaut corps. Ed Harris, who had portrayed John Glenn in *The Right Stuff,* delivers a riveting performance as flight controller Gene Kranz, who leads his NASA team of "steely-eyed missile men" to the ultimate victory over the perils of outer space. Kathleen Quinlan's brilliant portrait of Lovell's long-suffering wife Marilyn offers an earthbound emotional counterpoint to her husband's travails. A sequence in which Marilyn has a nightmare about her husband being sucked out of the Command Module was inspired by a similar scene in *Marooned,* which the Lovells had seen three months before the Apollo 13 launch.

Director Howard decided early on that he would not use any NASA documentary footage in his recreation of the event. Replicas of the Command and Lunar Modules were constructed, using some original Apollo components, and installed inside a Boeing KC-135 aircraft. The KC-135, known affectionately as the "vomit comet," flies in huge parabolic arcs and is used to train astronauts by simulating zero gravity for short periods. The actors were filmed while inside this airborne set, to realistically simulate weightlessness during the scenes that take place in space. The movie's copy of the Houston Mission Control facility was so realistic that a former NASA employee who had worked there once became momentarily confused as to whether he was back in Houston or on the movie set. The actor's spacesuits were not merely costumes, but were precise replicas of the pressure suits worn by the Apollo astronauts. Like the real thing, they were airtight; air had to be pumped inside in order for the actors to breathe and to maintain a proper temperature. Ed Harris and the actors portraying the flight controllers were schooled by former NASA controllers and listened to archival audio tapes of the Apollo 13 mission to get a feel for the operations in Mission Control. There were two memorable tag lines in the film. The first was, "Houston, we've had a problem," which was actually said by Jim Lovell, although it's sometime transliterated as, "Houston, we have a problem" and "Houston, we've got a problem." The second was Grover Kranz's declaration "Failure is not an option," which was invented by the screenwriters. Lovell has a cameo as the captain of the recovery ship, the *Iwo Jima.*

A critical and popular success, *Apollo 13* was nominated for nine Academy Awards, including Best Picture, but only won in the categories of Best Sound and Best Editing. To this day, it remains the most realistic and fact-based account of a space mission and has affinities with *The Martian* in its depiction of survival against all odds in the hostile environment of outer space.

After the failed Apollo 13 mission, Apollo 14 through 17 successfully landed on the Moon. NASA had planned three more lunar missions, but these were cancelled for budgetary reasons, and the remaining Apollo hardware was re-directed toward the Skylab space station program in 1973 through 1974, and the Apollo-Soyuz Test Project in 1975. Yet conspiracy theories about the Apollo astronauts encountering an extraterrestrial presence on the Moon proliferated in UFO circles and elsewhere. There were stories about the discovery of alien artifacts on the Moon (*à la 2001*), as well as reports that the lunar explorers were "warned off" of territory that hostile E.T.s considered theirs.

These wild tales formed the basis for a fictional account of a clandestine mission to the Moon, *Apollo 18* (2011). The unlikely plot centers around a clandestine Moon landing narrative told via found footage allegedly uploaded to the site lunartruth.com. Astronauts Ben Anderson (Warren Christie), Nathan Walker (Lloyd Owen) and John Grey (Ryan Robbins) are dispatched on a top secret mission to the Moon, ostensibly to install an array of PSD-5 radar detectors designed to spy on Soviet ICBM launches. Anderson and Walker land their Lunar Module *Liberty* on the Moon's south polar region, while Grey remains in lunar orbit in the Command Module *Freedom*.

The astronauts go about their work while detecting anomalous noises and observing a rock moving by itself. During a moonwalk, Walker and Anderson find a set of human footprints that lead them to a Russian Proton lunar lander and a dead cosmonaut inside a crater. Things really get weird when Walker detects something moving inside his suit and a spider-like creature is seen crawling over his face inside his helmet. Anderson rescues him and brings him inside the Lunar Module, where a wound is discovered in Walker's chest. Anderson extracts a Moon rock from the wound and Walker smashes it with a hammer. Apparently the creatures can disguise themselves as Moon rocks.

Walker's wound becomes infected as he descends into mental confusion and paranoia. In the meantime, the astronauts lose all communication with both Houston and *Liberty*, and Anderson comes to believe that the radar detectors they have installed are designed to monitor the alien life forms rather than Soviet missile launches. As Walker descends further into delirium, he goes on a rampage and damages the Lunar Module so it cannot take off. Anderson decides that their only chance of returning home is to take off in the Russian Proton lander. He manages to get Walker into the lunar rover, but on their way to the Russian ship, Walker freaks out, crashes the vehicle and winds up in a crater where he is attacked by the spiders.

Anderson continues on alone to the Proton, where he establishes radio contact with *Liberty* and American authorities. A Defense Department official informs him that he will not be allowed to return to Earth because he has become infected by the lunar organisms. He is cynically told, "We'll let your family know you died a hero." Anderson rejects this directive and arranges to link up with *Liberty*, but as he is preparing to launch, Walker appears, now completely under the influence of the aliens, and attempts to damage the spacecraft. Anderson successfully launches the Proton and attains lunar orbit, but once the ship is in zero gravity, rock samples collected by the cosmonaut transform into the spiders and attack him. He loses control of the spacecraft as he is attempting to rendezvous with *Liberty*, destroying both the Proton and the Command Module and killing Anderson and Grey. In the aftermath, the astronaut's deaths are covered up and a postscript states that Moon rocks collected during previous Apollo missions have mysteriously gone missing.

This oddball exercise in Moon conspiracy theory is primarily a space-bound horror–sci-fi flick in the *Alien* (1979) mold. As such, it's reasonably entertaining for a low-budget production despite its bizarre premise. Director Gonzalo Lopez-Gallego exploits the current vogue for the found footage cinematic form with gusto, utilizing non-actors and Apollo-era footage of space hardware. The "secret" launch of the mission, for instance, was stock footage of the nighttime launch of Apollo 17 in 1972. The main problem with the film lies with the Brian Miller screenplay, which is so full of logical holes as to render it beyond absurdity. It is unclear in many instances who is actually doing the filming of the astronauts, and how the alleged found footage was obtained after the Command Module and Proton lander were destroyed. Additionally, the alien creatures pictured in the film, which are presumably some form of mineral-based life, strain credulity to the max.

The Science and Entertainment Exchange reportedly provided scientific consultation for the film, and NASA was initially involved with the production but later withdrew. A simulacrum of the Apollo Command Module looks realistic, but the interior of the Lunar Module is filmed using very wide angle lenses that make it look much larger than the confined space it really was. The astronauts' spacesuits look authentic, and the model of the Russian Proton lunar lander is historically accurate. *Apollo 18* performed well at the box office, especially in light of its modest production costs.

The film's tag line, "There's a reason we've never gone back to the Moon," places it squarely in the domain of space-age myths such as the Apollo 11 Moon landing hoax and the so-called "Face on Mars." After the conclusion of the Apollo program, a number of conspiracy theories concerning an E.T. presence or alien artifacts allegedly discovered on the Moon have circulated among UFO enthusiasts and the general public. In 1976, amateur astronomer George Leonard authored the book *Somebody Else Is on the Moon* that alleged that Apollo 11 astronauts Neil Armstrong and Buzz Aldrin had encountered UFOs on the Moon and that Aldrin had photographed them. This narrative was picked up by the supermarket tabloid the *National Enquirer*, which ran a story entitled "Aliens on Moon When We Landed" in 1979. Another conspiracy theory claims that the Apollo 17 astronauts were "warned off" the Moon by hostile aliens who felt we were invading their turf, which was why the program was discontinued. In the 1990s, science writer Richard Hoagland publicized blurry NASA photographs of what were purportedly massive alien structures on the lunar surface. Of course, the conspiracy mongers claimed that extraterrestrial presence on the Moon has been suppressed by NASA for almost half a century, but there is no basis for any of these lunatic theories.

As the 50-year anniversary of the Apollo 11 Moon landing approached in 2019, Hollywood filmmakers strove to commemorate this momentous event. A biopic about moonwalker Neil Armstrong had been in the production pipeline for several years before being realized as *First Man,* released in 2018. The film begins in 1961 with Armstrong (Ryan Gosling), a civilian NASA test pilot, flying the X-15 rocket plane to the edge of space. His piloting skills are called into question when the aircraft nearly skips off the atmosphere into space and he is grounded for being "too distracted." Armstrong has more serious problems, as his two-year-old daughter Karen (Lucy Stafford) is undergoing intensive treatment for a brain tumor, and the prognosis is not good. Karen dies, leaving Armstrong and his wife Janet (Claire Foy) awash in grief.

In the wake of the tragedy, Armstrong decides to apply for the Gemini program, and is accepted due to his piloting skills and engineering background. After undergoing rigorous astronaut training, he is assigned to the Gemini 8 flight, which will attempt the first docking maneuver in space, a procedure which will be essential for a lunar mission. He is launched on his first space flight along with Dave Scott (Christopher Abbott) and the Gemini 8 crew successfully performs the first docking with the Agena target vehicle that has been placed in orbit for that purpose. But then the docked spacecraft begins to roll uncontrollably, putting the astronauts in danger of blacking out. Armstrong deftly undocks from the Agena and brings the careening Gemini capsule under control by skillfully manipulating the craft's control thrusters. Armstrong is held blameless for the equipment malfunction.

In 1967, as the Apollo program moves into high gear, Armstrong is devastated by the deaths of Gus Grissom, Roger Chaffee and Ed White during a static ground test of the Apollo 1 spacecraft. Then he is nearly killed during a test flight of the Lunar Landing Research Vehicle when it malfunctions and he is forced to eject at a low altitude. The deadly risks of space flight begin to tear at the nerves of his wife Janet and his children. Despite these misgivings, Armstrong is selected to command Apollo 11 and is slated to be the first man to walk on the Moon. His crewmates are to be Lunar Module Pilot Buzz Aldrin (Corey Stoll) and Command Module pilot Michael Collins (Lukas Haas).

On July 16, 1969, Apollo 11 lifts off and four days later the astronauts are in orbit around the Moon. Armstrong and Aldrin enter the Lunar Module *Eagle* and separate from Collins in the Command Module *Columbia*. During their descent to the lunar surface, they are confronted by program alarms that threaten to abort the mission but they continue. Their pre-selected landing site is found to be strewn with large boulders, so Armstrong assumes manual control of the lander and touches down. He tells Mission Control, "The Eagle has landed."

The astronauts prepare for their spacewalk on the lunar surface. Armstrong steps out of the lander, descends the ladder and becomes the first human to walk on the Moon while uttering the historic words, "That's one small step for man, one giant leap for mankind." During one of his spacewalks, Armstrong drops Karen's hospital bracelet into a

Neil Armstrong (Ryan Gosling) contemplates the launch of the Apollo 11 Moon rocket in concept art for the biopic *First Man* (2018).

crater in an act of somber remembrance. After the astronauts return to Earth, they are placed in quarantine to guard against possible infection from space germs. Neil silently greets Janet from the other side of a glass barrier.

Directed by Damien Chazelle, who had lensed the musical *La La Land* (2016), the film purports to be a paean to America's crowning accomplishment in space and a tribute to the first man on the Moon, but comes up short on both counts. The Josh Singer screenplay, based on an Armstrong biography by James R. Hansen, is solid and covers the key points in the astronaut's career, but is compromised by Chazelle's visual treatment of the theme. The events portrayed, whether on the ground or in space, are filmed in dark, murky tones, casting ominous shadows that tend to dull the dramatic edge. The walls of Armstrong's home are painted in a sickly-looking ochre, and for some reason the couple are frequently shown in long shot in a square in the middle of the frame surrounded by a zone of blackness. Lighting setups are dull and uninteresting, and hand-held camera is frequently employed; both techniques are hallmarks of low-budget TV production. Spacecraft interiors are rendered so dark that it would be impossible for the astronauts to see the instruments or controls. Critics have noted that the Gemini and Apollo cockpits look grimy and rusted as if well-worn from use when in reality they were pristine and factory-fresh. The Apollo 11 launch is depicted as taking off in pre-dawn darkness, when it actually occurred at 9:32 on a bright Florida morning.

Filming an Armstrong biography proved to be a problematical task, as capturing the essence of the astronaut's quiet, self-effacing persona is all but impossible. Despite his well-deserved fame, he remained an enigma to both the public and his NASA colleagues, one of whom once remarked, "I knew him, but I didn't know him." Under the circumstances, there was little that Ryan Gosling could do to characterize Armstrong's elusive personality. Claire Foy provides an emotional foil to his remoteness in her intense portrayal of his wife. His Apollo crewmates Collins and Aldrin, played by Corey Stoll and Luke Haas, are pushed far into the background, while the rest of the cast turn in unremarkable performances. All in all, the film is flat and lacking in emotional effect.

The film's $59 million budget was insufficient to encompass the full scope of its epic subject matter. Apollo 11's voyages to and from the Moon are not shown, truncating the mission while freeing the filmmakers from the expense of depicting the actors floating in zero gravity. On the other hand, the odd-looking Lunar Landing Research Vehicle (dubbed the "flying bedstand" by the astronauts) is accurately and realistically recreated, and the Gemini 8 and Apollo 11 launches are replete with screaming vibrations and bone-shaking violence without musical accompaniment. The lunar landing is the dramatic climax of the film and is depicted with all the suspense and drama inherent in the actual event. Instead of using standard "green screen" projection techniques to simulate vistas of outer space, Chazelle chose to employ large LED displays that enabled the actors to perform while watching the space images that would appear in the finished film. Scenes taking place on the Moon's surface were filmed at night in a rock quarry near Atlanta, using a custom-made 200,000-watt lighting system to simulate the harsh lunar sunlight. Former Apollo astronauts Al Worden and Alan Bean were hired as technical advisors to ensure verisimilitude for these scenes.

First Man received mostly positive critical reviews and was nominated for four Academy Awards in technical categories, but only won for Best Visual Effects. It performed poorly at the box office due to a number of factors, including its understated performances and its excessive 141-minute running time. It was also plagued by controversy over its failure to depict the astronauts planting the American flag on the Moon. Domestic audiences perceived this as an anti–American gesture, and it was denounced by conservative politicians. The film is inferior in most respects to the similarly themed *Apollo 13*, especially its dramatic potency.

While the Apollo missions represent the zenith of America's technological prowess (tens of millions watched humankind's historic first steps onto another world), enthusiasm for our space program proved to be short-lived. *First Man* contains a performance of social critic Gil-Scott Heron's anti–Apollo screed "Whitey's on the Moon," which expresses the misgivings many Americans had about the cost of the program and sentiments that these funds could be better spent on social programs for the poor. Hollywood seems to have reflected, and continues to reflect, anti–Apollo sentiments in its filmic depictions of the program. The roster includes a perilous one-man lunar landing (*Countdown*), astronauts lost in space (*Marooned*), hoaxed landings (*Capricorn One, Operation Avalanche*), a failed Moon mission (*Apollo 13*), aliens killing astronauts (*Apollo 18*) and a desultory account of America's finest moment in space (*First Man*). Only *Apollo 13* showed the program in a positive light.

In 2019, *Apollo 11*, a documentary about the first Moon landing, was released in connection with its 50-year anniversary. It included previously unseen 70mm footage of the mission that had been discovered in NASA vaults. As humanity contemplates a return to the Moon, films like this can provide inspiration for our future as a spacefaring species.

FIVE

Red Star in Space:
Russian Space Films

The late 1950s and early 1960s were heady times for the Soviet Union's space program. The space race had commenced with the launch of Sputnik, the first artificial satellite to orbit the Earth in November 1957 in a Soviet engineering feat that stunned the world and challenged America's perceived technological superiority. A string of Russian successes in space followed, including the first cosmonaut in orbit, the first three-man spaceship, the first woman in space and the first spacewalk. America struggled to play catch up, but by the end of the Mercury program the Soviet female cosmonaut Valentina Tereshkova, as previously noted, had spent more time in space than all of the U.S. astronauts combined.

Cold War Soviet propagandists trumpeted these early space triumphs as the dawn of a new era of a cosmic period of mankind and proof of the technological superiority of Communism over capitalism. Yet Soviet cinema did not move to exploit the idea of space exploration, and produced a mere handful of films on the subject during this period. Meanwhile, Hollywood produced a plethora of space-themed movies during the 1950s.

Prior to the advent of the space race, Russian cinema had delved into the topic in only two films. As discussed in Chapter One, *Aelita* (1924) was a stylish interplanetary fantasy about a trip to Mars, while *Cosmic Voyage* (1936) chronicled a more scientifically accurate trip to the Moon based on the musings of the great Russian space pioneer Konstantin Tsiolkovsky. Neither film was looked upon with favor by Soviet propagandists, who considered them escapist fluff, at odds with the artistic tenets of "socialist realism."

The new space age was heralded by the film *Road to the Stars* (*Doroga K Zvezdam*, 1957), which was released a month after the launch of Sputnik. This 48-minute semi-documentary is divided into two parts. The first follows Tsiolkovsky (Georgi Solovyov) during his early years in the Kaluga province as he formulates the basic theories of space flight as the principles of celestial mechanics are explained to the audience in detail. The second half depicts speculative future events in the exploration of space such as the first manned launch, the construction of an orbital space station and the first Moon landing.

Director Pavel Klushantsev begins the second part with the launch of a three-man crew into orbit from a sprawling space complex. The cosmonauts, clad in leather flying outfits rather than pressure suits, wave farewell before entering the spacecraft. The first two stages propel the winged third stage into orbit as the spacefarers cavort about the roomy, padded cabin in freefall. One cosmonaut dons a spacesuit and ventures out of the ship to witness a dramatic sunrise in outer space. When their mission has been completed, the ship is brought back to Earth and glides to a water landing in the Black Sea. A motor launch transports the triumphant cosmonauts to shore, where they are greeted by cheering crowds.

The next sequence depicts multiple cargo ships being launched from the cosmodrome. Once in orbit, teams of spacesuited cosmonauts begin the construction of a circular space station. When the station is completed, crews are shown relaxing within its hallways, enjoying all the comforts of home. A pet cat basks in the starlight shining through one of the station's windows, illustrating the everyday domesticity of the space environment. Horticulturists create a lush garden to provide food for the cosmonauts. Meteorologists and astronomers utilize the station's high vantage point to make observations, and engineers devise unique materials in microgravity that cannot be fabricated on Earth.

Soon a lunar landing craft, a tall spacecraft with four landing legs, is launched into orbit and docks with the station. A two-man crew departs for the Moon and achieves lunar orbit. The forbidding lunar surface passes by until the cosmonauts execute a de-orbit burn and land. A crewman exits the lander and descends to plant the first human footprints on the Moon. In a postscript, a future lunar base is shown, along with expeditions to Mars, Venus and the outer planets as humankind sets off on its journey to infinity and beyond.

Part educational film, part futurist documentary and part space travelogue, *Road to the Stars* was an impressive achievement in special effects for its time. The miniature work is superb and the spacecraft interiors are realistically depicted. Its orb-like space station conforms to technological notions of the early space age and has been compared to a similar structure in *2001.* Stanley Kubrick and co-scripter Arthur C. Clarke reportedly viewed numerous science fiction films in preparation for filming their space odyssey, and *Road to the Stars* was probably among them.

Director Klushantsev held up the film's release for a month in order to incorporate material about the launch of Sputnik 1. The space hardware pictured in the film, however, differs markedly from the real-life Soviet rocketry and spacecraft of the time, such as the Proton launchers used to loft Sputnik and Yuri Gagarin into orbit, and the manned Vostok and Voskhod spacecraft. Instead, the film's rockets resemble the finned craft typical of science fiction imagery, although the Moon landing vehicle bears a resemblance to the Apollo lunar module. In 1988, the Russian version of the space shuttle, the Buran (*not* a manned spacecraft), duplicated the feat of gliding back to Earth from orbit and landing on a runway. Of course, grandiose circular space stations were never built by any nation, and a permanent base on the Moon is still a long way off.

The space race between the Soviets and the U.S. was dramatized in *The Heavens Call* (*Nebo Zovyot*, 1959). A framing story leads off the narrative, as young Soviet writer Troyan (Sergey Filimonov) seeks inspiration for a story about space exploration by visiting a rocket institute. He is shown around by engineer Yevgeny Kornev (Ivan Pereverzev) and cosmonaut Andrei Gordienko (Alexander Shvoryn). Troyan is shown replicas of the first and second Sputniks and models of a space station and a sophisticated spacesuit. Beguiled by the hardware, he returns home and begins to work on a science fiction story.

As the film's actual narrative begins, Kornev and Gordienko travel by rocketship to an orbiting, wheel-shaped Soviet space station. The station is a palatial affair containing laboratories and greenhouses, along with spacious cabins and common areas. Docked at the station is an advanced spacecraft, the *Rodina* (*Homeland*), that is being readied for the first expedition to Mars. Kornev and cosmonaut Grigory Somov (Valentin Chernyak) have been assigned to fly the mission.

Things get dicey when an American spaceship, the *Typhoon*, arrives at the station and is permitted to dock. The *Typhoon* is piloted by youthful astronaut Robert Clark (Constantine Bartashevich) and senior commander Herman Verst (Gurgen Tonunts). During a conference with the Russians, Verst announces that the *Typhoon* is also bound for the Red Planet. As the *Rodina* is scheduled to depart in a matter of days, the American crew is instructed by their superiors to launch as soon as possible, in order to beat the Soviet ship to Mars. Accordingly, the *Typhoon* takes off prematurely, before their preparations are complete. Somov, who has been assigned to fly the *Rodina*, is injured during the impetuous maneuver; Gordienko replaces him. Days later, Gordienko and Kornev depart from the space station bound for Mars.

Clark and Verst's haste comes back to bite them: Their navigation system fails and the Americans find themselves off course and low on fuel. Things go from bad to worse as they encounter a meteor storm. They send out an SOS and the *Rodina* is obliged to answer the distress call for humanitarian reasons. The Russian crew maneuvers to a rendezvous with the *Typhoon* in deep space and Gordienko performs a spacewalk to bring Verst and Clark aboard the *Rodina*. The derelict American ship is left to drift off into the void.

The *Rodina* has used up too much fuel during the rescue and is unable to land on Mars. They must set down on the asteroid Icarus to await the arrival of a supply ship that will bring them the extra fuel needed to return them to Earth. The cosmonauts and astronauts work together to erect radar towers that will guide the unmanned cargo ship to the asteroid while observing Mars close-up and lamenting the fact that they cannot fulfill their missions. The arriving cargo ship crashes into the radar towers and destroys them in a terrific explosion.

With no radar guidance system, the next supply ship must be flown by a human pilot, and Somov volunteers for the suicidal mission. In an act of supreme self-sacrifice, he manages to land on Icarus but perishes from exposure to cosmic radiation. The Russian and American crews return to Earth in the *Rodina* and land on a floating platform.

This pulp fiction excursion into interplanetary adventure is enlivened by the brisk direction of Aleksandr Kozyr and Mikhail Karyukov and the futuristic hardware devised by production designer Yuriy Shvetz. The rocketships and space station miniatures are impressive by late 1950s standards, and its panoramic vistas of the universe have a distinctly poetic quality. The storyline by Aleksey Sazonov involving the Soviet rescue of a disabled American spacecraft was echoed in *Marooned* (1969). Sazonov's screenplay emphasizes the superiority of the cooperative Soviet approach over the capitalist motivation of the competitive Americans. For instance, when the *Typhoon* takes off for Mars, commercials for various Mars-related products are heard blaring on the soundtrack over stock footage of Times Square billboards and advertisements. Thus, the crass opportunism of the American crew is contrasted with the idealistic attitude of the Soviets. *The Heavens Call*, set during some unspecified time in the future, documents the idealistic phase of Russian space exploration during the early years of the space race.

In terms of its space hardware, the rocket that conveys the cosmonauts to the space station is a direct ascent, single-stage rocket rather than the multi-stage vehicle depicted in *Road to the Stars.* The elaborate, wheel-shaped space station has similarities to the one in *Conquest of Space* (1955). It is equipped with an imposing horizontal platform on which the cosmonauts embark and disembark from docked spacecraft in spacesuits and presumably use magnetized boots to secure themselves to the metal deck in the zero gravity environment. On its interior, it contains a vegetable garden, spacious conference rooms and lavish living quarters. As was usual in space films of the period, the spacefarers reach Mars in a brief span of screen time rather than the months an actual journey would take. The film's most impressive visual is the view of the Red Planet hanging like a giant crimson orb as seen from the vantage point of Icarus. Released at the time that the Soviet Luna 3 probe circumnavigated the Moon and transmitted the first photographs of the Moon's far side, *The Heavens Call* gave the impression that humankind would be colonizing the solar system in the near future.

The next Soviet interplanetary excursion took place two years later in *Storm Planet* (*Planeta Bur*, 1962). The plot: Some time in the future, the Soviet news agency TASS announces that three "astro ships," the *Vega*, the *Capella* and the *Sirius*, are in orbit around Venus and preparing to send expeditions down to the planet's surface. The *Capella* is hit by a meteor and destroyed, leaving only two ships to complete the mission. A relief ship, the *Arcturus*, is dispatched from Earth, but will not arrive for four months. The remaining cosmonauts prepare to send teams to explore Venus. One group from each ship will descend to the planet's surface. Cosmonauts Vershinin (Vladimir Yemelyanov), Bobrov (Georgiy Zhzhonov) and Alyosha (Gennadi Vernov) are due to depart from the *Sirius*, while Kern (Georgi Teich) and Shcherba (Yuri Sarantsev) and robot Iron John (Boris Prudkovsky) comprise the *Vega* team. The lone female cosmonaut, Masha Ivanova (Kyunna Ignatova), is assigned to remain in orbit on board the *Vega* in order to transmit the expedition's data back to Earth. Observing the cloud-shrouded planet surface from orbit, Alyosha spies a mysterious red glow that may indicate the presence of intelligent life.

The *Vega* team departs first in a glider craft piloted by Robot John but strong winds on the storm planet blow it off course. They land in a swampy area where radio contact is lost. Vershinin, Bobrov and Alyosha land the *Sirius* on a rescue mission. They find themselves confronted by a landscape of bare rock and swirling fog. Alyosha is promptly attacked by a giant carnivorous plant and must be rescued by his crewmates, but at least they have discovered that there is some kind of life on Venus. From time to time, they hear a woman's mellifluous voice somewhere in the distance. Meanwhile, Misha radios the *Sirius* to report that she has discovered the location of the *Vega* crew on the other side of a lake.

A group of ferocious lizard men attack the *Vega* team out of the fog, but are driven off by the Earthmen's firepower and the might of Robot John. Afterwards, they become infected by a Venusian germ and take refuge in a cave. The *Sirius* team runs into an alien brontosaurus, and Bobrov obtains a blood sample from the obliging beast. They set out to cross the lake in their hovercar, but are attacked by a pterodactyl and driven under the water, where they discover a stone idol that indicates the existence of intelligent beings.

The *Vega* men resume their overland trek, but are threatened by a new danger as a volcano erupts and streams of magma block their way. Kern and Shcherba must be carried through the lava on Robot John's shoulders, but the extreme heat activates the machine's self-preservation circuits and it suddenly begins trying to shed the excess weight of the men by hurling them into the lava. Fortunately, Kern is able to short circuit the robot's programming before it can accomplish this task. The rescuers from the *Sirius* arrive in time to transport their fellow cosmonauts to safety as the disabled Robot John falls into the magma and is consumed by its heat. Once reunited, the crews head back to the *Sirius*, and on the way they observe various prehistoric beasts as they continue to collect rock and water samples. They reach the ship and are preparing to embark when Alyosha discovers a carving of a female alien's head and tries to convince his crewmates to remain on Venus, but he is summarily hauled up into the spacecraft and the *Sirius* takes off to rendezvous with the *Vega* for the trip home. After the launch, the haunting song is heard on the soundtrack once more as the camera pans over to a pool of water, where the image of a robed, female alien being is reflected.

Like *The Heavens Call, Storm Planet* is an adventure story set in the exotic locale of outer space. Written by Aleksandr Kazantsev from his novel and directed by Pavel Klushantsev, the creative force behind *Road to the Stars*, the film represents the aspirations of the spacefaring Soviet state that was certain to explore and colonize the solar system in the future. "The migration of life in space is as natural," one of the cosmonauts muses, "as seed swept by the wind on Earth." The perils of space exploration are expressed in Communist ideological jargon. "Be on the lookout for any and all counterrevolutionary one-celled organisms," a message from Earth warns, "which must be compelled to join into collective dialectic action." Although Soviet dogma supposedly embraced gender equality, Misha, the lone female cosmonaut, is treated with a thinly concealed contempt. At one point, Vershinin states, "Bringing a girl into space is like bringing a little monkey with his own spacesuit. When it starts chittering and engaging in mindless hijinks, you can't really blame the monkey."

In contrast to the earlier Russian space epics, there's little in the way of space hardware in evidence, as most of the action takes place inside the spaceships and on the planet's surface. The cosmonaut's spacesuits look realistic, however, and the futuristic hovercraft is a nice bit of 1960s sci-fi tech. Robot John, who was perhaps inspired by Robby the Robot in MGM's *Forbidden Planet* (1956), is clunky and utilitarian rather than stylish and resembles a walking refrigerator. The Russians apparently had never heard of science fiction writer Isaac Asimov's "laws of robotics," cybernetic programming that prevents robots from harming humans, as John attempts to save himself by ejecting Kern and Shcherba into the lava flow. John cuts a sympathetic figure as he topples into the flaming river to his destruction.

Storm Planet seems hardly different from much of the sci-fi fare of the period, such as the similarly themed East German–Polish production *First Spaceship on Venus* (1959). Critics have pointed out that *Storm Planet*'s glimpse of the alien being in its last reel is where most Western science fiction films begin. The notion of dinosaurs inhabiting alien worlds makes a mockery of evolutionary theory, but extraterrestrial dinos were also featured in *King Dinosaur* (1955) and *Planet of the Dinosaurs* (1978). Romantic notions about our sister planet persisted into the early 1960s. Venus, being closer to the Sun, was depicted as an exotic hothouse world inhabited by all manner of alien life forms. These illusions were shattered when the Soviet Venera 7 probe landed on the planet in 1970 and transmitted data showing that its crushing atmospheric pressure and extreme temperatures were completely inimical to the existence of life.

Neither *The Heavens Call* nor *Storm Planet* was seen in the West in their original forms until recently, but they did reach American audiences in a roundabout way. Hollywood producer-director Roger Corman bought the rights to exhibit these films in

America and assigned some of his up-and-coming directors to devise English-language versions. In 1965, director Curtis Harrington converted *Storm Planet* into *Voyage to a Prehistoric Planet* by splicing in footage of American actress Faith Domergue to replace scenes featuring the female cosmonaut Misha, plus additional footage of Basil Rathbone talking to the expedition members from a lunar base. To add insult to injury, *Storm Planet* was further sliced and diced by director Peter Bogdanovich into a second version entitled *Voyage to the Planet of the Prehistoric Women* (1968). This iteration featured sex goddess Mamie Van Doren leading a bevy of scantily clad Venusian glamor girls who keep the Earth expedition away from their planet with their telepathic powers.

As for *The Heavens Call*, Corman assigned a young Francis Ford Coppola to produce an American version, which was re-titled *Battle Beyond the Sun* (1962). Coppola rewrote and dubbed the dialogue, obscured the Cyrillic lettering on the Russian spaceships, and added scenes of the crew battling space monsters on the asteroid Icarus. Footage from the Soviet film was also used in Curtis Harrington's science fiction horror flick *Queen of Blood* (1965).

These Russian science fiction space excursions were nowhere near as popular as their American counterparts. None of them were produced by the premier Soviet studio, Mosfilm, but were the product of regional production companies. By the mid–1960s, the American space program had overtaken the Soviet efforts, and the glory days of Sputnik and Gagarin had been eclipsed by the anticipation of the Apollo Moon landing. The Apollo 8 mission that flew around the Moon in December 1968 effectively ended the space race, and films on the subject quietly disappeared from Russian movie screens for a decade.

During the 1960s, the works of Polish science fiction writer Stanislaw Lem began to be published and appreciated in the West. They were also popular within the Soviet bloc, and his 1951 novel *The Astronauts* was adapted for the screen as the aforementioned *First Spaceship on Venus*. In that film, an international crew comprises an expedition to Venus that discovers evidence of a vanished alien race that had been poised to invade the Earth.

Lem's 1961 novel *Solaris* was lensed by the acclaimed Russian director Andrei Tarkovsky and was the first space film produced by the prestigious Mosfilm studios. *Solaris* (*Solyaris*, 1972) takes place in some future era in which humankind has achieved interstellar space flight and established a permanent space station orbiting Solaris, a planet completely covered by a roiling ocean and drifting banks of fog. As the film opens, communications with the space station have ceased, and authorities suspect that its scientists have suffered mental breakdowns. Psychologist and "Solaricist" Kris Kelvin (Donatas Banionis) is assigned to travel to the station to assess the mental condition of the crew and determine whether the Solaris project should continue. On the eve of his departure, Kelvin pays a visit to his elderly father (Nikolai Grinko) at his country home, a visit that is especially poignant because, due to the time involved in interstellar flight, it is the last time that the two will see each other alive. Also on hand is Henri Burton (Vladislav Dvorzhetsky), a former cosmonaut who plays a video recording in which he describes his encounter with a 12-foot-tall infant while cruising over the surface of Solaris. As no images of the apparition were captured on video, Burton's experience was judged to be a hallucination. Burton warns Kelvin that the planet is capable of producing such bizarre mental effects.

Kelvin travels to Solaris, where he finds the station in a chaotic state. His friend Dr. Gibarian (Sos Sargsyan) has committed suicide, and the remaining scientists, Snaut

(Juri Jarvet) and Sartorius (Anatoli Solonitsyn), are uncommunicative and show signs of mental illness. Kelvin soon learns that the station is also inhabited by "visitors" when he catches glimpses of a surly, bearded dwarf and a scantily clad young woman lurking about the premises. A rambling, incoherent video left behind by Gibarian does nothing to resolve the mystery.

In his living quarters, Kelvin falls asleep and awakens to find a double of his dead wife, Hari (Natalya Bondarchuk), in bed beside him. Hari had committed suicide ten years earlier, after the failure of their marriage. The replica is a perfect physical copy of Hari, down to the wound from her fatal injection, but is in a state of mental confusion. Shocked and confused, Kelvin sends the pseudo–Hari on a one-way ride into the void inside a space capsule. He learns from the others that the "visitors" began appearing on the station after the research team bombarded Solaris with high energy X-rays. They theorize that the entire planet constitutes a vast alien intelligence that is able to probe their minds and construct the visitors from their memories, in order to study the humans. They are not flesh-and-blood people, but artificial "neutrino systems" that cannot die.

Another Hari doppelgänger appears in Kelvin's chambers that evening. This time he seems to accept her, but this iteration of Hari cannot tolerate being parted from him and injures herself when left alone. He watches as her wounds heal in a matter of moments and she is restored to wholeness. During a demented birthday party celebration, Sartorius confronts Hari with the fact that she is not real. In response, she drinks liquid oxygen and "dies," only to be resurrected once more. Kelvin falls into a deep sleep, and when he awakens he finds that she has persuaded the scientists to destroy her by using a device called the "annihilator" that scrambles her neutrino structure.

Psychologist Kris Kelvin (Donatas Banionis) is confronted by a doppelganger of his deceased wife Hari (Natalya Bondarchuk) in Andrei Tarkovsky's *Solaris* (1972).

When the "visitors" stop appearing at the station, Kelvin decides that it is time to return to Earth. Now Kelvin is shown approaching his father's dacha in a repeat of the film's early scenes. As he observes his father, who is supposedly dead, through a window, the camera pulls up and back to a wide shot to reveal that he is actually on an island on the surface of Solaris where an illusion is being generated from his memories.

Considered by critics to be the most important science fiction film in Russian cinema history, *Solaris* was awarded the Grand Prix Spécial du Jury when it was shown at the Cannes Film Festival in 1972. The film was credited with bringing a new level of intellectual, psychological and philosophical depth to the SF genre. Donatas Banionis lends a stolid and serious screen presence to his lead role as Kelvin, while Natalya Bondarchuk portrays Hari's doppelgänger with a combination of sensitive frailty and inhuman strangeness. Cinematographer Vadim Yusov contributed the lush visuals, and art director Mikhail Romadin designed the space station set with distinctive curvilinear passageways. The station is crammed with realistic-looking scientific equipment, plus a real mainframe computer on loan from an aerospace company.

All this having been said, with a three-hour running time, *Solaris* is overlong and director Tarkovsky's pacing is ponderous and static. Like much European cinema, it seems overly talky by American movie standards. Tartovsky's direction is often arty and pretentious; for example, a seemingly interminable sequence showing a car driving down a freeway, an annoying tendency to shift the imagery between black-and-white and color for no particular reason, and a scene in which the camera endlessly pans around a 16th-century landscape painting by Brueghel the Elder.

The film's major flaw lies in its screenplay, co-written by Tarkovsky and Friedrich Gorenstein, which emphasizes the dramatic relationship between Kelvin and Hari over the theme of an enigmatic encounter between human and alien intelligences that is the core of Lem's book. Lem had collaborated on early treatments with Tarkovsky, but later disparaged the finished film and expressed the opinion that the director had lensed *Crime and Punishment* rather than his novel. Still, the film contains some compelling imagery, especially the final shot of Kelvin alone on his island, completely beguiled by the illusions created by the alien ocean. The research station has the semblance of a haunted house in space where revenants and hallucinations are rampant.

The film is frequently compared to *2001*, as both films revolve around an encounter between an astronaut and a mysterious and superior extraterrestrial intelligence symbolized by the black monolith in *2001* and the swirling, bilious ocean in *Solaris*. Both films largely take place in outer space environments, but *Solaris* eschews Stanley Kubrick's vistas of the universe in favor of a reductionist environment inside the claustrophobic environment of the dysfunctional space station. Tarkovsky mostly dispenses with the space hardware that enlivened *2001*, as there's nary a spaceship in evidence. Kelvin's interstellar journey is shown via an extended tight close-up of the actor's face. The bulk of the film's narrative could be performed as a theatrical stage play, as the dramatic interplay of a small group of characters constitutes the soul of the plot. In a 1970 interview, Tarkovsky was dismissive of *2001*, calling it "phony" and a "lifeless schema." In 2002, Steven Soderbergh wrote and directed an American remake of *Solaris* that featured 21st-century special effects but was inferior to the original. George Clooney starred as Kelvin.

Another one of Stanislaw Lem's works provided the basis for *The Trial of Pilot Pirx* (*Doznaniye pilota Pirksa*, 1979). This Polish-Russian production was based on *Inquest*, one of Lem's short stories about Pirx the Pilot, a cosmonaut who has many sci-fi adventures while exploring outer space. The film begins with Commander Prix (Sergei Desnitski) being recruited by UNESCO official Mr. Green (Ferdynand Matysik) for an unusual mission: He is to travel to Saturn with a crew that includes some androids (referred to as "non-linears") manufactured by the firm United Atomic Laboratories in order to evaluate their performance during the flight. UNESCO's ultimate aim is to replace humans with androids to avoid exposing people to the dangers of space flight. As part of the experiment, Pirx will not be told which of his crewmates is human and which is a non-linear.

Pirx is introduced to his four crew members, Calder (Zbigniew Lesien), Nowak (Aleksandr Kaidanovsky), Otis (Boleslaw Abart) and Brown (Vladimir Ivashov), and peppers them with questions, and cannot distinguish the humans from the androids. The crew blasts off for a rendezvous with a space station where a deep space ship, the *Goliath*, is docked. Transferring to the *Goliath*, they depart for Saturn, where their mission is to launch two space probes through the Cassini Division, a gap between the planet's rings. The crew seems to function efficiently, but they behave in a robotic fashion that makes it impossible to tell who is human and who's not.

As the *Goliath* approaches Saturn, Pirx finds a video cassette containing a grim message from one of the non-linears. Wearing a grotesque disguise, the android informs Pirx that it intends to sabotage the mission to prove that the non-linears are superior to humans. Once their ship is in orbit around Saturn, Pirx orders the firing of the first probe, which negotiates the gap between the planet's rings without a hitch. The second probe, however, fails to fire and remains attached to the ship, so Pirx orders that the *Goliath* go through the Cassini Division and launch the probe on the other side. It turns out that the probe's malfunction is the result of sabotage performed by the non-linear, who hopes that the human crewmen will be killed when the ship accelerates during the dangerous maneuver. As the *Goliath* races through the planet's rings, the saboteur tries to increase its speed, but is destroyed by high G forces in the attempt.

The second probe is launched manually, and the mission is successful, but when the ship returns to Earth, there are questions about Pirx's performance during the crisis and he is put on trial before a United Nations court. The issue is decided when Nowak, the ship's surgeon, comes forward with video data recovered from a recording device discovered during an autopsy of the renegade android's body. Pirx is exonerated by the evidence, and in a final irony Nowak reveals that he was the other non-linear crewman aboard the *Goliath*.

Directed and co-written by Marek Piestrak, this Lem adaptation comes off as a fairly typical European space drama of the period. It was made two years after the release of *Star Wars* and the special effects are cheesy by comparison, giving the film an antiquated look. The film's pacing is robust, and the uncertainty about the identity of the android crewmen adds an element of mystery. Sergei Desnitski portrays the title character as a dour professional, while his fellow crew members all act in a mechanical fashion. Pirx's trial, rather than constituting the soul of the plot, only occupies a short interval during the third act.

In the scene just prior to the mission's launch, Pirx is shown framed by the business end of a Russian Proton rocket; this footage was likely shot at the Soviets' Biakonur Cosmodrome. When the actual takeoff is depicted, however, the filmmakers inexplicably chose to use NASA stock footage of a Saturn V rocket launch. During their time on the space station and on the *Goliath*, the cosmonauts do not experience weightlessness, but function entirely in normal gravity. A voyage to Saturn's environs using rocket propulsion would take years in real life, but is accomplished in mere minutes of screen time.

This Lem adaptation is as much about robotics and artificial intelligence as it is about space travel. Its opening scenes depicting the construction of the androids recall similar ones in *Westworld* (1973). There is also an uncanny similarity to two science fiction films by the acclaimed director Ridley Scott. In *Alien* (1979), made during the same year, one spaceship crew member turns out to be an android who attempts to kill off all the humans aboard. Similarly, in *Blade Runner* (1982), artificial humanoids called "replicants," indistinguishable from humans, are used to perform dangerous tasks in outer space colonies.

The 1980s produced a new crop of space-themed movies. *Per Aspera ad Astra* (1981), a title based on a Latin phrase meaning "through thorns to the stars," was a sci-fi melodrama set during the 23rd century. It begins with the starship *Pushkin*'s discovery of a derelict vessel containing a number of dead alien humanoid clones. One of the beings is found to be still alive, taken aboard the ship and transported back to Earth. The ship's head scientist, Sergei Lebedev (Uldis Lieldidz) adopts her and names her Neeya.

The blue-skinned femalien (Yelena Metyolkina) is suffering from amnesia and is found to possess powers of telepathy and teleportation. Eventually Neeya recovers her memory and travels back to her home world of Dessa in the starship *Astra* to lead a crusade against a cartel that is polluting the planet. The film is much more in the realm of space opera adventure fantasy than a reality-based exercise in space exploration.

Return from Orbit (*Vozvraschenie s orbiti*, 1984), on the other hand, was a unique Soviet effort that contained footage actually filmed in space by cosmonauts aboard the Salyut 7 space station. It opens with the two-person cosmonaut team consisting of Pavel Kuznetsov (Juozas Budraitis) and Vyacheslav Mukhin (Vitaly Solomin) anticipating their first joint flight to the Salyut space station. Just before the launch, Kuznetsov's wife dies unexpectedly. Consumed by grief, he is unable to participate in the upcoming flight and decides to leave the cosmonaut corps. Mukhin flies to the space station with co-pilot Valery Romanov (Valery Yurchenko).

Romanov is seriously injured during the docking procedure and needs to immediately return to Earth. But their damaged Soyuz spacecraft is unable to undock from the station. Kuznetsov is persuaded to fly into space to rescue his friend Mukhin and the wounded cosmonaut. He and Alexei Evgenievich Sviridov (Aleksandr Porokhovshchikov), head of the cosmonaut program, fly to the Salyut, spacewalk Romanov onto the second Soyuz and return him to Earth with Sviridov. Kuznetsov and Mukhin remain on the station and attempt to stabilize it, but a meteor strike causes further problems and the need for a *second* rescue mission.

This film has never been released in the West, and details about it are sketchy. Some scenes were reportedly shot in space aboard the Salyut 7 station and a Soyuz T-9 spacecraft by cosmonauts Vladimir Lyakhov and Aleksandr Aleksandrov. Short clips from the film posted on YouTube show documentary footage of a Soyuz launch, two cosmonauts inside the spacecraft, and one cosmonaut in weightlessness. Additional footage was shot in the Yuri Gagarin Cosmonaut Training Center and the RKA Mission Control Complex. The film has been compared to *Apollo 13*, the recent space survival movie *Gravity* (2013) and the similarly themed Russian feature *Salyut 7* (2016).

On April 12, 1961, one of the most momentous events in the history of space exploration took place when cosmonaut Yuri Gagarin became the first human being to orbit the Earth. The film *Gagarin: First in Space* (*Gagarin*, 2013) offered a recreation of this proud moment in the history of the Soviet space program in the context of a Gagarin biopic that unrolls in a series of flashbacks. The film opens at the Soviet space center of Biakonur in Central Asia, where Gagarin (Yaroslav Zhalnin) and his backup, cosmonaut German Titov (Vadim Michman), prepare for the first manned flight. The men, friendly rivals, don orange pressure suits and bulky space helmets and are driven to the launch site, where Yuri is installed inside the spherical Vostok spacecraft as the countdown commences. The multi-stage rocket performs flawlessly and Gagarin is launched on his journey.

As the space flight unfolds, various incidents from Yuri's life are interspersed in random sequence, including his initial qualification as a student pilot, the birth of his first child, his training as a cosmonaut, his early life with his parents and the courtship of his wife. The most extensive sequences document his testing for the cosmonaut corps. He was one of 20 finalists selected to participate in the program. The fledgling space cadets are subjected to trials in a centrifuge, in a high altitude pressure chamber and a battery of psychological tests under the strict tutelage of program leader Nikolai Kaminin (Vladimir Steklov).

Reaching orbit, Gagarin gazes out of the Vostok's porthole at the glories of the Earth from space. Observing some stray water droplets floating about the spacecraft, he is the first human being to experience weightlessness. Meanwhile, back at Biakonur, Kaminin and rocket scientist Sergei Korolev (Mikhail Filippov) worry about the functioning of the Vostok's automatic re-entry system. Their fears prove groundless, however, as the Vostok descends toward Earth, leaving a fiery trail after one orbit and 108 minutes in space. When the spacecraft reaches an altitude of 23,000 feet, Gagarin activates an ejection seat that propels him out of the Vostok into the sky. Descending on parachutes, he lands in a Russian farmer's field, where the spaceman identifies himself as a Soviet citizen. Word of the triumph quickly spreads through the U.S.S.R. and Gagarin is greeted by joyous mass celebrations in Moscow. The movie ends with film and audio clips of the real Gagarin extolling the glories of space flight for all humankind.

Gagarin: First in Space offers up a re-enactment of one of the milestones of manned space flight and the heroism of the first individual to brave the dangers of the high frontier. His achievement has long been overshadowed by the Apollo Moon landings, so it's nice to see him finally get his due in this biopic. Another figure that the film draws out of the shadows is that of Sergei Korolev, chief designer of the Soviet space hardware who, unlike Gagarin, was deliberately kept in obscurity over fears of assassination. Yaroslav Zhalnin's endearing performance as the modest, self-effacing Gagarin drives the film, along with Mikhail Filippov's portrayal of the stolid, avuncular Korolev. Director Pavel Parkhomenko has a fine grasp of the material and delivers a stirring evocation of a bygone era, and George Kallis composed an aggressive orchestral score that provides a stirring backdrop to the visuals. The special effects are stunning and sophisticated and compare favorably to the Hollywood product.

Many critics, however, took issue with the screenplay by Andrey Dmitriev and Oleg Kapanets, which was thought to whitewash Gagarin's character by deleting details of his later life. After the flight, Gagarin was declared a Hero of the Soviet Union and achieved rock star status among the Russian populace. He hobnobbed with international celebrities and was elected to the Soviet legislature, but there were complaints about his overindulgence in alcohol. Five years after his historic space flight, he attempted to return to the cosmonaut corps, and despite having gained weight and let his flying skills deteriorate, he was assigned as backup pilot on the first flight of the Soyuz spacecraft. The Soyuz malfunctioned, killing its pilot Vladimir Komarov, and in the aftermath Gagarin was deemed too valuable to risk and was never allowed to fly in space again. On March 27, 1968, he was killed during a routine flight of a MiG-15 UTI fighter jet. Numerous conspiracy theories about his untimely death were later shown to be unfounded.

Despite these factors, the film offers a realistic and accurate depiction of Gagarin's flight. International moviegoers were afforded their first glimpse of Russian space technology circa 1961, which seems rough-hewn and low-tech compared with its American counterpart, a factor that makes their achievement even more impressive. The sequences depicting the rigors of cosmonaut training parallel those of the American astronauts as shown in *The Right Stuff*. *Gagarin*'s 108-minute running time approximates the time the cosmonaut spent in space during the Vostok 1 mission.

Produced under the auspices of the Russian state, *Gagarin* plays upon nostalgia for the vanished glories of the Soviet space program. This trend continued with *The Spacewalker* (*Vremya Pervykh*, 2017), an account of the first spacewalk performed by cosmonaut Alexei Leonov during the Voskhod 2 space flight on March 18, 1965, another milestone for the Soviets. The film begins with test pilot Leonov (Yevgeny Mironov) conducting a test flight of a MiG fighter. The plane's engine flames out, but rather than eject from the aircraft he opts to perform a daring maneuver. He puts the plane into a steep dive that restarts the engine, allowing Leonov to regain control. General Nikolai Kaminin (Anatoly Kotenyov), head of the cosmonaut corps, arrives in time to see Leonov land the MiG and realizes that the pilot has the right stuff to fly in space.

Leonov becomes a cosmonaut and is paired with Pavel Belyayev (Konstantin Khabensky) in training for the Voskhod 2 mission, which is scheduled to include the world's first spacewalk. Chief designer Sergei Korolev (Vladimir Ilyin) is frantically striving to maintain Soviet dominance in space and is driving his team hard to complete work on the Voskhod, the first multi-man spaceship. The mission's first setback occurs when Belyayev is injured while skydiving and is replaced by another cosmonaut who is not to Leonov's liking. Then the unmanned test flight of the Voskhod 1 spacecraft malfunctions, casting doubt on the ship's novel design. Belyayev recovers fully and is re-instated on the flight, and Korolev and his team work out the kinks in their craft.

Voskhod 2 is launched from Biakonur Cosmodrome on a snowy day in March. Once it is in orbit, Leonov prepares for his extravehicular activity. The cosmonauts activate the Voskhod's inflatable airlock and Leonov clambers into the cylindrical chamber and seals the hatch behind him. Then he opens the forward hatch and emerges into space. Confronted by the glorious sight of the Earth from orbit, he is transported to ecstasy, but is soon absorbed by his assigned tasks during the EVA. He slips out to the end of the tether that secures him to the ship but has a difficult time getting back into the airlock when he finds that his spacesuit has overinflated. Deflating his suit by bleeding off some of the pressure, he must enter the airlock head first, then turn around in the cumbersome suit in order to close the hatch manually, which he manages to do just before his oxygen supply runs out. Another problem arises when the cosmonauts jettison the inflatable airlock, causing the craft to spin and creating a minor leak in the air supply. In response, the spacecraft's safety system begins flooding their cabin with pure oxygen, causing a toxic reaction that brings on hallucinations, blurred vision and loss of consciousness. Belyayev passes out but Leonov keeps his head clear just long enough to locate a wire that cuts off the excess oxygen flow and stabilizes the spacecraft's atmosphere.

Their troubles are far from over. They are scheduled to complete another 22 orbits, but the Voskhod is spinning too rapidly for ground controllers to activate the automatic re-entry system. The cosmonauts are instructed to land the ship manually. In addition, they are obliged to bring the ship down somewhere in Soviet territory to prevent the West from obtaining secret Russian space technology. The cosmonauts complete the difficult maneuver, but the spacecraft comes down hundreds of miles from their landing site in a remote, heavily forested area of the Ural Mountains that prevents their radio beacon signal from being detected. A frantic search ensues as Leonov and Belyayev struggle to survive in the frozen taiga. A ham radio operator in Sakhalin province picks up the signal and informs the authorities. A rescue helicopter is quickly vectored to the site, where the cosmonauts have just enough strength to fire a flare gun that alerts the pilot to their presence. The film ends on a happy note as Leonov and Belyayev are united with their families after their harrowing ordeal in space.

A gripping story of survival in space in the vein of *Apollo 13* and *Gravity, The Spacewalker* is a handsomely produced historical drama. Unlike *Gagarin*, the film's screenplay by Andrey Dmitriev and Oleg Kapanets is a straightforward narrative that proceeds in a linear fashion rather than jumping around in time and space. Most of the film was directed by Yuri Bykov; he was fired by the producers and replaced with Dmitriy Kiselev, who lensed the last third of the movie and received full credit as director, but there was no variance in cinematic style. Solid performances by Yevgeny Mironov and Konstantin Khabensky as the Voskhod cosmonauts, Vladimir Ilyin as the harried chief designer Korolev and Anatoly Kotenyov as the unflappable Kamanin give dramatic heft to the production. Russia's premier visual effects studio CGF worked on over 1200 computer graphics shots that are as impressive as anything in Western productions.

Cosmonaut Leonov acted as technical advisor on the film, which offers a fascinating recreation of a crucial event in the history of space exploration. In contrast to American space launches made in the balmy climes of Cape Canaveral, the Voskhod 2 launch is shown taking place during a snowstorm on the steppes of Baikonur. The imperative of maintaining Soviet dominance in the space race is very much in evidence as Korolev and Kamanin rush to develop the new spacecraft. Although *Spacewalker* is historically accurate in most respects, there is one glaring discrepancy. In the film, the Voskhod 1 flight is depicted as an unmanned test flight that malfunctioned, while in reality it was another Soviet milestone in space. Lifting off on October 12, 1964, it was the first multi-manned space vehicle that lofted three cosmonauts into orbit and set a new altitude record of 209 miles. It would seem that the filmmakers wished to simplify the narrative and create a sense of danger posed to the cosmonauts.

Leonov's feat was duplicated by astronaut Ed White, who performed the first American spacewalk during the Gemini IV mission four months later. The flight of Voskhod 2 was the last Soviet triumph in space as the Americans surpassed them when the Gemini program swiftly progressed into new levels of technological sophistication. Leonov (who died in 2019) became one of the principals in the Russian space effort, and reportedly was slated to pilot the lunar landing vehicle before the Soviet Moon program collapsed in the late 1960s due to Korolev's untimely death.

After the Apollo 11 landed on the Moon and the U.S.S.R. lost the space race, the Soviet space program shifted its focus to building a series of space stations beginning

Cosmonauts Alexei Leonov (Yevgeny Mironov, top) and Pavel Belyayev (Konstantin Khabensky, bottom) are pictured before and after their historic flight in this poster for *The Spacewalker* (*Vremya Pervykh*, 2017).

in the mid–1970s with Salyut 1. In 1985, the Soviets lost contact with the Salyut 7 station when all its systems inexplicably shut down; cosmonauts Viktor Savinykh and Vladimir Dzhanibekov were sent to save the station from orbital decay and eventual destruction. This harrowing space endeavor was the subject of the film *Salyut 7* (2017).

It opens in outer space in 1983, aboard the Salyut, where Vladimir Fyodorov (Vladimir Vdovichenkov) and Svetlana Savitskaya (Aleksandra Ursulak), the second woman in space and the first woman to perform an EVA, are working on a welding job outside the station. A tear on Savitskaya's glove puts her in danger of asphyxiation from loss of air in her spacesuit. Fyodorov coolly takes charge of the situation and guides his colleague to safety, but while she is entering the hatch he observes an anomalous light phenomenon in space. Upon returning to Earth, he reports it to his superiors and asks, "What if I saw angels?" He is promptly grounded for his remark.

Two years later, the station suddenly shuts down for unknown reasons, and flight director Valery Shubin (Aleksandr Samoylenko) briefs members of the Soviet space community and military brass about his concerns that the station could de-orbit over a populated area of the United States and cause casualties that would lead to an international incident. Shubin also claims that the Americans are poised to launch the space shuttle *Challenger* with an empty payload bay and speculates that their Cold War adversaries may execute an audacious plan to capture the Salyut, which could lead to a confrontation between the two superpowers. In consideration of these factors, the Russians decide to authorize a mission to reactivate the station, which represents the apex of Soviet space technology.

Shubin reinstates Fyodorov's flight status and teams him with engineer-cosmonaut Viktor Alyokhin (Pavel Derevyanko) for the mission. In preparation, Fyodorov spends many hours in the Soyuz flight simulator hoping to master the art of docking with the wildly gyrating Salyut. When he considers himself equal to the task, the cosmonauts are launched aboard the Soyuz spacecraft and rendezvous with the Salyut. After some frantic maneuvering, Fyodorov manages to achieve docking. Entering the dormant station, they find atmosphere inside but little else. Globules of frozen water droplets float around the frigid interior like a hailstorm of crystals.

The cosmonauts have their work cut out for them as they struggle to prevail against the severe cold and malfunctioning equipment. Dials and gauges are covered with a layer of ice, and a meteor strike has disabled a key piece of equipment, a sensor that controls the deployment of the solar panels that provide the station's electrical power. Using electricity from the Soyuz, they heat the station, but the water that had frozen over everything melts and creates new hazards. Things are not going well back on Earth, either, as Fyodorov's wife Nina (Mariya Mironova) is having severe nightmares about her husband not returning from space. Alyokhin's spouse Liliya (Lyubou Aksyonova) goes into labor and gives birth.

While Fyodorov is conducting an EVA to inspect the damaged sensor, a fire breaks out inside the station and Alyokhin is severely burned. The fire consumes much of the oxygen needed to continue the mission, and there is only enough to allow one of the cosmonauts to return to Earth. Faced with the probability of total failure of the mission, the authorities order Alyokhin to return, stranding Fyodorov on the Salyut. The decision prompts Shubin to hurl a chair through a glass partition. Alyokhin refuses to leave his comrade, and insists that they keep trying to rescue the station. The two cosmonauts perform a strenuous spacewalk during which they remove the damaged sensor

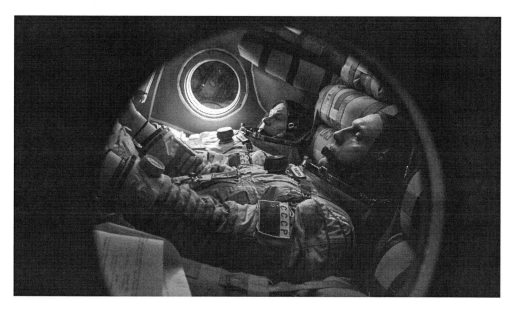

Vladimir Fyodorov (Vladimir Vdovichenkov, right) and Viktor Alyokhin (Pavel Derevyanko) ride their Soyuz spacecraft to a crippled space station in *Salyut 7* (2017).

and restore power to the Salyut. At their moment of triumph, the space shuttle *Challenger* performs a flyby, and the cosmonauts and astronauts salute each other in a gesture of mutual admiration and respect.

Another harrowing tale of survival and triumph in space, *Salyut 7* is very much in the mold of *Apollo 13, Gravity* and *The Martian*. Although it's not an actors' film, Vladimir Vdovichenkov and Pavel Derevyanko's performances as the cosmonauts tasked with salvaging the station provide the movie's main dramatic focus, as Vdovichenkov's maverick pilot character contrasts with Derevyanko's calculating engineer persona. The strongest dramatic performance is provided by Aleksandr Samoylenko as flight director Valery Shubin, whose hot-headed personality contrasts with the steely-eyed portrayal of his American opposite number Gene Kranz (played by Ed Harris) in *Apollo 13*.

The real stars of *Salyut 7* are the special effects, which are highly realistic, wonderfully crafted and more than equal to anything produced in Western effects studios. The film's producers claim that this realism was due to several sequences being shot in outer space, presumably at the International Space Station, but this claim is highly dubious. Director Klim Shipenko moves the action along briskly and doesn't let the stunning special effects overwhelm the drama of the life-or-death situation. There are affinities with the 1985 film *Return from Orbit*, which also featured a crisis, albeit a fictional one, aboard the Salyut 7 station. The film offers one of the most realistic depictions of the challenges and triumphs of space travel, although some details, such as the fire aboard the station and the plan to abandon one of the cosmonauts, were likewise melodrama concocted by the screenwriters (director Shipenko, Natalya Merkulova and Aleksey Samolyotov). Their screenplay is generally accurate in its depiction of the facts of the rescue operation, but there is also a strong element of Russian nationalism and nostalgia for the Soviet Union, as well as anti–American sentiment.

The most egregious example is the subplot in which the space shuttle *Challenger* is on a mission to capture the Salyut and thereby pilfer Russian scientific and military

Flight director Valery Shubin (Aleksandr Samoylenko) is featured in this production still from *Salyut 7* **(2017).**

secrets. This preposterous scenario first appeared in the Russian TV documentary "The Battle for Salyut: A Space Detective," which aired on November 1, 2011, on Teleradiostudiya Roskosmosa, the Russian equivalent of NASA TV. This conspiracy theory is easily debunked by considering a number of facts. *Challenger* was not launched in June 1985 and was not in space at the same time as the Soyuz T-13 mission to rescue the station. The shuttle's cargo bay was just large enough to accommodate a skyjacked Salyut, but numerous spacewalks would have been required to remove solar panels, antennae and other appurtenances in order to make it fit. The shuttle's maximum payload return capability was 14.5 tons, but the Salyut weighed in excess of 20 tons. These and other technical considerations make this conspiracy scenario entirely unfeasible. *Challenger* makes a brief guest appearance in a flyby scene in the film, but American-Soviet rescue missions were prohibited by the Russians' refusal to conduct such operations in 1984 and 1985.

For most of the 20th century, America and Russia were the only two spacefaring nations, and long before humans ventured off the planet, Russian cinema embraced space travel. Inspired by the works of pioneering theorist Konstantin Tsiolkovsky, the silent films *Aelita* and *Cosmic Voyage* pictured rocket voyages to other worlds. When Tsiolkovsky's theories were realized during the nascent years of the Soviet space program, their movies pictured a future in space in *Road to the Stars, The Heavens Call, Storm Planet* and *Solaris*. While space-themed science fiction films have never been as popular in Russia as they have in the United States, the 21st-century crop of fact-based, effects-laden space extravaganzas such as *Gagarin: First in Space, The Spacewalker* and *Salyut 7* will perhaps lead to a renaissance of big-screen Russian space odysseys.

Six

Working in Space

Having established techniques for traveling in space, futurists posit that the next step will be to establish a permanent human presence on the Moon, in orbit, and other places in the solar system. Once this has been accomplished, commercial interests can exploit the natural resources found in these exotic locales for profit. Space enthusiasts have theorized that asteroids could be mined for rare earth elements that are currently in great demand for industrial uses, and that the Moon could provide a source for Helium-3, an isotope that might provide fuel for the fusion power reactors of tomorrow. A small number of films have considered this possibility and constructed dramatic narratives set in these hostile environments where spacefarers must not only survive but accomplish complex and demanding tasks.

Many of these films take place during some future time, when humanity has established functioning commercial facilities on the Moon or other heavenly bodies. A common theme is covert corporate malfeasance that exploits space workers and places them in dangerous situations in the interest of higher profits. Some films depict the perils facing astronauts working in the hostile environment of low Earth orbit. Oddly, the first movies featuring off-planet working stiffs were billed as being "space westerns," a rather unlikely genre meld.

Moon Zero Two (1969) was a product of Britain's Hammer Films. The company was best known for its horror flicks, but they also dabbled in the science fiction genre with entries such as the *Quatermass* trilogy, *X—The Unknown* and *The Abominable Snowman of the Himalayas*. *Moon Zero Two* is set in the far future year of 2021, when frontier settlements have been established on the Moon and expeditions have landed on Venus and Mars. Former astronaut Bill Kemp (James Olson), the first human to set foot on the Red Planet, has been reduced to operating the salvage vessel *Moon Zero Two*, an antiquated space tug, with his partner Dan Korminski (Ori Levy). While collecting a fee for a salvaged satellite on the largest lunar settlement Moon City, Kemp is approached by millionaire speculator J.J. Hubbard (Warren Mitchell) about a scheme to salvage a small asteroid composed of ceramic sapphire in lunar orbit by crashing it onto the Moon's far side. Hubbard hopes to corner the market on this heat-resistant substance for building advanced rockets that will enable the further colonization of the solar system.

Kemp has doubts about this scheme because of its dubious legality, but Hubbard makes him an offer he can't refuse, as he threatens to have Kemp's operating license with the Space Corporation revoked. While cooling his heels in Moon City waiting for the mission to commence, Kemp is approached about another job by Clementine Taplin (Catherine Schell), a young woman whose brother Wallace went incommunicado while staking a mining claim on the Far Side. Clementine hires Kemp to transport her to the

Farside 5 settlement, where they will rent a Moon buggy to continue over the rough terrain to reach Wallace's claim at Spectacle Crater.

Upon reaching the crater, Kemp and Clementine discover Wallace's corpse and are promptly attacked by three spacesuited thugs. A gunfight ensues and the attackers are killed, but the pair's Moon buggy is disabled, forcing them to use their assailants' vehicle to return to the settlement. They cope with power and life support problems as they negotiate the treacherous terrain and must trek the last few miles on foot in their spacesuits. When they arrive at Farside 5, they find Hubbard waiting for them, along with his henchmen Whitsun (Dudley Foster) and Harry (Bernard Bresslaw). Hubbard threatens to kill Kemp and Clementine unless they do his bidding.

Moon Zero Two promptly lifts off and sets course for the sapphire asteroid. Once they are in orbit, Kemp, Hubbard and his men spacewalk over to the asteroid and attach rocket engine thrusters that will de-orbit the rock. During the operation, a gunfight breaks out. Hubbard and his men, trapped on the asteroid, are killed when the rockets are lit and it impacts on the Moon's surface. In the aftermath, it turns out that Hubbard had Wallace murdered because his claim occupied the space where he planned to bring the asteroid down. Because the precious sapphire material is now on Wallace's claim, Clementine is going to be a very rich woman.

This 1960s–era filmic artifact is a fun romp with an entertaining *Austin Powers* vibe. The costuming and set designs have a cartoonish, plastic and vinyl pop art flavor, while Don Ellis' frothy jazz-oriented score seems inappropriate for a serious science fiction picture. Hammer veteran Roy Ward Baker directs this unusual material with all the skill he can muster and does a workmanlike job in this distinct departure from Hammer's usual horror product. The film's most egregious sins are two ridiculous dance numbers staged by the Fabulous Go-Jos troupe. Star James Olson cuts a staid, heroic figure, glam actress Catherine Schell is easy on the eyes, and Warren Mitchell's J.J. Hubbard is a stock comic opera Teutonic villain complete with monocle. Billed as "the first Moon western," the film takes place in a rough'n'tumble frontier environment where, as in the Old West, miners stake claims on virgin territory, fights break out in the local saloon and citizens tote pistols holstered on their hips, but the attempt to juxtapose the two disparate genres is problematic at best.

To their credit, screenwriters Frank Hardman and Gavin Lyall adhere to scientific fact (with a few exceptions). The *Moon Zero Two* "space tug" resembles a souped-up version of the Apollo Lunar Module, and a briefcase-sized computer used for its navigation system recalls a similar device employed during the Apollo missions. The Moon's far side is correctly depicted as having much rougher terrain than the near side, and the surface rovers function in a realistic fashion. While there are no known mineral resources on the Moon, space futurists have theorized that asteroids could be mined for rare earth elements that are essential for the manufacture of hi-tech devices such as computers and smart phones, and some have suggested deliberately crashing the asteroids onto the lunar surface in order to harvest these materials. Oddly, the heat-resistant ceramic substance found in the movie's asteroid predates the ceramic tiles used on the space shuttle to deflect the enormous temperatures generated during the vehicle's atmospheric re-entry.

On the other hand, Wallace's corpse is discovered to be a skeleton, an impossibility in the airless environment of the Moon, and the film's Moon City employs the hoary pseudo-scientific device of "artificial gravity" to bring the Moon's one-sixth gravity up to an Earth-like 1G. The film takes place in a post–Cold War milieu in which the space race is a relic of the past. A multinational "Space Corporation" administers all off–Earth commercial ventures on the Moon and elsewhere in the solar system.

While *Moon Zero Two* attempted a generic evocation of the Western genre, *Outland* (1981) transported a specific Western movie into outer space, namely Fred Zinnemann's acclaimed *High Noon* (1952). Written and directed by Peter Hyams, lenser of the 1978 space-themed thriller *Capricorn One*, the film is set on Io, one of Jupiter's moons, where the Conglomerates Amalgamated Corporation operates a titanium mining outpost designated Con-Am 27. The workers labor under harsh conditions, working long shifts, wearing spacesuits in the reduced gravity. Con-Am 27 is managed by Mark Sheppard (Peter Boyle), who must keep up productivity while insuring that his workers are happy.

William O'Neil (Sean Connery), the outpost's new law enforcement officer, arrives with his wife Carol (Kika Markham) and son Paul (Nicholas Barnes). Living conditions on Con-Am 27 are not much to Carol's liking and she abruptly decides to return to Earth with Paul, leaving O'Neil in isolation. O'Neil has his hands full with the mining personnel, who are behaving in a psychotic fashion. One of them has the delusion that spiders are crawling over him and rips his spacesuit open while he is on Io's surface, causing him to die from decompression. Another worker enters an airlock without a pressure suit, causing his body to explode. In another incident, a knife-wielding worker takes a prostitute hostage and has to be killed by police.

Conferring with Dr. Marian Lazarus (Frances Sternhagen), O'Neil ascertains that these psychotic episodes are being caused by a synthetic amphetamine called

Marshall William O'Neil (Sean Connery) dispenses frontier justice at a deep space mining colony in *Outland* (1981).

polydichloric euthimal. It enables the miners to work long shifts, but the downside is that it causes its users to experience bizarre hallucinations. O'Neil learns that Sheppard is permitting the drug to be imported into the colony because it boosts productivity. When the lawman intercepts a shipment, Sheppard realizes that his nemesis must be eliminated or his corporate superiors will eliminate him. He places a call to the nearest space station and hires a trio of assassins to dispose of the troublesome cop.

O'Neil intercepts the call, and thus forewarned he makes plans to counter the killers by hiding weapons in various strategic places. Word soon gets around the colony that O'Neil is a marked man, and not even his fellow officers will risk their necks to help him. The shuttle takes 70 hours to reach Con-Am 27 from the space station, and the ship's flight time counts down on a giant digital display. Just before the ship's arrival, O'Neil pleads with the miners for help and is refused. Only Dr. Lazarus is willing to aid him. Amid a blare of klaxons, the shuttle arrives and the three assassins disembark. O'Neil engages in a deadly game of cat and mouse with the killers both inside and outside the station, and with the help of Dr. Lazarus, he ultimately triumphs, leaving Sheppard to his fate. As an added bonus, he and his family reconcile, and he plans to return with them to Earth.

In *High Noon*, the marshal of a western town must face a trio of bad guys who are arriving on the 12 o'clock train to kill him, but despite his pleas, no one in the town will help him. The similarities with the plot of *Outland* are obvious and intentional. Hyams reportedly wanted to make a Western, but was dissuaded because the genre was no longer commercially viable. He then came to the conclusion that the Western was not dead, but had merely been transplanted into outer space. Like many Westerns, *Outland* is set in a grungy frontier outpost that is poised on a knife edge between law and anarchy, and where the only morality is provided by an upright, courageous marshal. Sean Connery plays this part to perfection. His terse exchanges with Frances Sternhagen's acid-tongued Dr. Lazarus provide the film's dramatic (and comedic) backbone, while Peter Boyle's portrayal of the corrupt corporate lackey Sheppard comes off as blandly villainous.

Critics have pointed out many similarities between *Outland* and Ridley Scott's science fiction–horror megahit *Alien*, which was released two years earlier (1979). Both films take place in space and have a gritty, industrial sci-fi ambience. Although they took pains to deny it, Hyams and his production designer Malcolm Middleton reportedly sought to emulate what was called the "Ridley look" from Scott's sci-fi hit *Alien* (1979).

Another connection was that veteran composer Jerry Goldsmith scored both films. *Outland*, shot at Pinewood Studios in the U.K., was the first film to utilize a process called Introvision, a sophisticated front projection technique that allowed the actors to interface with the background sets and miniatures without using blue screen optical superimposition. Cinematographer Stephen Goldblatt made liberal use of the Steadicam, a device that allowed the camera to get fluid, moving shots without the use of cumbersome tracks and dollies, to swoop through the maze-like corridors of the mining facility.

The film takes place during a time in the future when humans have expanded their commercial operations into the solar system's outer planets. The Con-Am 27 mining colony is convincingly portrayed as a self-contained, fully functioning frontier town in space. Although Io, like the Moon, has one-sixth Earth gravity, the film makes no effort to depict this condition, and seems to rely on the hoary sci-fi plot device of "artificial gravity." The notion of humans establishing a mining facility on Io also strains credulity, as the moon is constantly being warped by Jupiter's enormous gravity and is highly volcanic. Humans on Io's surface would also be subject to intense radiation that is continually streaming out of the giant planet.

German-born director Roland Emmerich has sometimes been referred to as the "German Spielberg" due to his output of blockbuster science fiction films. After leaving his native country for Hollywood in the 1990s, Emmerich directed a string of big-budget sci-fi crowd pleasers, a list that includes *Universal Soldier* (1992), *Stargate* (1994), *Independence Day* (1996), *Godzilla* (1998), *The Day After Tomorrow* (2004), *10,000 B.C.* (2008), *2012* (2009) and *Independence Day: Resurgence* (2016). The last film he directed in Germany, however, was *Moon 44* (1990), a production that established his bona fides as a science fiction director.

The film takes place in the year 2038, when humans have achieved interstellar travel and corporations are able to exploit the resources of other star systems. An outfit called the Galactic Mining Corporation operates a mining outpost on Moon 44, a world in the Outer Zone. The Pyrite Defense Company, has been hijacking Galactic's shuttles and their cargoes, so Galactic recruits Internal Affairs agent Felix Stone (Michael Paré) to investigate. Galactic uses helicopters to guard their shuttles, but since pilots are scarce, the company has resorted to using prisoners to fly the aircraft.

Navigators Tyler (Dean Devlin, front) and Cookie (Stephen Geoffreys, rear) direct attack helicopters against enemy corporate aircraft in *Moon 44* (1990).

Stone arrives at the outpost incognito and goes undercover as a prison inmate. He confers with helicopter navigator Tyler (Dean Devlin), who fingers Major Lee (Malcolm McDowell) and his assistant Master Sergeant Sykes (Leon Rippy) as the culprits who are reprogramming the flight computers on the stolen shuttles. During his investigation, Stone catches Sykes in the act of modifying one of the shuttle's navigation co-ordinates. When Sykes attacks Stone with an axe, Major Lee appears and shoots Skyes dead.

Thinking that the case has been solved, Stone is preparing to return to Earth when the outpost is attacked by a wave of Pyrite robot drones. The real culprit turns out to be Major Lee, who has sabotaged the base's defense systems and programmed all of the Galactic shuttles except one to return to Earth. Stone mans the base's defenses and shoots down the drones as Lee attempts to blow up the last remaining shuttle with a bomb. Stone traps Lee in an elevator, and he is killed when the bomb explodes. The rest of the base's personnel are evacuated from Moon 44 in the shuttle and return to Earth, where Stone reports to his corporate superiors that Lee had been working for Pyrite all along.

Obviously inspired by *Outland*, the film emulates its grungy sci-fi *misè en scene* on another off-world mining colony. Director Emmerich does a workmanlike job with this derivative material, but the plot, as devised by screenwriters Oliver Eberle and Dean Heyde, is predictable, with its obvious villains and anti-corporate thematics. Emmerich

Terry Morgan (Lisa Einhorn) confers with Major Lee (Malcolm McDowell) in *Moon 44* (1990).

does manage to achieve decent special effects on a modest budget. Dean Devlin, who acted in the film, subsequently collaborated with Emmerich as a screenwriter on many of the director's most successful productions.

The notion that humankind would have to seek out new sources for vital materials on far-off worlds is a plot element that appears in a number of sci-fi flicks. In *Alien* (1979), an enormous space freighter transports loads of mineral ore across interstellar distances, while in *Avatar* (2009), Earth spaceships travel to the moon of Pandora to mine the scarce anti-gravity mineral "unobtainium." Some critics chided the film's use of helicopters on a moon (they would not be able to fly due to the absence of an atmosphere); but some satellites are known to have an atmosphere, such as Saturn's moon Titan.

An outpost on the Moon's far side is the setting for the British science fiction thriller *Moon* (2009). In the year 2035, an energy shortage on Earth is being mitigated by machines that harvest Helium–3, a fuel for nuclear fusion reactors, from rocks on the lunar surface. Giant automated harvesters grind up the lunar regolith, which is then placed into containers and propelled down to Earth using a rail gun device. Sam Bell (Sam Rockwell) oversees a mining operation for the energy consortium Lunar Industries Ltd. at Sarang Station, a facility on the Moon's far side. The job is undemanding and mostly consists of troubleshooting and repairing the harvesters when they malfunction. His existence at the station is lonesome but pleasant, and he spends his time working in a garden, constructing an elaborate model and watching reruns of TV sitcoms.

Sam's only companionship is provided by an intelligent computer, GERTY 3000 (voiced by Kevin Spacey), that efficiently runs all of the station's systems. A satellite link provides sporadic communications with Eve (Kaya Scodelario), his wife on Earth.

Sam Bell (Sam Rockwell) performs his daily rituals in a lonely lunar mining station in *Moon* (2009).

Within the next two weeks, Sam will complete his three-year assignment at Sarang. His long isolation seems to have led to a bout of cabin fever, and one day he sees a hallucination of a teenage girl that startles him so badly that he burns his hand.

When one of the harvesters malfunctions, Sam is obliged to put on a spacesuit and roll out to the machine in a lunar rover to investigate. The Moon buggy crashes, trapping Sam inside. The next thing he knows, he is back in the station's infirmary, where GERTY informs him that he has sustained brain damage that has led to amnesia about the accident. Sensing that something about the situation is bogus, Sam commandeers another rover and returns to the scene of the accident, where he discovers an injured double of himself trapped inside the crashed vehicle.

Sam transports his twin back to Sarang and resuscitates the double with GERTY's help. When the second Sam returns to full consciousness, the two grapple with the enigma as to which of them is the real Sam Bell. The rescued Sam Bell has a wound on his hand, while the other Sam seems younger and more robust. The two Sams eventually discover the grim truth that they are both clones of the original Sam Bell, who returned to Earth some time ago. Rather than sending workers to the Moon every three years, the company found it simpler and cheaper to man the station with a workforce composed entirely of clones. Each of the two Sam clones has a three-year life span and possesses the memories of the real Sam Bell. When the two Sams learn that a team of company technicians is en route to the station, ostensibly to repair the harvester, they realize they will both be killed if they are found together. They devise a plan wherein one of them will sacrifice himself and the other will stow away inside an ore canister and return to Earth to expose the illegal cloning practices of the company.

First-time director Duncan Jones delivers a hard science fiction *tour de force* that is

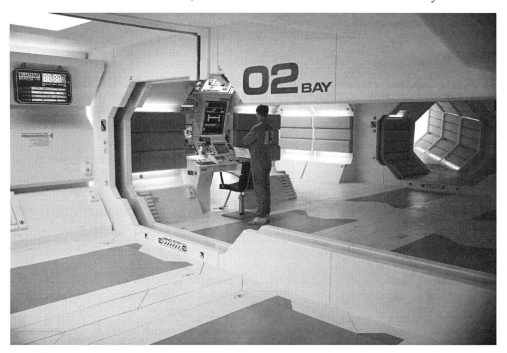

Tony Noble's economical but highly effective production design is showcased in this still from *Moon* (2009), featuring Sam Rockwell.

all the more remarkable for being produced on a modest budget of $5 million. Jones and production designer Tony Noble conjured up a white, antiseptic environment in which the film's astronaut vainly struggles to retain his sanity. The filmmakers reportedly recycled sets from the BBC-TV series *Red Dwarf* to keep costs down. Sam Rockwell, playing multiple variants of a single individual, sustains the dramatic action admirably in what is in essence a one-man show, with the off-screen voice of Kevin Spacey offering needed support. *Moon* depicts the crushing loneliness of an individual confined to a virtual prison on an alien world. The bleak lunarscape of the Moon's far side provides a hauntingly empty backdrop to the proceedings.

Extracting Helium-3 from the lunar surface has long been proposed as a reason for establishing commercial mining ventures on the Moon. This isotope is rare on Earth, but has been found in lunar dust and minerals that have been bombarded by the solar wind for millennia. It is thought that it could provide fuel for the nuclear fusion reactors of the future to efficiently produce electrical power, but this idea is highly controversial. Such reactors do not currently exist, and the use of this substance to provide power is purely theoretical. Many researchers believe that mining Helium-3 on the Moon and transporting it to Earth in sufficient quantities would not be economically feasible.

While these films postulated commercial ventures on various moons in the solar system and elsewhere, a couple of more recent films explored the dangers and stresses of working in low Earth orbit, and both of these films had female astronauts as protagonists. *Gravity* (2013) begins with a spectacular shot of the Earth from space as the space shuttle *Explorer* comes into view. The shuttle is mated to the Hubble Space Telescope, which is being repaired by engineer Ryan Stone (Sandra Bullock) as Commander Matt Kowalski (George Clooney) zooms around in a manned maneuvering unit in an effort to break a world record for a spacewalk. Stone, who is on her first space mission, is standing at the end of the shuttle's manipulator arm installing new circuit boards when she is joined by Kowalski, who assists her with the difficult task as he makes jocular remarks. Gorgeous vistas of the planet revolve slowly beneath them.

This idyllic scene is abruptly interrupted by an urgent message from NASA. The Russians have deliberately blown up one of their own satellites, an event that has caused a chain reaction that is propelling debris through space at an estimated 50,000 miles per hour. As the two astronauts strive to undock from the Hubble, they watch in horror as a debris swarm slams into the *Explorer* and devastates it. Stone is flung away from the shuttle and helplessly tumbles head over heels into the void.

When things seem darkest, Kowalski jets into view to rescue Stone. He attaches a tether to her spacesuit and propels them both back to the shuttle. They are horrified to find the corpses of their crewmates floating in microgravity inside the now derelict spacecraft. Their only means of survival is to reach the International Space Station and return to Earth in one of the two Soyuz lifeboats.

Kowalski and Stone jet toward the ISS as their oxygen supplies run low. As they approach the ISS, it becomes evident that the station has also been heavily damaged and that the crew has abandoned it in a Soyuz. The remaining Soyuz is damaged and cannot be used for re-entry, but Kowalski suggests that it can still be used to reach the Chinese Tiangong space station, and they can use one of its escape capsules to return to Earth. Hurtling toward the ISS, the astronauts struggle to obtain a handhold on the station's superstructure. Stone becomes entangled in some wires. Kowalski realizes that the wires are too loose to hold them both, and deliberately untethers himself in order to

Astronaut Dr. Ryan Stone (Sandra Bullock) attempts to return to Earth in a Soyuz lifeboat in *Gravity* **(2013).**

save her. As he drifts away into space, he coaches her through the airlock until his voice can no longer be heard on her headset radio.

Objects float around the forlorn interior of the ISS and broken equipment emits sparks as Stone struggles to find her way to the Soyuz. Once inside, she is devastated to discover that there is no fuel in the spacecraft, rendering it unusable. To make matters worse, a fire aboard the ISS destroys the station and she barely manages to undock, but she is still trapped in space and descends into despair as she contemplates her death. Just when things seem hopeless, Kowalski returns and enters the Soyuz, and in his usual joking manner he suggests that she use the spacecraft's soft landing rockets, which will no longer be needed for re-entry, to propel the Soyuz toward the Tiangong. After imparting this advice, the astronaut abruptly vanishes.

Taking Kowalski's suggestion, Stone separates the landing module from the rest of the Soyuz and fires the jets that propel it toward the Chinese station 100 kilometers away. As she approaches, she sees that the station is descending into the stratosphere and is starting to disintegrate. She manages to gain access as it falls to pieces around her and finds her way into the Shenzhou spacecraft. Although it is similar to the Soyuz, the controls are all in Chinese characters as she struggles to initiate the undocking procedures. She succeeds, perhaps through sheer luck, as the station plunges into the atmosphere and starts to burn. Stone's parachute deploys and she makes a safe water landing. She swims to shore and stands up with the good Earth beneath her feet.

Like *Apollo 13* and *Salyut 7*, *Gravity* is a harrowing narrative of survival in space. An opening title states, "Life in space is impossible," and this view sums up the theme of the film. The audience is meant to experience a profound sense of relief when the movie's protagonist returns to the safety of Earth. Director Alfonso Cuaron, who co-scripted with his son Jonas, delivers a rollicking thrill ride as the film's vulnerable heroine struggles to stay alive while undergoing a series of ordeals that threaten her at every turn, yet manages to beat the odds. The film's space hardware is beautifully and accurately realized, and the 3-D space environment is exquisitely rendered.

Gravity makes do with only two actors, one of whom is quickly removed from the narrative. George Clooney's relentlessly upbeat Matt Kowalski provides an emotional anchor not only for the distraught Dr. Stone, but for the audience as well, and his timely advice from beyond the grave saves the day. It is Sandra Bullock's riveting,

Oscar-nominated performance, however, that dominates the film. In its most moving sequence, Stone is trapped in the disabled Soyuz and contemplates her death in space while listening to the amateur broadcast of a man singing to his baby on the ship's radio. She muses, "No one will mourn for me."

The film's other major character is space itself, which is depicted as alternately beautiful and threatening. From the early spacewalking scenes that feature dazzling vistas of the Earth in the background, the film progresses to show a darkened void of stars as Stone spins helplessly into infinity. The movie's $100 million budget allowed the filmmakers to invent new techniques to render the exotic environment of space. Cinematographer Emmanuel Lubezki invented a "light box," a 20 foot-high enclosure containing 4096 LED lights that projected moving images of the Earth and space around the actors, who were filmed by robotic cameras. The production crew nicknamed the rig "Sandy's cage," as Bullock was obliged to spend up to ten hours a day inside the contraption during shooting. A 12-wire suspension system was used to simulate the actors moving in zero gravity, while in other scenes they were filmed underwater with backgrounds filled in using computer graphics during post-production. Nominated for seven Academy Awards, *Gravity* won in the categories of Best Director, Best Cinematography, Best Visual Effects and Best Original Score.

Many critics praised the verisimilitude of the movie's depiction of the space environment, including Apollo moonwalker Buzz Aldrin and Space Shuttle astronaut Michael Massimino, who had performed repairs on the Hubble Space Telescope. Others pointed out certain discrepancies, such as the fact that the Shuttle program was retired in 2011, two years before the film was released. One of the movie's most prominent critics

Sandra Bullock undergoes the rigors of hi-tech filmmaking in this production still from ***Gravity*** **(2013).**

was astronomer Neil de Grasse Tyson, host of the PBS series *Cosmos*, who made a number of criticisms regarding what he felt were details that were inconsistent with the realities of space travel. Most of these were minor, but he did point out that traveling from the Hubble, which orbits at an altitude of about 559 kilometers, to the ISS, which is parked at approximately 420, would be highly improbable at best. The laws of celestial mechanics dictate that an object in a lower orbit moves at a higher velocity than one in a higher orbit due to the effects of gravity, so that it would not be a simple matter to travel between them, especially in a spacecraft with limited motive power as shown in the film. Director Cuaron responded to these criticisms by stating that he was making a fiction film, not a documentary.

One aspect of *Gravity* that rings true, however, is the plot element wherein the Russians destroy one of their own satellites with a missile, an act that causes debris to hurtle through space in a chain reaction that destroys the Shuttle and two space stations. This scenario has a firm basis in reality and has been named the Kessler Syndrome after scientist Donald Kessler, who first proposed such a possibility in 1978. As objects large and small accumulate in low Earth orbit, the odds that a collision between them could precipitate a destructive chain reaction that could make space activities impossible due to the kinetic energy of debris travelling at high speed that can damage spacecraft. In January 2007, the Chinese deliberately destroyed one of their defunct weather satellites with a missile, an act that could have led to a Kessler Syndrome event similar to the disaster depicted in the film. This did not happen, but space scientists are currently keeping an eye on the European Space Agency's Envisat satellite, which is on an orbital path that could put it on a collision course with other objects in orbit.

The plight of another female astronaut provided the basis for *Lucy in the Sky* (2019). Like *Gravity*, it begins with a mission specialist, Lucy Cola (Natalie Portman), performing a spacewalk while tethered to the International Space Station. She is dazzled by the glories of space and so moved by the sights that she has a type of mystical experience. After returning to Earth aboard the Space Shuttle from a ten-day mission on the ISS, she has difficulty adjusting to life on the ground, as her first venture into space seems to have changed her psychologically. A hard-charging overachiever, she becomes obsessed with her desire "to be up there," and continually daydreams about being back in space. Her husband Drew (Dan Stevens), a PR specialist at NASA's Johnson Space Center in Houston, provides what moral support he can, and she's also close to her elderly grandmother, Nana Holbrook (Ellen Burstyn), who offers up her own brand of earthy wisdom.

Lucy is in competition for a slot on the upcoming Polaris mission that will utilize the new Orion spacecraft to install new solar arrays on the ISS. One of her chief competitors is another female, Erin Eccles (Zazie Beetz). Lucy undergoes a series of physical and psychological tests, along with sessions in the Orion simulator, to earn a place on the mission, and her psychological obsession with returning to space drives her to her limits. During the evaluation, she aggressively enters into an affair with the square-jawed, charismatic Shuttle pilot Mark Goodwin (Jon Hamm), which severely complicates her home life. Another complication is provided by her niece Blue Iris (Pearl Amanda Dickson), whom she and her husband are obliged to accept into their household due to a family crisis.

Things begin to go south for Lucy during a session at NASA's Neutral Buoyancy Lab, essentially a large swimming pool where astronauts train for operations in full EVA gear underwater in an environment that simulates floating in zero gravity. While she is performing a panel-removal simulation on an ISS mockup, her spacesuit begins to fill

Rival astronauts Erin Eccles (Zazie Beetz, left) and Lucy Cola (Natalie Portman) compete for a spot in an upcoming space flight in *Lucy in the Sky* (2019).

with water. Despite the danger, she ignores safety protocols and continues to work at her task until her helmet is completely filled. This does not sit well with her NASA evaluators, who begin to question her readiness to fly again. Lucy had been deprived of oxygen for two minutes during the test, and had this occurred in space, another astronaut would have been imperiled while trying to rescue her. NASA bumps her from the Orion mission and informs her that she will not be able to fly again for three years. This severe setback devastates her.

Lucy endures another psychological jolt when she discovers that Mark is having an affair with her rival Erin. She confronts him about it, and he ends their relationship. At the same time, Lucy's husband knows that something is going on and becomes estranged from her. When Lucy's grandmother dies from a stroke, the event precipitates the end of her marriage. She moves into her grandmother's house with Blue Iris as she spirals downward into mental illness.

Learning that Mark betrayed her by providing a negative appraisal to NASA brass that led to her being grounded, she begins to plot her revenge as meticulously as if it was a space mission. Accompanied by Iris, she purchases a blonde wig, a gun, a can of bug spray and other items as the pair departs on their road trip to San Diego, where Mark and Erin are vacationing. When they arrive at San Diego Airport, Lucy cannot find her weapon, which has secretly been confiscated by Iris who fears that Lucy will commit homicide. Donning the wig, Lucy stalks Mark into the airport's car rental lot and confronts him, spraying him in the face with the insecticide as he attempts to drive away. Alerted by Iris, the police arrive, and Lucy is pursued and taken into custody. In an epilogue, Lucy is seen three years later working on a bee farm in France, having finally abandoned her dreams of space and reconciled to life on Earth.

Unmercifully panned by critics, *Lucy in the Sky* had a limited release and was a major box-office failure. The film is severely flawed, but nowhere near the disaster that critical consensus has made it out to be. One major problem is that its astronaut protagonist is an unpleasant person who is overly aggressive and promiscuous, and her obsession fails to engage the audience's sympathy even as she is betrayed, endures personal loss and descends into mental illness. Natalie Portman's intense performance dominates the film and paints a portrait of a driven, ambitious woman that should have appealed to a feminist sensibility. Another defect is the screenplay by Brian C. Brown, Elliott DiGuiseppi and director Noah Hawley, which is overlong and lacks focus. The script is "inspired by a true story" (the criminal exploits of NASA astronaut Lisa Nowak) and it attempts to meld this with a narrative about a space traveler obsessed with the mystical experience of being "up there," but the two story threads don't quite mesh. Critics also groused about director Hawley and cinematographer Polly Morgan's use of varying screen aspect ratios, but this minor affectation is barely noticeable. Jon Hamm's portrait of a macho astronaut offers an effective foil to Portman's obsessive persona, while screen veteran Ellen Burstyn steals every scene she's in as the curmudgeonly grandmother. Pearl Amanda Dickson shines in her supporting role as Blue Iris.

The launch vehicle in the film is that most photogenic of spaceships, the Space Shuttle (even though it was retired eight years before the movie's release), but the film's NASA crews are training for the Orion spacecraft. Essentially a ramped-up successor to the Apollo Moon ship, Orion has been in development by Lockheed-Martin for quite some time and is designed to transport astronauts to the ISS, the Moon, Mars and other deep space destinations. A mockup of the Orion Crew Module is seen in the background in one scene. The sequence taking place in the Neutral Buoyancy Lab was not filmed at the actual site in the Johnson Space Center in Houston, but in a college swimming pool in San Carlitas, California.

While some critics decried the depiction of an astronaut having a spiritual experience during an excursion into space, a number of astronauts have reported having similar feelings. Apollo 11 Command Module pilot Michael Collins is quoted in the film regarding his expansive emotions while orbiting the Moon alone. Collins later wrote, "I am alone now, truly alone, and absolutely isolated from any known life.... I feel this powerfully—not as fear or loneliness—but as awareness, anticipation, satisfaction, confidence, almost exultation. I like the feeling."[1] During the Apollo 14 mission, moonwalker Alan Shepard, America's first man in space, known as the "Icy Commander" in NASA circles for his severe reserve, experienced a similar epiphany. As related by space historian Andrew Chaikin,

> He took a moment to lean back so that he could look up into the black sky, and near the zenith his gaze found a small and lovely blue-and-white crescent. Suddenly he was overcome by the beauty of the earth.... Shepard cried. For several long moments, while the checklist went unnoticed, his tears flowed in spite of himself.[2]

Similarly, Apollo 17 astronaut Gene Cernan was transfixed by the sight of his home planet from the Moon. Chaikin writes that Cernan thought, "It was simply too beautiful to have happened by accident. He felt as if he were seeing the earth as it had appeared in the moment before creation, in the mind's eye of God."[3] So far, *Lucy in the Sky* is the only filmic treatment of this psychological aspect of space travel.

As previously stated, the movie was "inspired by true events," namely the scandal surrounding astronaut Lisa Nowak. A Navy flight officer and robotics mission special-ist, Nowak flew aboard the Space Shuttle *Discovery* for 12 days during the STS-121 mis-sion in July 2006. Although she had been married for 19 years, she subsequently entered into an affair with fellow astronaut William Oefelein, and suffered a mental breakdown when he broke off the relationship and took up with Air Force Captain Colleen Ship-man. In February 2007, Nowak packed up a wig, a BB gun, a folding knife, pepper spray and several other items and drove 900 miles from Houston to Orlando, Florida, to con-front her rival. She caught up with Shipman at the Orlando Airport parking lot and pep-per sprayed her while she was inside her car. Nowak was promptly arrested and charged with burglary, assault and attempted kidnapping. After a plea deal, she was convicted of felony burglary and misdemeanor battery. As a result, she was terminated by NASA, reduced in rank by the Navy and received a less than honorable discharge. A psycho-logical evaluation revealed that Nowak suffered from obsessive-compulsive disorder, Asperger syndrome, and had experienced a psychotic break during the incident. This led to an internal review of mental health issues within the astronaut corps, but nothing came to light regarding psychological problems associated with space flight as depicted in the film.

As humankind continues to expand into space, spacefarers will enter into com-mercial ventures to exploit the resources found within this realm. Whether harvesting Helium-3 on the Moon, mining rare earth metals on nearby asteroids or searching the solar system for as-yet-undiscovered materials, these industrial space pioneers will face unique challenges in their quest for off-world profits.

SEVEN

The Allure of Mars

Mars has always held a particular fascination in the human mind. Along with Venus, it's our closest neighbor, but *unlike* Venus, the Red Planet is not covered by a dense layer of clouds that obscure its surface. During the 19th century, astronomers Sir William Herschel and Giovanni Schiaparelli observed that Mars had Earth-like polar caps and posited that intelligent beings had constructed a series of canals designed to transport water around the desiccated desert world. The advent of more powerful telescopes and Mars space probes eventually disabused scientists of these fanciful ideas, but beginning with H.G. Wells' 1898 novel *The War of the Worlds*, Mars was invested with a fantastical mystique that inspired a raft of science fiction works.

In the cinema, Martian invaders populated movie screens for decades in sci-fi fare such as *The War of the Worlds* (1953), *Invaders from Mars* (1953), *The Day Mars Invaded Earth* (1962), *Martians Go Home* (1990) and *Mars Attacks!* (1997). Mars was the interplanetary destination of choice in thee early features *Heaven Ship* (1917), *Aelita* (1924), *Just Imagine* (1930) and the serial *Flash Gordon's Trip to Mars* (1938). The sci-fi movie craze of the 1950s and early '60s produced a number of journeys to the Red Planet. In *Rocketship X-M* (1950) and *Flight to Mars* (1951) astronauts discovered humanoid inhabitants living there. *Conquest of Space* (1955) featured a more realistic, science-oriented expedition to Mars. Spacefarers encountered monstrous life forms such as a "bat-rat-spider" and a humongous amoeba in *The Angry Red Planet* (1960). *The Wizard of Mars* (1964) transplanted elements of *The Wizard of Oz* into outer space.

The Mariner space probes in 1965 and the Viking Mars landers in 1976 began the process of the de-mythologizing of Mars. It was revealed to be a lifeless world devoid of liquid water, with a thin atmosphere composed mainly of carbon dioxide. No longer could filmmakers conjure fanciful creatures or alien civilizations there. But the notion of life on Mars was briefly resuscitated during the 1990s when a group of scientists announced that they had discovered evidence of microbial life in a Martian meteorite. This news item caused a stir in media outlets, but the claim is still considered highly controversial and was probably premature. In a parallel development, the Viking orbiters' low resolution photographs of the Cydonia area of Mars purportedly showed evidence of a Sphinx-like "face," pyramids and other artificial structures thought to be the remains of a vanished civilization. But subsequent, higher resolution photos of Cydonia by the Mars Global Surveyor showed that these features were geological in nature. Still, these much-publicized ideas found their way into popular culture, including the cinema.

While the outdated visions of Mars gave way to scientific reality, the real Mars would eventually come into focus as a romantic and imaginative landscape all its own. As revealed in photographs from the Opportunity and Sojourner rovers, Mars is the most Earth-like world in the solar system. It has an atmosphere that scatters light into the brightness of a sky (unlike the Moon, whose sky is the deep black of space), and a day that is just one hour longer than ours. It has polar ice caps composed of water ice and frozen CO_2, sand dunes, canyons, mountains and volcanoes similar to ours. The surface is not heavily cratered like Mercury or the Moon. Space visionaries like Elon Musk are intent on colonizing Mars as a hedge against a future catastrophe that might destroy the human race.

Robinson Crusoe on Mars (1964) takes place some time in the future, as NASA astronauts Christopher "Kit" Draper (Paul Mantee) and Dan "Mac" McReady (Adam West) conduct a survey of the planet's gravitational field from their orbiting spacecraft, the *Elinor M.* An oncoming meteor forces them to take evasive action and their ship plunges into a dangerously low orbit. Lacking the fuel for further maneuvers, the astronauts have to abandon ship, departing the *Elinor M.* in separate lifeboats.

Draper survives a rough landing on a surface engulfed in volcanic flames and attempts to contact Mac via a communication device but receives no reply. He salvages any undamaged equipment, including a spare oxygen tank, supplies of food and water, along with an all-purpose device that functions as a television, radio, tape recorder and radar unit. Donning a survival suit equipped with one of the O_2 tanks, he fashions a makeshift harness and proceeds to haul his equipment over the Martian surface, searching for Mac's escape pod. After spending a night on the planet's cold desert, he locates a cave where he takes shelter and ignites some yellow colored rocks for warmth. Oxygen consumption proves to be problematical in the thin Martian air, so he must carefully ration the oxygen in his tanks.

The next day, he locates the escape pod and finds that Mac has not survived the crash. He buries his fellow astronaut, but then notices what appears to be a tentacle poking out from behind a rock. Thinking it is an alien life form, he draws his pistol, but it turns out to be the tail of Mona, the monkey that was brought along on the mission. He is glad to have the animal for companionship. Back in the cave, he loses consciousness from asphyxiation. When he revives, he discovers that the yellow rocks he has been burning for warmth emit oxygen, and he devises a method to pump the released gas into his tanks to replenish them. He also invents a "sand clock," an hourglass contraption designed to awaken him during sleep periods when he will need to inhale oxygen from his tanks.

While he has solved the oxygen problem, he is rapidly running out of food and water. Noticing that Mona is not drinking from his supply, he follows the monkey to a pool of water. He also finds Mona eating some bulbous plants growing in the pool, and finds that they are edible. One night when he prepares the plants into a stew, he has a vivid dream in which Mac's ghost visits him in the cave. He awakens frightened and confused because of the plant's hallucinogenic effect. He also discovers that fibers from the plants can be woven into clothing.

His basic needs for food, clothing, shelter, air and water having been met, Kit settles down to a routine domestic existence. He keeps an audio diary of his day-to-day experiences on his tape recorder. One day when he is out exploring, he comes across a human skeleton with a pair of hi-tech bracelets attached to its wrists and realizes he is not alone on the planet. Fearing discovery by an unknown adversary, he carefully covers up his tracks and destroys the *Elinor M.* Several weeks later, he observes a ship landing in the distance. Hoping that it's a rescue mission he treks out to the landing site to investigate.

When he arrives, he videotapes a number of strange-looking alien craft engaged in a mining operation, along with a group of human workers overseen by armed, space-suited figures. Kit shoots a video of the scene from hiding, and is startled when one of the workers (Victor Lundin) suddenly appears behind him. Seeing that the man is wearing the same bracelets he had found on the skeleton, Kit surmises that he is an escaped slave and leads him back to the cave.

At first Kit is suspicious of his new companion, with whom he cannot communicate. Little by little, however, a bond begins to form between them and he names the stranger Friday, after the character in *Robinson Crusoe*. Friday has oxygen pills that enable slaves like him to function in Mars' thin atmosphere without an oxygen tank. Eventually the pair learns to communicate, and Kit learns that Friday hails from a world orbiting Alnilam, a star in the constellation Orion.

The alien slave masters are able to track Friday via the bracelets. As Kit tries to remove them, the ships return and blast the cave entrance with their rays, trapping Kit, Friday and Mona inside. Friday leads them through a series of underground caverns that he explains are the remnants of the canal system built ages ago by a vanished Martian race. During the journey, Kit manages to remove Friday's bracelets, which prevents the alien slave masters from continuing to track him. Their water supply exhausted, they finally emerge from underground near one of the planet's polar ice caps, which will provide them with all the water they need. To avoid freezing to death, they build an igloo. But a meteor crashes nearby and melts the ice with the heat of the impact. Kit detects a blip on his radarscope, which turns out to be a NASA vessel that sends down a lander to rescue them.

Intelligently directed by Byron Haskin, who helmed *The War of the Worlds* (1953), the film is an exercise in "hard" science fiction in the mode of *Destination Moon* and *Conquest of Space*, as the protagonist must confront the scientific challenges of surviving in a hostile alien environment. Haskin frequently shoots Kit in extreme long shots that accentuate his aloneness in the barren landscape, and he reportedly considered Mars one of the film's major characters. Outdoor scenes were filmed in the rugged terrain of Death Valley National Park in California, which does bear a resemblance to the barren wastes of the Red Planet. In addition, Haskin instructed his special effects expert Lawrence Butler to use optical printing mattes to change the blue sky to an orange hue to realistically simulate the extraterrestrial skies of Mars.

Inspiration for the film arose in the mind of veteran sci-fi scenarist Ib Melchior during a trip to Death Valley, where the forbidding desert landscape conjured imaginative visions of an alien world. His screenplay is divided into two parts, the first dealing with Kit's struggle to survive on Mars and the second with involving Kit and Friday's ordeal while being pursued by the alien slave masters. Many critics opined that the second half descended into a fantastical scenario that detracted from the realism of the first half. This dichotomy probably arose from having to emulate the plot of the Defoe novel. The film must get by with only three actors (four if Mona the monkey is counted). Adam West, best known as the star of TV's *Batman* series, is removed from the plot early in the film and has his best scene as an apparition. Paul Mantee carries most of the film on his broad shoulders and plays the part of Kit with stolid heroism and occasional humor. Victor Lundin's portrayal of Friday must struggle through stretches of silence and dialogue in pidgin English. The alien spaceships were recycled war machines from *The War of the Worlds*, while the slavers' spacesuits were from *Destination Moon* leftovers. Made during the tumultuous days of the civil rights movement in the early 1960s, the film's subplot involving Friday's liberation from slavery reflects the tenor of the times.

The first half of *Robinson Crusoe on Mars* bears a resemblance to Ridley Scott's crowd pleaser *The Martian* (2015). Both films focus on the struggles of a lone astronaut marooned on Mars, who must find ways to survive, and both films feature an extensive space travelogue as their protagonists explore the exotic alien world. Of course, the second half of *Robinson Crusoe* descends into the realm of space opera and confrontation with hostile extraterrestrials. *Robinson Crusoe* and *The Martian* both posit a robust NASA space program that is able to mount expeditions to the far reaches of the Red Planet.

Outside of the alien issue, the main difference between the two films is that *Robinson Crusoe* was informed by the science of the times and still adheres to romantic notions about Mars. Over 50 years after the film was made, we know that liquid water cannot currently exist on the planet's surface, and that the Martian polar caps are composed primarily of frozen carbon dioxide mixed with water ice. Its thin atmosphere contains only CO_2 without any breathable oxygen, and fires cannot burn there as depicted in the film. While microbial life might have existed there in the past, there is currently no evidence of complex plant life. The astronaut is shown wearing nothing but a T-shirt in the planet's balmy clime, and Friday goes shirtless during most of the proceedings, but in reality Mars' surface temperatures are colder than those on Antarctica. Finally, the film still clings to the notion of a system of Martian canals built by a vanished alien race, something we now know to be nothing more than a 19th-century fantasy. Amusingly in the 21st century, the movie's posters featured the phrase "This film is scientifically authentic … it is only one step ahead of present reality."

The year 1968 saw the ascendency of the American space program over the Soviet Union as NASA's Apollo program began a series of successful flights that culminated in the first lunar landing the following year. The Apollo 7 mission tested the viability of the spacecraft in Earth orbit, but Apollo 8 stunned the world by flying around the Moon that Christmas. Against this backdrop of spectacular NASA feats, the first landing on Mars was depicted in the low-budget space adventure *Mission Mars* (1968).

Intrepid astronauts Mike Blaswick (Darren McGavin), Nick Grant (Nick Adams) and Duncan (George De Vries) blast off on a nine-month mission to the Red Planet aboard the *Mars One*. After docking with a crayon-shaped "supply ship" in space, they settle down for the long journey to their destination. The spaceship is roomy and comfortable and the astronauts don't have to struggle with zero gravity as they cook their meals on a full-sized kitchen stove and keep in shape on an exercise machine. While en route, they come across the frozen bodies of two Russian cosmonauts tumbling through the void, victims of the fatal accident that befell a Soviet Mars mission launched four months earlier.

Reaching Mars orbit months later, the astronauts undock from the supply ship, which tumbles away to land off course on the planet's surface. The men land without incident, don their spacesuits, and step out of the spacecraft to explore Mars and locate their supply ship. Inflating a series of balloons to guide them back to *Mars One*, they trudge over the bleak terrain, but they are startled to discover the frozen corpse of yet another Russian cosmonaut. Blaswick orders Grant to take the body back to the ship as he and Duncan continue their search. When they locate the supply ship, they find their supplies scattered about. The ship has been burned by an infrared heat ray.

Then they discover that their trail of balloons has disappeared, and the reason becomes apparent when they are attacked by a group of one-eyed plant-animal creatures who shoot heat rays out of their eyes. The astronauts fight back with their own ray guns and disintegrate the aliens, then flee back to the safety of the ship. They report their close encounter to NASA, whose scientists dub the creatures "polarites" for some reason, and warn that the beings are transmitting data to an unknown source on Mars.

NASA orders the men to abort the mission and take off immediately, but a new conundrum arises as a sphere suddenly appears outside the spacecraft and exerts a force field that prevents them from firing their rocket engines. Duncan goes outside the ship and attacks the sphere with his weapon, but the sphere fires back, zaps him and then drags his body inside of it. The frozen cosmonaut (Bill Kelly) revives and says that the sphere can only be neutralized by getting inside it and destroying a disc. Deciding to sacrifice himself, Grant goes out to attack the sphere, which obligingly opens up to allow him to train his blaster on its innards. Grant is killed in the explosion and the force field is eliminated, allowing Blaswick and the cosmonaut to blast off for Earth. The film ends on a happy note: NASA informs Blaswick that his wife is pregnant as *Mars One* speeds toward home.

Released the same year as the groundbreaking *2001*, *Mission Mars* presents a pathetic counterpoint to Kubrick's masterwork. Director Nick Webster, whose previous association with the Red Planet was the notoriously awful kiddie flick *Santa Claus Conquers the Martians* (1964), fares little better in this low-rent space odyssey. The special effects are dreadful; the *Mars One* lander resembles a soda can mounted on stilts, and Mars, viewed from space looks like a pockmarked rubber ball. Likewise, the astronaut's spacesuits are ludicrous, tight-fitting white garments with radio antennae atop their helmets. The alien globe looks like it's made out of aluminum foil. Dialogue penned by screenwriter Mike St. Clair consists of astronaut jargon like "All common systems are go!" and "Flight trajectory A-OK," and the recitation of boring statistics about Mars. Arguably the silliest aspect of the film is the soundtrack, which consists of bad 1960s–era psychedelic guitar riffs that accompany *Mars One* on its journey through space. Hollywood stalwarts Darren McGavin and Nick Adams demonstrate they have the wrong stuff as a couple of hapless astronauts.

Like *Robinson Crusoe on Mars,* the film conflates a scientific model of the planet with a fantasy scenario involving aliens. The film's bleak Martian landscape gives no clue about how these indigenous life forms obtain food, water or other sustenance, and the film's "polarites" look as if they were copied from the cover art on a 60s–era sci-fi paperback. A flurry of stock footage clips of Saturn launches depicts the launch of the Mars mission. Models of the film's spacecraft are crude and leave much to be desired, especially in comparison with the exquisite miniatures that so enlivened *2001*. The astronauts are not obliged to cope with zero gravity on their long journey. The crew's radio communications with Mission Control are instantaneous rather than taking the real-life 40 minutes for a two-way chat. Mars, as pictured in the film's sets, is on the low-tech level of the alien landscapes appearing on TV sci-fi shows like *Star Trek*.

During the succeeding decades, NASA's Mars probes (especially the 1976 Viking landings) thoroughly de-mythologized the Red Planet as it was revealed to be a frozen, airless desert world devoid of life, past or present, except for the controversial furor over the so-called "Face on Mars." As a consequence, filmmakers were forced to more accurately depict their Martian odysseys. In addition, movie special effects technologies became orders of magnitude more sophisticated after the advent of *Star Wars* in 1977, a quantum leap that enabled filmmakers to picture outer space environs with much more verisimilitude.

It took several decades and a new millennium before humans returned to off-world exploration with *Red Planet* (2000). The film opens with a monologue that informs the audience that by 2000, the Earth had become so overpopulated and polluted that humanity's survival was in question. By 2025, governments were implementing a plan to colonize Mars as a lifeboat, and started sending unmanned probes there containing algae designed to terraform the planet by producing oxygen to make Mars habitable. In addition, nuclear bombs have been exploded on the planet's polar caps to release the carbon dioxide contained therein, in an effort to create a greenhouse effect that would raise the planet's surface temperature. But oxygen levels on the Red Planet began declining, and in 2057 a team of astronauts and scientists was assigned to go to Mars and study the problem.

The spaceship *Mars One* is set to depart from a high-orbit space station on the first manned mission. The crew consists of pilot and commander Bowman (Carrie-Anne Moss), hotshot co-pilot Santen (Benjamin Bratt), mechanical systems engineer Gallagher (Val Kilmer), science officer Chantillas (Terence Stamp), bio-engineer Burchenal (Tom Sizemore) and terraforming scientist Pettengill (Simon Baker). The seventh member of the crew is AMEE (an acronym for Autonomous Mapping Exploration and Evasion), a sophisticated military robot resembling a large mechanical dog. On loan from the Marine Corps, it will help the crew navigate and explore the new world. A habitat (food and life support supplies), sent ahead of the expedition, will sustain the astronauts once they reach Mars.

Once the ship is in orbit around Mars, a burst of gamma energy from a solar flare disables the power and life support systems on the spacecraft. Bowman decides to stay with the mother ship and orders the crew to evacuate in the lander. The astronauts launch and endure a rough landing, bouncing over the terrain as the lander's cluster of impact bags deploy. Chantillas suffers a ruptured spleen and must be left behind to die. AMEE has also been disabled. Gallagher, Santen, Burchenal and Pettengill depart on their trek to the habitat.

Bowman strives to restore power and must deal with a dangerous fire that has engulfed the mothership. She manages to snuff out the fire by donning a spacesuit and opening the ship's airlock, which sucks the flames out into the vacuum of space. When she restores full power, she finds that she is unable to communicate with the others (their radio is damaged). Meanwhile, AMEE reactivates itself—in military mode. The robot sets out to stalk the astronauts in a war fighting protocol.

The astronauts hike over the Martian surface, the air in their spacesuits running out. Gallagher gets into a tussle with the hotheaded Santen and accidentally causes him to plunge off a cliff to his death. The remaining three crewmen are forced to remove their helmets and are surprised to find they can breathe in the planet's atmosphere. This is puzzling, because they have so far seen no sign of algae growths.

When the three men arrive at the habitat, they are horrified to find it in tatters and its supplies scattered. They are only able to salvage some rocket fuel, which they ignite for warmth during the chilly night. The fire allows AMEE to locate the men. It attacks but stops short of killing them and instead vanishes into the night, acting in accordance with a pre-programmed military routine that compels it to play a cat-and-mouse game with its prey. In the morning, Gallagher comes up with the idea of using the radio from a Mars probe that landed on the planet back in 1997. They hike to the landing site and get the device up and running, but its signal can't be picked up by *Mars One* because it is broadcasting on a different frequency. But NASA picks up the signal and notifies Bowman, who hones in on the new frequency and is now able to communicate with the team.

The brain trust at NASA also comes up with a plan to return the astronauts to the mothership using *Cosmos*, a Russian probe that landed on Mars 30 years ago but failed to take off. *Cosmos* is 100 kilometers from the men's location, and they must reach it within 19 hours, when *Mars One* must leave the planet's orbit. The Russian scientist who designed *Cosmos* devises a routine to jumpstart the spacecraft's engines. The plan is communicated to Bowman, who passes it on to Gallagher, but there is a hitch: The craft will only accommodate two people. While the men deliberate over who should stay behind, Pettengill, who does not trust the others, steals the radio and runs out into the night so he can return alone while leaving the others behind. Before he can reach the *Cosmos*, he is intercepted by AMEE and killed.

Gallagher and Burchenal retrieve the radio and continue their trek. Burchenal notices that there is algae growing on the rocks around them, and incendiary insects crawling around on the rocks. Burchenal theorizes that the bugs are responsible for creating the planet's oxygenated atmosphere. He takes samples of the insects, but is trapped by a swarm of them. Sacrificing himself, he passes the samples on to Gallagher, who continues on alone.

Reaching the *Cosmos*, Gallagher struggles to initiate the launch sequence while Bowman radios instructions. His task is complicated by the spacecraft's controls being printed in Russian Cyrillic lettering. He also finds that the spacecraft needs a power boost in order to take off. AMEE appears and attacks him, but he cleverly disables the robot and extracts a power cell, which he uses to start the ship's engines. He crawls inside the spacecraft and initiates the launch sequence, hurling *Cosmos* into Mars orbit.

In *Mars One*, Bowman watches the *Cosmos* craft approach, but realizes that it will fall short of achieving her orbit. As the craft gets nearer, she dons an EVA spacesuit and attaches a tether. She propels herself into space, grabs hold of the *Cosmos*, retracts the cable and pulls the small craft into *Mars One*'s airlock. Gallagher has suffered cardiac arrest from the launch, but is soon revived by Bowman. He has brought the insect specimens with him, and the two remaining astronauts prepare for the six-month trip back to Earth with their mission accomplished.

A competently made science fiction thriller, *Red Planet* melds a realistic space exploration narrative with a fantastic action movie plot into an uneven whole. The Chuck Pfarrer-Jonathan Lemkin screenplay posits an idealized, terraformed Mars with a breathable atmosphere and mild temperatures, and throws in well-worn sci-fi tropes such as a killer robot and swarms of carnivorous insects. The script also assigns oddball names (Chantillas, Santen, Burchenal, Pettengill) to the astronauts, an eccentricity that distances them from the audience. Note that the mission commander's name is Bowman, which seems to reference the name of one of the spacefarers in *2001*.

Director Anthony Hoffman does a decent job orchestrating the film's visual effects by Jack Geist and art direction by Hugh Bateup and gives the production a slick techno-ambience. His direction of the actors is another matter. The characters are one-dimensional. Santen is an egotist with anger management problems, while Chantillas is a philosopher scientist. Their personalities are poorly drawn and lack depth. Star

Val Kilmer performs his leading role with a curious lack of affect, and seems to be channeling his role as the reserved jet pilot "Iceman" in *Top Gun*. Sci-fi heroine Carrie-Anne Moss delivers a similarly flat performance as the commander, while British veteran Terence Stamp does little to enliven the proceedings and is removed from the plot early on. The rest of the cast members don't fare any better, which is the film's major flaw. There was reportedly bad blood between Kilmer and co-star Tom Sizemore on the set.

Red Planet was one of the first films to depict a realistic image of Mars that was informed by NASA's orbiters, landers and rovers, and it ushered in a new visual paradigm for cinema portrayals of the planet. The joint U.S.-Australian production was budgeted at $80 million and shot at the Wadi Rum area of Jordan and in the Australian outback, with the Martian sky digitally tinted red. The film also reflects current notions about the need to colonize Mars as a hedge against the devastation of the human race through overpopulation, pollution or natural disasters such as a planet-killing asteroid impact. These scenarios are currently providing the impetus for interplanetary exploration championed by Elon Musk and others. The idea of terraforming Mars is problematical, however, as the process would take generations, and any atmosphere produced would probably bleed out into space by the solar wind, as, unlike Earth, Mars has no magnetic field to preserve it. Of course, growing algae and mutant bugs on Mars as shown in the film is highly fanciful at best, and as any high school science student knows, animals breathe in oxygen and exhale carbon dioxide, not the other way around. The space hardware pictured in the film comports with real-world NASA technology, especially the bouncy house lander that has been used to land unmanned probes on the planet's surface.

While *Red Planet* was a commercial flop and has faded into obscurity, it appears that several of its plot elements re-appeared in *The Martian*. These include NASA detecting the presence of the astronaut on Mars, the use of a decades-old, defunct probe to communicate, NASA's devising a plan to use a previously landed spacecraft to launch an astronaut into orbit and a female mission commander performing a spacewalk to bring the stricken astronaut safely into the mother ship.

The other big-budget Mars odyssey released that year was *Mission to Mars* (2000). In the year 2020, NASA launches the first manned expedition to the Red Planet, Mars One. The four-member crew is commanded by Luke Graham (Don Cheadle). The astronauts erect a habitat in the Cydonia region and set about exploring the new world. A robotic rover, sent out to map the environs, detects anomalous electronic signals, which the team believes indicates a subsurface geothermal column of water that might provide life support for future colonists. Initial radar probes reveal that the formation from which the signals emanate is metallic underneath, but when they send out another radar burst, there is a violent reaction. A huge, snakelike vortex of sand and stone arises and kills all of the crew except Luke and reveals a metallic, Sphinx-like face under the rubble. Luke sends a cryptic message back to Earth before an electromagnetic pulse fries the communication equipment and the electronics on the mission's ERV (Earth Return Vehicle).

In the light of these events, a hastily organized rescue mission, Mars Two, departs during the next launch window. The crew consists of Commander Woody Blake (Tim Robbins), his wife Terri Fisher (Connie Nielsen), Phil Ohlmyer (Jerry O'Connell) and Jim McConnell (Gary Sinise), who recently lost his spouse. Among other supplies, the rescue ship is transporting a replacement set of circuit boards for the ERV. Mars Two is about to begin orbiting Mars when a meteorite storm causes multiple breaches in the hull. Two of the holes that are bleeding the ship's atmosphere out into space are located and quickly patched, but unbeknownst to the crew, the spacecraft's fuel lines have also been punctured.

When the main engines are fired for orbital insertion, the leaking fuel explodes, forcing the astronauts to abandon ship. Their only chance of survival is to perform an EVA to reach a Resupply Module (REMO), a ship that has previously been placed in orbit around Mars, and use it as a landing vehicle. Woody manages to reach the REMO and attach a tether cable, but slips off the craft's surface and drifts away from the others. Terri launches a valiant attempt to rescue her husband, but he has moved out of range and sacrifices himself so that she will not pursue him further and imperil her own life. As she watches in horror, he removes his space helmet and his corpse slowly drifts away.

Terri, Phil and Jim commandeer the REMO and ride it down to the planet's surface. Trekking overland, they reach the Mars One expedition's habitat and link up with Luke, who has survived by using greenhouse plants to generate oxygen. Luke fills them in concerning the signals emanating from the Face, which he believes represents an incomplete molecule of human DNA. He speculates that the transmission was a test, one that the Mars One's explorers failed, and that it is necessary to beam a signal containing a complete schematic of human DNA at the Face to avoid a repeat of the tragedy.

While Jerry stays behind to repair the ERV, Luke, Jim and Terri ride a rover to the Face, which opens up an aperture to admit them. Inside, they find a breathable atmosphere and a holographic model of the solar system that depicts an Earth-like Mars devastated by a cataclysmic impact from a huge asteroid. An alien being, one of Mars' original inhabitants, emerges to explain via imagery that in the wake of the disaster, the Martians departed their home planet to colonize new worlds. One ship went to Earth and was responsible for propagating life there. The Martian extends an invitation to the humans to voyage to the stars, but only Jim accepts. In the meantime, a severe sandstorm is about to engulf the ERV, and Jerry warns the others that they must return at once, before he is forced to take off without them. Terri and Luke struggle through the storm and reach the ERV in time, and as the ship blasts off on the return trip to Earth, the alien spacecraft streaks away bearing Jerry on its journey.

Directed by Brian De Palma, best known for horror fare such as *Sisters* (1973), *Carrie* (1976) and *Dressed to Kill* (1980), the film transitions from a space exploration extravaganza in the first half to a highly derivative alien contact movie in the second, as De Palma crafts a workmanlike but not particularly inspired effort. The most memorable sequence is the spacewalk from their disabled craft to the Resupply Module as the Red Planet's surface revolves far below them. Woody's self-sacrifice to save the mission is the dramatic high point, but this serves to remove star Tim Robbins from the narrative prematurely and renders the remainder of the movie anticlimactic. Most of the film's shortcomings can be laid at the feet of scripters Jim Thomas, John Thomas and Graham Yost, who recycle plot elements from some earlier science fiction classics. An encounter with an alien artifact in space was likely cribbed from *2001*, while an astronaut invited to join an alien on an interstellar journey seems to have been lifted from the ending of *Close Encounters of the Third Kind* (1977). Robbins and Connie Nielsen perform a charming dance routine in zero gravity while the rest of the cast members deliver earnest performances and Jerry O'Connell provides weak comic relief.

The film's $100 million budget provided state-of-the-art effects from Industrial

Light & Magic, Dream Quest Images and Trans FX. Extensive use of miniatures and CGI animation reportedly involved over 400 technicians in post-production, although the film did not receive any award nominations. While praising the film's visuals, most critics balked at its clichéd dialogue, mediocre performances and sappy ending. *Mission to Mars* did poorly at the box office, bringing in only $10 million in domestic and international profits over its production costs.

Unlike the International Space Station, the film's World Space Station in orbit around the Earth has a wheel-like structure spinning around its center that provides a fraction of terrestrial gravity through centrifugal force, a feature that counters the long-term effects of zero gravity on the human body. The Mars Two spacecraft also has a rotating section in the crew compartment for similar purposes. This "artificial gravity" effect also relieves the filmmakers from having to show the actors floating around in zero G on wires or by other means. Having the astronauts perform an EVA to rendezvous with a spacecraft going faster in a lower orbit poses problems in celestial mechanics maneuvering similar to those that would later crop up in *Gravity*. While global sandstorms are not uncommon on Mars, the planet's atmospheric pressure measures only six millibars as compared to Earth's 1013 millibars, which means that a storm on Mars would have a barely perceptible effect on a spacecraft trying to take off. The Wadi Rum area of Jordan, known in Arabic as the Valley of the Moon for its dramatic sandstone formations, was used to film the scenes taking place on Mars, and this same location, a UNESCO world heritage site, was also used for the same purpose in *Red Planet* and *The Martian*. NASA astronaut Story Musgrave, veteran of several Space Shuttle missions, cameos as a space station worker.

A controversy addressed in the film is the theory of *panspermia*, which, in its classic form, posits that life on Earth was seeded from somewhere else in the universe. According to this theory, extraterrestrial micro-organisms originating on another world survived in the harsh environment of space and fell to Earth inside meteorites; here they found benign conditions and "seeded" life on our planet from elsewhere. A variation of this theory is called *directed panspermia*, in which life was deliberately sent here by an alien intelligence, as depicted in *Mission to Mars* and *Prometheus* (2012). While these theories remain unproven, they were embraced by scientists (including Fred Hoyle and Stephen Hawking) and continue to be investigated by researchers.

Note that all of these Martian odyssey films have featured extraterrestrial life forms existing on the Red Planet. In *Robinson Crusoe on Mars,* interstellar aliens are mining minerals there, while "Polarites" and a mysterious sphere menaced astronauts in *Mission Mars*. *Red Planet* had oxygen-breathing mutant insects evolving on the terraformed planet, and *Mission to Mars* featured an alien presence inhabiting a monumental artifact. In 2015, *The Martian* finally offered a reasonably accurate and extraterrestrial-free portrait of an expedition to Mars.

The Martian takes place in 2035, when NASA's Ares III mission is exploring Mars' Acidalia Planitia region. Six astronauts have set up a base camp that includes a habitat (or Hab) to house them during their 31-sol (Martian day) mission. Parked nearby, the Mars Ascent Vehicle (MAV) is a shuttlecraft that will transport the crew back to the *Hermes*, a giant spaceship in Mars orbit, for their return to Earth. The explorers go about their tasks until sol 18, when a massive dust storm approaches the base camp. Mission commander Melissa Lewis (Jessica Chastain) orders the crew to evacuate into the MAV. One astronaut, botanist-engineer Mark Watney (Matt Damon), is injured by a flying piece of debris and gets separated from his crewmates. Commander Lewis, believing him dead, reluctantly orders the MAV to take off before the intense storm winds can topple it. The crew returns to the *Hermes*, which leaves Mars orbit for the return trip. Watney is stranded on the alien world.

Watney regains consciousness to find he has sustained a serious abdominal puncture wound and his spacesuit is leaking oxygen. He returns to the Hab, where he treats his wound and takes stock of his situation while recording his ruminations in a video log. Lacking a radio, he is unable to communicate with NASA. The Hab is well-stocked with life support essentials, including power, air and water, but he is without a food supply that will last him until the Ares IV mission is scheduled to return in four years. Using his botany skills, he sets up a potato farm in the Hab with a batch of spuds the crew had planned to cook for Thanksgiving dinner; potatoes will supplement the rations left behind by the other astronauts. Bags of freeze-dried human excrement are used as fertilizer and stored hydrogen and oxygen are combined to produce water as he successfully grows and harvests his crops.

Back on Earth, NASA imaging analyst Mindy Park (Mackenzie Davis) notices changes in the vicinity of the Hab while reviewing photos from a Mars orbiter that indicate that Watney is still alive. She brings the images to the attention of NASA director Teddy Sanders (Jeff Daniels), who announces the startling discovery to the press. Watney's plight is deliberately kept from the crew of the *Hermes*, however, as Sanders fears that it will interfere with their mission. Stung by adverse publicity over the incident, but also motivated by humanitarian concerns, NASA scientists and engineers scramble to save Watney's life and bring him back to Earth.

On Mars, Watney uses his ingenuity to travel to the Pathfinder probe, which became disabled in 1997, in his Mars rover vehicle. He rigs up the Pathfinder's video and gear and a system of written letter signs to transmit and receive messages using ASCII symbols in hexadecimal mode. NASA sends him a software modification that enables him to communicate directly using text via a computer link with the rover. He is told that they will send a supply rocket as soon as possible. He is chagrined to learn that his crewmates aboard the *Hermes* have not been told that he is still alive.

A major setback occurs when the Hab's airlock accidentally depressurizes and Watney's potato farm is wiped out by the Martian cold and carbon dioxide atmosphere. He is now unable to grow more food, making the resupply mission more essential to his survival. NASA's Mars mission director Vincent Kapoor (Chiwetel Ejiofor) and Jet Propulsion Laboratory engineer Bruce Ng (Benedict Wong) pull out all the stops in assembling the supply rocket by cutting corners with the pre-flight safety protocols. When the rocket is launched, it explodes seconds after liftoff.

Just as things seem hopeless, JPL astrodynamicist Rich Purnell (Donald Glover) has a brainstorm. He proposes to have the *Hermes* resupplied for a return trip to Mars and use the Earth's gravity to fling it back on a return trajectory to Mars to rescue Watney. Sanders is against the idea, but *Hermes* flight director Mitch Henderson (Sean Bean) makes the decision to inform the crew on his own. Once they are apprised of the situation, the astronauts unanimously vote to return to rescue Watney and they change course to rendezvous with a Chinese resupply rocket. Once the supplies are loaded on board, the *Hermes* heads back to Mars.

To reach the rescue ship, Watney must travel 2000 miles to the Schiaparelli Crater, where the Mars Ascent Vehicle (MAV) for the Ares IV mission has been pre-positioned.

Mark Watney (Matt Damon) contemplates the Red Planet's bleak environment in *The Martian* (2015).

The trip in the rover will take 90 sols, and Watney must make frequent stops to recharge the vehicle using solar panels he is hauling behind him in a trailer. The astronaut marvels at the vast empty spaces of the Red Planet as he observes, "Everywhere I go, I'm the first." Upon reaching the MAV, he must remove all excess weight from the launcher in order to lighten it so it can reach the *Hermes* as it swings around Mars. Timing is critical because the ship will not go into orbit around the planet, and he will only have one chance to get it right.

When the *Hermes* is in position, Watney fires up the MAV and ascends through the planet's atmosphere wearing a Manned Maneuvering Unit spacesuit. The MAV doesn't gain enough velocity to rendezvous with the ship, so Commander Lewis orders a controlled explosion to slow down the *Hermes*. Even this desperate measure doesn't quite do the trick, so Lewis dons a Manned Maneuvering Unit and performs a spacewalk to reach Watney, but her tether falls short. Watney then punctures his suit and uses the escaping air to propel him toward Lewis. The successful rescue is watched by cheering crowds around the world. A brief epilogue shows Watney instructing a new generation of astronauts in off-world survival techniques.

Helmed by producer-director Ridley Scott, who had directed the science fiction classics *Alien* (1979) and *Blade Runner* (1982), *The Martian* was a brilliant exercise in scientifically accurate hard sci-fi. Scott's magnificent visuals, shot in the Wadi Rum area of Jordan, beautifully conjure the Martian landscape from photographs of Mars supplied to the director by NASA. His mastery of all aspects of the production, including special effects, art direction and acting, combined to produce a *tour de force* that proved to be an enormous critical and popular success. Faithfully adapted from Andy Weir's popular novel by scenarist Drew Goddard, the film exemplifies a can-do optimism as its protagonist "works the problem" of survival in concert with the unflagging efforts of NASA and the cooperation of the Chinese space program. Like *Gravity,* the main thrust of the narrative is a lone individual coping with the unforgiving environment of space. Although the members of the large supporting cast turn in fine performances, Matt Damon's portrayal of the upbeat Mark Watney dominates the film. The psychological effects of isolation during his 560 sol ordeal on Mars are not addressed. It received praise from most critics, enjoyed success at the box office and was nominated for seven Academy Awards, including Best Picture and Best Actor but did not win in any category.

Scott and his production crew received an almost unprecedented degree of cooperation from NASA, who viewed the film as an excellent opportunity to promote Mars exploration. James L. Green, director of the Planetary Science Division, was the space agency's main liaison with the film's production team, and NASA provided hundreds of photographs of Mars and images of actual space hardware to Scott's production designer Arthur Max. Allowed to tour the Johnson Space Center, Max got a first-hand feel for real-life interplanetary technology. NASA even plugged the film on its website and designed a web tool that tracked Watney's journey from the Acidalia Planitia region to Schiaparelli Crater.

While the filmmakers took pains to present realistic hardware, much of the movie's technology and space science is speculative. The *Hermes* is approximately the size of the International Space Station, and it would be a daunting and expensive task to construct it in Earth orbit. It would presumably be equipped with heavy radiation shielding to protect the astronauts from high energy cosmic rays and solar flares during long-duration space flights. Such a vehicle, sometimes called a Mars Cycler, was popularized by Apollo 11 moonwalker Buzz Aldrin. The *Hermes* would be placed on a permanent trajectory between the two planets to facilitate transportation between the Earth and Mars using gravity assist and minimal propellant.

As previously noted, atmospheric pressure on Mars is so feeble in comparison with that of Earth that it could not topple the heavy MAV as depicted in the film. The movie also does not accurately portray the conditions of severe cold that prevail on the planet. Director Scott reportedly did not attempt to picture the reduced gravity conditions in the Martian environment, as he deemed it too problematical to present convincingly. The film also dispenses with the 40-minute back-and-forth radio transmission time between Earth and Mars, as adhering to this reality would not be practical in a two-hour film. Perhaps the most controversial plot element concerns the growing of crops in Martian soil. Unlike soil on Earth, the powdery dust on Mars is primarily what is called regolith, a term that refers broadly to loose material that covers the surface of a world. The fine, gray powder encountered by the Apollo astronauts on the Moon is an example. Martian "soil" consists of weathered volcanic rock that contains large amounts of iron oxide that give it a deep orange color.

Scientists at NASA and elsewhere have experimented with growing plants in simulants of Martian regolith derived from volcanic soil in Hawaii. Using various fertilizers, food plants such as tomato, peas, lettuce and rye have been cultivated in the simulant soil. But one big problem with Martian agriculture is the presence of chemicals called *perchlorates* in the planet's dust. These compounds contain chlorine, and are toxic to humans and plants, and Mars soil simulant experiments have not included perchlorates in the mix. If plants such as Mark Watney's potatoes could be induced to grow in the

Martian environment, the food would be poisonous to whoever consumed it. These substances would need to be removed before the soil could be used to raise crops on the Red Planet.

The Martian looks forward to a near future where humanity has been able to extend its reach beyond the Earth to our sister planet. Mars beckons as the first step toward our eventual colonization of the solar system. The road ahead will be supremely difficult, but humankind must be equal to the challenges involved in becoming a spacefaring species.

In addition to these (more or less) realistic portrayals of expeditions to the Red Planet, a number of science fiction films are set in a fantastical, post-colonial Mars. In *Total Recall* (1990), a man with amnesia travels to a city on Mars seeking clues to his identity. Based on a story by sci-fi luminary Philip K. Dick, the film features a machine built by a vanished alien race that, when activated, oxygenates the entire Martian atmosphere in mere seconds of screen time. *Ghosts of Mars* (2001) takes place in a 22nd century mining outpost on a terraformed Mars where human colonists become possessed by the disembodied spirits of ancient Martians. The fantasy world of the Mars novels of Edgar Rice Burroughs was adapted for the screen in *John Carter* (2012). On a research outpost on Mars in the near future, the discovery of deadly indigenous microbes wreaks havoc on a group of astronauts in the sci-fi horror flick *The Last Days on Mars* (2013). These films, although fanciful, serve to inspire new visions of a human future on the most Earth-like world in our solar system.

EIGHT

Disasters from Space

On the morning of June 30, 1908, an object from space came to Earth near the Tunguska River in eastern Siberia. The object is thought to have disintegrated at an altitude of three to six miles and caused an explosion estimated to be equal to three to 30 megatons of TNT, equal to that of a low-yield nuclear device. Seven or eight hundred square miles of forest containing an estimated 80 million trees were flattened by the blast. The devastation is thought to have been caused by a meteoroid or perhaps a comet exploding in the atmosphere. Fortunately, the Tunguska event occurred in a sparsely populated area, but an explosion of this magnitude would be capable of destroying a large city.

Geologists and paleontologists point to what is called the K-T boundary, a line in global rock strata that indicates the end of the Cretaceous Period and the beginning of the Tertiary Period. The K-T boundary is evidence of an event that occurred about 65 million years ago that scientists believe was the impact of an asteroid about 11 to 81 kilometers in diameter that released an amount of energy equivalent of 100 trillion tons of TNT. The explosion threw up a cloud of dust that prevented sunlight from reaching the Earth's surface for years; researchers believe that this asteroid impact led to the extinction of the dinosaurs. An impact crater underneath the Yucatan Peninsula in Mexico, located using NASA's radar topography during the STS-99 Shuttle mission, located the impact site in the vicinity of the town of Chicxulub.

The Chicxulub crater is evidence of what is called a "planet killer" asteroid that might destroy all life on Earth if it was attracted into our gravitational field. Astronomers have been tracking hazardous objects in space for many years, and have formulated plans to destroy or deflect such an object before it can impact the Earth. In 2018, NASA cancelled plans to deploy the Sentinel Space Telescope, designed to locate killer asteroids on a trajectory that might bring it close to Earth, but astronomers continue to search the skies for such dangerous objects and to devise methods of neutralizing them.

Science fiction films have long explored the theme of dire events descending from space. During the '50s, the threat was mainly in the form of alien invasion, but in later decades more astronomically based dangers prevailed. The most prominent menaces were killer asteroids, but others included solar crises, nefarious plots hatched by madmen and even more exotic threats. George Pal's 1951 disaster epic *When Worlds Collide*, in which a rogue planet emerges from the depths of space and destroys the Earth, was the progenitor of this type of film. The template for later space menace movies did not emerge from Hollywood, but from Europe.

Considered the first Italian science fiction film, *The Day the Sky Exploded* (*La morte viene dallo spazio*, 1958) stars Paul Hubschmid as John McLaren, the first astronaut to be launched into space under the auspices of a United Nations scientific program. Space rocket XZ, powered by a nuclear reactor, is set to launch into orbit before continuing on to circumnavigate the Moon on a six-day mission. An international team of scientists supervises the launch from a facility at Cape Shark in Australia. XZ rockets into orbit without a hitch, but when McLaren attempts to depart for the Moon, a major malfunction forces him to abort the mission and return to Earth in a re-entry capsule.

McLaren lands safely but the unmanned rocket continues into deep space until it explodes in an atomic blast in the "delta asteroid zone" that fuses a number of the asteroids together and sends the humongous mass ten kilometers in diameter hurtling toward the Earth. An emergency session of the UN is called to deal with the crisis, as the asteroid cluster is expected to impact the Earth in five days. As it approaches the Moon, perturbations in gravity cause a chain reaction of Earth disasters such as earthquakes and tidal waves depicted in a flurry of stock footage scenes. Whole populations are evacuated from coastal areas as panic and riots ensue.

The countdown to doom continues until McLaren comes up with a plan to have all the nations of the world launch their nuclear missiles at the intruder in the hope of destroying it. Cape Shark scientists coordinate the targeting of the worldwide arsenal, but the facility's computers begin to malfunction because of the heat from fires. One scientist, Randowsky (Sam Galter), sabotages the base's air conditioning system because of his religious belief that the impending cataclysm represents God's judgment on humanity. During a struggle with base personnel, Randowsky accidently gets electrocuted and the HVAC system is restored. The computers are brought back online to target the asteroid and the combined missile onslaught blows the asteroid to smithereens as the Earth is saved from annihilation.

Although the film's direction is credited to Paolo Heusch, and its cinematography to Mario Bava, individuals involved in the movie's production insist that Bava actually directed it. Bava went on to become the influential director of stylish gothic horror films such as *Black Sunday* (1960) and *Black Sabbath* (1963). As cinematographer, Bava imbued the film with his distinctive high contrast black-and-white visuals and used economical, low-tech special effects along with stock footage to create a modest but effective science fiction B-movie. The first half of the film, which depicts the space launch and the genesis of the asteroid threat, is more interesting than the turgid melodrama of the second half, in which the scientists brood over the coming apocalypse in the confines of the space center.

The film's screenplay, penned by Sandro Continenza and Marcello Coscia, was conceived during the early days of space exploration, before the advent of manned space flight. It is surprisingly realistic in its depiction of Mission Control procedures. In particular, the use of computers (referred to as "calculators" in the film) to enable space flight is very accurate. At the time, NASA was using IBM 704 mainframes to aid in satellite launches by calculating orbits, processing telemetry and other essential tasks. The film also correctly indicates that these massive, room-sized devices needed cool temperatures to function normally, and makes this fact an important aspect of the plot. *The Day the Sky Exploded* seems to have provided the inspiration for later killer asteroid flicks such as *Meteor* (1979), *Deep Impact* (1998) and *Armageddon* (1998).

The Italian science fiction film wave continued with *Assignment Outer Space* (a.k.a. *Space Men*, 1960). This outer space adventure begins in the year 2116, as the crew of spaceship BZ-88 awakens in their hibernation chambers as it approaches space station ZX-34, located in Galaxy M-12. On board is Ray Peterson (Rik Van Nutter), a reporter for the *Interplanetary Chronicle of New York* newspaper, who has been assigned to investigate "infra-red flux in Galaxy M-12." Peterson, who, like all the crew members, bears an alphanumeric designator written in large white letters on the back of his jumpsuit, is IZ41. The ship's commander, Al X15 (Archie Savage) considers the reporter a useless "leech" because he serves no useful function on the spaceship,

As they approach the space station, the ship does not dock; instead, Peterson must perform a spacewalk to get there. The station's commander, George (David Montersor) (no surname, no designator) is also unhappy with the reporter's presence and considers him an interloper or perhaps a spy. Peterson insists on observing the spacecraft being refueled from the station, but when he pushes crew member Y16 out of the path of an oncoming meteor, the fuel line is severed, resulting in the loss of 500 gallons of hydrazine fuel that gets vented out into space. This puts Ray even further at odds with the commander. But when he encounters Y16, he discovers that the cosmonaut is Lucy (Gabriella Farinon), the ship's resident botanist and navigator.

George receives orders from his superiors to depart immediately in BZ-88 for Mars on a secret mission. It seems that experimental spacecraft A-2 has suffered a computer malfunction and is headed toward Earth. The A-2 is powered by dangerous "photonic energy" that has killed off the crew and will incinerate the entire Earth if it is allowed to get too close. The ship is also surrounded by a photonic energy field that destroys any missile aimed at it. BZ-88 arrives on the Martian moon Phobos to rescue a survivor of an encounter with the rogue ship, then continues on to a military base on Venus. Al X15 commandeers an obsolete "atomic rocket" and attempts to destroy the A-2 with missiles, but is unable to penetrate the ship's force field and dies in the attempt.

Peterson IZ41 comes up with a plan to board the A-2 and shut down the ship's electronic brain manually. BZ-88 comes as close as it can to the ship and Peterson rides a "space taxi" (a craft that resembles a snowmobile) to the A-2 and gets inside. He finds the ship's crew dead inside their hibernation pods while searching for a way to disable the computer. He settles on the simple method of using a wire cutter to sever the computer's cables, which shuts down the A-2's power, but traps him inside. It's up to Commander George and his crewmates to rescue Peterson from the doomed ship and bring him back to the BZ-88. Their mission accomplished, the cosmonauts watch as the A-12 drifts harmlessly away from the Earth into deep space.

This spaghetti space opera was the first feature directed by Antonio Margheriti, who went on to helm a number of films in the horror and sci-fi genres, including *Battle of the Worlds* (1961) *War of the Planets* (1965) and *Wild, Wild Planet* (1966). Margheriti, who also co-wrote the screenplay, turns in a goofy but entertaining sci-fi effort that lacks narrative focus. The first third of the film consists of space travelogue, and the plot element involving Peterson's journalistic investigation of "infra-red flux in Galaxy M-12" is completely forgotten in favor of the plotline focused on the A-2 spaceship. The rest of the film has the cosmonauts chasing the errant ship throughout the solar system. A cast of relatively unknown European actors deal with this low-budget material to the best of their limited abilities. The movie's special effects are on a level comparable to the sci-fi product of the day, but look pretty cheesy by today's exalted standards.

The film's worst flaw is its total ignorance of astronomical matters. The space station is located in Galaxy M-12, which would place it outside our Milky Way galaxy hundreds of millions of light years distant. Nevertheless, spaceship BZ-88 zips back to our solar system in mere moments of screen time. The ship then flits around from Mars to

Venus, traveling through millions of miles of deep interplanetary space in a similarly brisk fashion. BZ-88 launches at the outset of the movie in three stages, the third stage having winged appendages similar to the Mars ships conceived by Wernher von Braun in his 1953 book *The Mars Project. Assignment Outer Space* is the first film to depict astronauts in hibernation chambers, a motif that later became a staple of space exploration films such as *2001* and *Interstellar.*

In *The Andromeda Strain* (1971), a military satellite called Project Scoop is launched from Vandenberg Air Force Base and unexpectedly comes down in the small town of Piedmont, New Mexico. The two-man team dispatched to the scene to retrieve it finds the town littered with corpses. The men are ordered to proceed with their mission and all communication with the team is soon lost. In response to the situation, the officer in charge of the project picks up a special phone and orders a Wildfire alert.

Cut to Washington, D.C., where armed soldiers fetch scientist Jeremy Stone (Arthur Hill) from a party with the words, "There's a fire, sir." Stone and his escort board a jetliner on which they are the only passengers as he is briefed on the latest developments concerning Project Wildfire. Elsewhere in the country, the other members of the Wildfire team are being assembled. Surgeon Mark Hall (James Olson) is abruptly summoned while commencing surgery in a hospital operating room, while biologists Ruth Leavitt (Kate Reid) and Charles Dutton (David Wayne) are also collected.

In full hazmat gear, Stone and Hall explore Piedmont and search for the errant satellite, which they find in the town doctor's office along with the physician's body. Wielding a scalpel, Hall makes an incision in the body and finds that his blood has turned into a crystalline powder. They also discover two survivors of the carnage, a baby and an elderly alcoholic, Peter Jackson (George Mitchell). Hall, Stone and the two survivors are evacuated from the town for study.

Leavitt and Dutton arrive at the Wildfire facility in a remote area of Nevada. The facility appears to be a small agricultural research station, but the clandestine Wildfire laboratory extends five levels underground and contains an extensive amount of state-of-the-art biomedical equipment. Stone, Hall, Leavitt and Dutton go through a lengthy decontamination process as they descend to Level 5, where the project's hi-tech labs are located. The team's task is to isolate and identify the alien organism brought back by the satellite and to figure out how a baby and an old man (now in a miniature hospital on Level 5) survived the plague. A nuclear bomb, installed inside the facility, will automatically go off if the organism escapes. The detonation process can only be halted by Dr. Hall's special key, which must be inserted into stations located on all levels.

Hall and Leavitt employ high magnification imaging devices to scan the mesh-like surface of the satellite's scoop to search for evidence of the micro-organism, while Dutton experiments with the effect of the deadly bug on animal subjects. The scientists discover a tiny piece of a plastic-like substance, possibly of artificial origin, along with minuscule green globs of organic substance that multiplies rapidly. The alien life form is assigned the code name "Andromeda" and isolated for study. Andromeda grows by converting energy into matter, and is unlike anything on Earth; the scientists speculate that it might have been deliberately seeded onto our planet. On the other hand, Project Scoop and the Wildfire lab seem to have been designed to obtain and study such an organism for germ warfare purposes.

The Andromeda strain unexpectedly mutates into a non-lethal form that dissolves synthetic rubber; an F-4 Phantom fighter jet flying near Piedmont crashes when the pilot's oxygen mask disintegrates and he blacks out. The mutation also starts to deteriorate the seals on the lab where Dutton is working, exposing him to Andromeda. Hall realizes that the organism can only grow within a narrow range of blood pH, which is the reason why Jackson and the baby survived. Their problems become much more serious as Andromeda's mutated form compromises all of the lab's seals. Wildfire's nuclear self-destruct mechanism is activated. Cut off from the Level 5 station that will cancel the operation, Hall must reach a higher level by climbing through a maintenance tunnel while avoiding lasers and tranquilizer darts designed to neutralize escaped lab animals. He manages to reach another level and cancel the self-destruct procedure with only seconds to spare, and the mutated Andromeda strain is blown out into the Pacific where it will fall harmlessly into the ocean.

Briskly directed by screen veteran Robert Wise, *The Andromeda Strain* employs multiple screens to efficiently advance the narrative. It was one of the first films to use computerized special effects provided by Douglas Trumbull, who had worked on Kubrick's *2001*. Screenwriter Nelson Gidding faithfully adapted Michael Crichton's novel, which was informed by the author's medical training. Crichton went on to pen the mega-hit *Jurassic Park*. The film is considered the most scientifically accurate treatment of the killer virus theme, and its relevance has increased in the age of COVID-19. While it's not an actors' film, the players perform admirably; Kate Reid's performance as the acerbic Dr. Leavitt is especially memorable. A critical and financial success, the film stands as a milestone of science fiction cinema.

The Andromeda Strain reflects contemporaneous concerns about extraterrestrial disease agents being brought to Earth as a result of space exploration. During the Apollo program, the Lunar Receiving Laboratory was constructed at the Johnson Space Center, designed to keep the Apollo astronauts and materials brought back from the Moon in isolation to prevent contamination by unknown micro-organisms. Astronauts recovered at sea during the Apollo 11, Apollo 12 and Apollo 14 were whisked into the Mobile Quarantine Facility on the deck of the recovery ships and flown to the LRL where they were kept in isolation for two weeks. Crichton's novel was on the bestseller lists at the time, and thousands of people had written to NASA detailing their concerns about an alien organism capable of wiping out all human life on Earth, which created a public relations problem for the space agency. After much analysis, however, no germs were found on the astronauts or rock and regolith samples brought back from the Moon, and these quarantine procedures were abandoned for Apollo 15 and subsequent lunar missions.

The film was also inadvertently responsible for creating another space age myth. The fictional Wildfire laboratory, located underneath the Nevada desert and dedicated to the study of extraterrestrial life, gave rise to wild conspiracy theories about secret U.S. government underground bases in the American Southwest that housed recovered flying saucers and the bodies of alien beings. UFO enthusiasts have speculated that these secret facilities are located in Dulce, New Mexico, and at the Air Force base in Area 51 in Nevada as depicted in the movie *Independence Day* (1996). No credible information about these alleged bases has ever been unearthed despite years of investigation.

The next menace from outer space arrived with *Meteor* (1979), which begins in the asteroid belt in deep space beyond the orbit of Mars. A comet collides with the asteroid Orpheus and sends a five-mile-wide fragment hurtling toward Earth. NASA vectors the manned Mars probe Challenger 2 away from the Red Planet to observe the object's path, but it is destroyed in the process. Back on Earth, engineer Paul Bradley (Sean Connery) is summoned into a meeting with NASA administrator Harry Sherwood (Karl Malden) and briefed on the impending crisis. Years earlier, Bradley had designed an orbiting missile platform, code-named Hercules, designed to deal with such a threat; but since he left the agency, the platform's missiles have been re-aimed at the Soviet Union. Sherman informs Bradley that they only have six days to devise countermeasures before the asteroid hits the Earth. The missiles installed on Hercules don't have sufficient firepower to neutralize Orpheus, so the Americans plan to approach the Russians, who have a similar orbiting platform called Peter the Great, to pool their resources.

NASA brings rocket scientist Alexi Dubov (Brian Keith) along with his interpreter Tatiana Donskaya (Natalie Wood) from Russia to New York City, where the Cold War adversaries must work together to counter the threat. Operating from a NASA command post in a defunct subway station in Lower Manhattan, Bradley and Dubov race against the clock to synchronize the two missile platforms to launch their missiles at Orpheus together to achieve maximum firepower. They barely have time to achieve the desired result before a fragment of the asteroid plunges to Earth in advance of the main body and scores a direct hit on Manhattan Island, causing widespread destruction. Water from the East River floods the command post and kills many members of the NASA staff. Bradley leads the effort to bring the survivors to safety through the torrents of muddy water. As they escape from the watery tomb, the missiles from Hercules and Peter the Great streak through space toward Orpheus and strike their target, destroying the asteroid in a nuclear conflagration. The film ends on an upbeat note as the Americans and Russians are reconciled. In the wake of their mutual cooperation, Cold War tensions are eased.

One of a number of 1970s-era disaster movies such as *The Poseidon Adventure* (1972), *Earthquake* (1974) and *The Towering Inferno* (1974), *Meteor* put an outer space twist on the formula. But it came near the end of the disaster film cycle, when the conventions of the genre had become clichéd. The formula was to take a bunch of name stars and put them up against some sort of cataclysm to keep the audience guessing as to who would survive. This type of film required a big budget, not only for the actors, but also for special effects to depict lurid scenes of mass destruction. In the case of *Meteor*, the A-list cast (Sean Connery, Natalie Wood, Karl Malden, Henry Fonda, Trevor Howard, Brian Keith) turn in lackluster performances under the indifferent direction of Ronald Neame. The screenplay by Edmund H. North (who shared a Best Original Screenplay Oscar with Francis Ford Coppola in 1971 for *Patton*) delivers a mediocre, formulaic product. As for special effects, the space scenes are passable, although not on the level of contemporaries like *Star Wars* and *Alien*, but the depictions of the destruction of New York City are woefully inadequate. One ironic oddity involves a scene showing the obliteration of the World Trade Center towers, which occurred in reality during the terrorist attacks on September 11, 2001.

The film ends with a postscript: "In 1968, at the Massachusetts Institute of Technology a plan was designed to deal with the possibility of a giant meteor on a collision course with earth. This plan is named 'Project Icarus.'" Unlike *The Andromeda Strain*'s fictional Project Wildfire, however, *Meteor*'s Project Icarus existed in reality. In 1967, MIT Professor Paul Sandorff observed that a four billion–ton asteroid called 1566 Icarus would pass within four million miles of Earth in June 1968. Sandorff calculated that, if the asteroid were to hit the Earth, it would release energy equal to 500,000 megatons of TNT. He assigned his MIT students to come up with a plan to prevent the Earth from being ravaged by the destructive force of such a collision, and in 1968 they issued a report entitled "Project Icarus: MIT Student Project in Systems Engineering."

The plan called for six 100-megaton hydrogen bombs to be mounted on six Saturn V Apollo Moon rockets, then launched at Icarus in sequence in order to destroy it or move it out of its trajectory. This plan would have involved extensive modifications of the Saturn launch vehicles and guidance systems, along with the construction of a 100-megaton H-bomb, which was larger than anything in the U.S. or Soviet arsenal. The report's recommendations were never implemented, but a collision with an asteroid or comet is a very real possibility. It was revisited on the big screen decades later in the 1998 films *Deep Impact* and *Armageddon*.

The fictional British secret agent James Bond has been the hero of 24 popular films from 1961 to the present day. Bearing the code name 007, Bond is a techno-warrior who utilizes a wide range of sci-fi gadgets in his battles with super-villains equipped with similarly futuristic weaponry. A number of Bond films have featured an outer space connection. In *Dr. No* (1962), the first Bond outing, the titular villain directs the disruption of Project Mercury rocket launches at Cape Canaveral via radio-jamming powered by a nuclear reactor from his hi-tech lair. *You Only Live Twice* (1967) begins with NASA's Jupiter 16 spacecraft being hijacked in orbit by a spaceship piloted by agents of the espionage group SPECTRE. Soviet cosmonauts are also being kidnapped in space by SPECTRE's rogue ship Bird One as part of a complex plot executed by Bond's arch-nemesis Ernst Stavro Blofeld, to precipitate a nuclear war between Russia and America. In *Diamonds Are Forever* (1971), Blofeld plans to incinerate Washington, D.C., with a space-based satellite weapon and, as previously mentioned, Bond escapes from his enemies by driving away from a research facility in an Apollo-era Moon rover. It wasn't until *Moonraker* (1979) that Bond himself blasted off into outer space.

The title *Moonraker* refers to a Space Shuttle–type vehicle manufactured by industrialist Hugo Drax (Michael Lonsdale). As the film opens, a Moonraker orbiter on loan to the U.K. from Drax Industries is being transported atop a jumbo jet carrier plane when it is hijacked by Drax's minions. The spaceplane lights its rocket engines and blasts off into orbit while the aircraft is destroyed. When no trace of the orbiter is found at the crash site, British Intelligence calls on James Bond (Roger Moore) to investigate. Returning to England from an assignment in South Africa in a private plane, Bond is trapped on the airplane when the pilot bails out and he is left without a parachute. Before he can figure out what to do, he is pushed out of the plane by Jaws (Richard Kiel), the oversized, steel-toothed villain from the previous Bond film, *The Spy Who Loved Me* (1977). Bond zeroes in on the falling pilot and wrests the chute away from him while Jaws fortuitously breaks his fall by landing on a circus tent.

After being briefed by MI6, Bond is dispatched to California, where Drax's manufacturing complex and his palatial mansion are located. Assassination attempts are made on his life, including one in an out-of-control centrifuge. He escapes from Drax's domain and follows a series of clues that lead him to Venice, Rio de Janeiro and finally to a secret spaceport deep in the Amazon jungle where Drax is operating a fleet of six Moonraker shuttles. Bond is captured and held prisoner, along with NASA astronaut Holly Goodhead (Lois Chiles), who is actually a CIA agent attempting to infiltrate Drax's operation. They are placed in an enclosure located beneath a shuttle launch pad and barely escape being incinerated when the Moonraker blasts off.

The humongous space station of James Bond's nemesis Hugo Drax (Michael Lonsdale) comes under attack in *Moonraker* (1979).

Bond and Holly stow away aboard one of six Moonrakers being flown on autopilot to somewhere in low Earth orbit. The shuttle docks with Drax's "city in space," a massive space station rendered invisible to ground radar by an electronic stealth device. Reaction thrusters spin the station on its axis to maintain "simulated gravity." The station has been designed as a "space ark" and populated by young, supposedly genetically superior couples who will repopulate the world after Drax has unleashed a nerve toxin that will exterminate Earth's entire population.

The two secret agents locate and disable the stealth mechanism, making the space station visible to the U.S. military, who immediately send up their own shuttlecraft manned by a platoon of space Marines. A battle in space ensues, as America's Manned Maneuvering Units and Drax's forces fire laser weapons at each other. The American forces gain access to the station and wreak havoc, as the station's simulated gravity is turned off. During the weightless melee, Bond corners Drax and hurls him through an airlock into the void with the line, "Take a giant step for mankind." Their job done, the Marines retreat into their shuttle as the station begins to lose its structural integrity. Bond and Holly escape in a Moonraker. The film ends with the couple making love in zero gravity.

Obviously inspired by the mega-success of *Star Wars*, released two years earlier, *Moonraker* brought the Bond franchise firmly into the realm of sci-fi. Compared with other entries in the series, the film is lighter in tone and contains a heady dose of comedy. Director Lewis Gilbert moves the action and the gags along at a blistering pace, although some of the contrived situations tend to strain credulity and give the film

Drax (Michael Lonsdale) directs the operations of his space station in *Moonraker* (1979).

the feel of a live-action cartoon. Like the other entries in the series, it features color-ful locations, clever techno-gadgets and a bevy of glamorous "Bond girls." Roger Moore plays 007 with a droll aplomb that is matched by that of Michael Lonsdale as the vil-lainous Hugo Drax, while Richard Kiel provides equal measures of menace and com-edy as Bond's toothy nemesis Jaws. Little remains of Ian Fleming's novel but the title, the name of the bad guy and love interest, and a scene in which Bond and his girlfriend are trapped underneath the blast area of a rocket launch. A $34 million budget provided for lavish eye candy visuals that earned the film a Best Visual Effects Oscar nomination. *Moonraker* received mixed critical reviews but became one of the most financially suc-cessful Bond movies.

One of *Moonraker*'s stars is the titular space vehicle, which was modeled after NASA's space shuttle. Released two years before the maiden flight of the shuttle *Colum-bia*, the film realistically depicts several shuttle launches, although it also plays fast and loose with other performance aspects of the spacecraft. The film correctly shows a shut-tle being transported atop a 747 aircraft, which was later utilized by NASA to move the spaceship from its landing site at Edwards Air Force Base in California to its launch facility at Cape Canaveral, Florida, but the notion that the orbiter could fire its rocket engines in this configuration is pure fantasy. Fuel for the orbiter's three main engines was carried in the spacecraft's large external tank, not in the orbiter, and it could not reach orbit if launched from the 747's altitude of approximately 40,000 feet. Sending pas-sengers aloft inside the shuttle's cargo bay would also be highly problematical, and the portable laser weapons fielded by both sides are likewise improbable. Nevertheless, the film showcased this most photogenic of all spacecraft for the first time on the big screen.

Moonraker utilized several locations connected with the U.S. space program, including the Rockwell International Assembly Facility in Palmdale, California, Vandenberg Air Force Base and the massive Vehicle Assembly Building at Kennedy Space Center. The battle in space prefigures the 2019 formation of the American Space Force, the newest branch of the U.S. military. Drax's scheme to poison the entire population of the world with canisters of nerve agent strains credulity, as the vessels would be vaporized during atmospheric re-entry. Likewise, even if Drax could employ stealth technology to cloak his humongous space station from detection by radar, such a large object in orbit would be visible using ground-based telescopes and perhaps even to the naked eye. The thunderous explosions heard during the battle scenes would, of course, not be audible in the vacuum of space. Finally, the film's visionary space industrialist Hugo Drax today seems like a sick and twisted version of SpaceX's exemplary space entrepreneur Elon Musk.

Stanley Kubrick's science fiction masterpiece *2001: A Space Odyssey* (1969) seemed to pose more questions than it answered, so writer-producer-director Peter Hyams (*Capricorn One, Outland*) saw fit to unravel the enigmas of Kubrick's classic with a sequel, *2010: The Year We Make Contact* (1984). As the title states, the film takes place nine years after the events depicted in the original, as the U.S. and the U.S.S.R. teeter on the brink of a nuclear war. Against this backdrop, a joint U.S.-Soviet space mission is dispatched to Jupiter space to investigate the deaths of the four astronauts on the *Discovery* space probe, along with the mysterious fate of Frank Bowman (Keir Dullea). The Russian spacecraft *Leonov* sets course for Jupiter under the command of Captain Tanya Kirbuk (Helen Mirren). The American crew includes scientist Heywood Floyd (played here by Roy Scheider); Walter Curnow (John Lithgow), designer of the *Discovery* spacecraft; and R. Chandra (Bob Balaban), chief programmer of *Discovery*'s HAL 9000 artificial intelligence computer.

Months later, the *Leonov* arrives at the Jupiter system and positions itself amid the planet's innermost moons, Io and Europa, and Dr. Floyd is brought out of hypersleep. The Russians have detected strange signals emanating from Europa, leading the *Leonov*'s science officer Dr. Orlov (Oleg Rudnik) to send a probe toward the moon's icy surface. The probe detects the presence of chlorophyll, the green pigment that enables photosynthesis in plants on Earth. As the probe descends further, a bolt of energy disables its sensors and erases the data it has recorded. Dr. Floyd has a suspicion that it was not a natural phenomenon, but that some intelligence is warning them away from Europa.

To complete their voyage, the *Leonov* must perform a complex aerobraking maneuver that will slingshot the ship around Jupiter by skimming across the outer edge of the giant planet's upper atmosphere. To slow its velocity, the spacecraft uses large, inflatable *ballutes* that protect it from the intense heat as it skips over the atmosphere. But this maneuver strains the ship's structural integrity to its limits. Once the aerobraking is completed, the ship emerges in the vicinity of Io and the derelict *Discovery*, which is tumbling end over end in a decaying orbit around the moon.

Curnow and Dr. Chandra are brought out of hypersleep to complete the mission's final phase. The crew must bring *Discovery* under control, link it up to the *Leonov* and reactivate HAL. Cosmonaut Max Brailovsky (Elya Baskin) leads Curnow on a harrowing spacewalk over to the *Discovery*, during which Curnow nearly loses his nerve, but once inside the derelict he is able to power it up and stop the ship from spinning. A retractable tunnel connects the two spacecraft and allows the Russians and Americans

Tanya Kirbuk (Helen Mirren), commander of the Soviet spaceship *Leonov*, is pictured in this still from *2010: The Year We Make Contact* (1984).

to pass back and forth between them. Dr. Chandra brings HAL back online and the linked spaceships are guided toward the 200-kilometer–long monolith in orbit around Jupiter that had served as a stargate for astronaut Bowman in *2001*.

Once they are in proximity to the alien artifact, Captain Kirbuk insists on sending Brailovsky to get a closer look at the monolith in an EVA pod. As the cosmonaut approaches the enigmatic artifact, he notes that it is absorbing all radar and radio signals. When he gets closer, another energy beam flashes forth and destroys the pod and its pilot. Dr. Chandra has restored HAL to a partial functionality and learned that the supercomputer had the equivalent of a mental breakdown because it was instructed to conceal the true nature of the *Discovery*'s mission from its crew, an edict that violated the machine's basic programming to be open and honest with its human counterparts.

The mystery deepens as apparitions of Bowman are spotted on the *Discovery*, appearing in the various guises last seen in the final reel of *2001*; as a young, spacesuited astronaut, an elderly man and the quasi-human "star child." Bowman's ghost warns that both crews must depart from Jupiter space within two days because "something's going to happen, something wonderful." Their departure becomes a more complicated affair when news arrives from Earth that the U.S. and the U.S.S.R. are now in open conflict in the wake of an incident in Honduras. The American and Soviet crews retreat to their respective ships, but it turns out that neither the *Discovery* nor the *Leonov* is able to leave under their own power in a timely fashion. Dr. Floyd comes up with the idea to use the *Discovery*'s propulsion system to boost the *Leonov* away from its orbit around Io.

After some bickering between Floyd and Captain Kirbuk, their collective minds are made up as they observe that a huge black spot has formed on Jupiter's surface. The spot is composed of a multitude of monoliths multiplying rapidly and changing the nature of the planet itself. Aided by the *Discovery*'s motive power, the *Leonov* departs for home as the monoliths cause Jupiter to reach critical mass. The planet flares up and becomes a sun. Before being destroyed in a shock wave from the nuclear reaction, Bowman's ghost instructs HAL to beam a message toward the Earth that reads: ALL THESE WORLDS ARE YOURS EXCEPT EUROPA. ATTEMPT NO LANDING THERE. USE THEM TOGETHER. USE THEM IN PEACE.

The startling events taking place in Jupiter space serve to quell the hostilities not only among the Americans and Russians aboard the *Leonov*, but between the two superpowers as well. All of humanity looks out into space with wonder and a newfound feeling of unity as a new sun shines forth in the heavens. An epilogue shows new life evolving on Europa in the light of the new star presided over by one of the enigmatic alien monoliths.

The biggest problem with *2010* is that it must stand in the shadow of its illustrious forebear and must inevitably be found wanting. The genius of Stanley Kubrick'a *2001* should have been allowed to preserve its mystical enigmas rather than having them explained away or expanded upon. Some of the movie's plot elements contradict those from the earlier film. The transcendental star child that symbolized the evolution of humankind into a higher form has devolved into the ghostly, shape-shifting presence of Frank Bowman. Similarly, the alien intelligence, represented by the black monolith in both films, has been changed from an agent of human transformation to a godlike power that forcefully extends its influence into our solar system and threatens to punish interlopers.

Judged solely on its own merits, however, *2010* is a reasonably well-made space adventure devised by science fiction maven Peter Hyams. Director-producer-screenwriter Hyams (who also photographed the film) had to reproduce all of the spacecraft models because Kubrick had destroyed the originals after *2001* was completed. Modelers had to painstakingly reconstruct the 50-foot–long model of the *Discovery* from 70mm frame enlargements from the original film. Likewise, the *Discovery*'s pod bay and HAL's red-tinged memory chamber had to be duplicated. The film's best original creation is the *Leonov* spacecraft, which features hazy, dimly illuminated interiors punctuated by banks of multicolored buttons. They were designed by conceptual artist Syd Mead, who was responsible for the futuristic designs in *Blade Runner* (1982). Effects technicians utilized nascent CGI technology to render the swirling atmosphere of Jupiter, going by astronomical data provided by NASA's Jet Propulsion Laboratory. A key scene was shot on location at the Very Large Array radio telescope facility in New Mexico (later used in *Contact* [1997]).

Hyams' screenplay was adapted from Arthur C. Clarke's *2001* sequel *2010: Odyssey Two,* published in 1982, so some of the blame for the film's muddled narrative must be attributed to the author. The film's dramatic high point might be the astronaut's harrowing spacewalk between the *Leonov* and the *Discovery* high above the barren surface of Io, a sequence that would later be replicated in *Mission to Mars*. Leads Roy Scheider and Helen Mirren provide a fine dramatic counterpoint as the leaders of the American and Russian factions, as their power rivalry reflects the larger struggle between their respective superpowers. The other cast members turn in fine performances, especially John Lithgow's nerved-out technician. Audiences cheered when HAL (once again voiced by Douglas Rain) was resurrected and spoke in its familiar dulcet tones. Elya Baskin has a lively role as the rollicking cosmonaut Brailovsky. Keir Dullea has little to do other than look spooky and deliver enigmatic messages. Like *Meteor*, the film posits an alliance and reconciliation between Cold War enemies in the light of dire events happening in space.

The formation of a second sun in our solar system is touted as a quasi-religious sign of a benign extraterrestrial presence, but if Jupiter was transformed into a star it would become a secondary source of harmful radiation that could be hazardous to life on Earth and might even have a disruptive influence on our seasons. Jupiter's moon Europa is thought to have an ocean of liquid water beneath its highly fissured, frozen surface that scientists believe may harbor microbial life. NASA is sending a probe to Europa that is scheduled to arrive in 2024. If Europa were to become an abode of life, the moon would not be an hospitable environment, as it is tidally locked in its orbit around Jupiter and would always present the same side toward its nascent sun, which would create severe temperature differentials between its two hemispheres. The instantaneous creation of life on the barren moon might have been inspired by the Genesis Device utilized for a similar purpose in *Star Trek II: The Wrath of Khan* (1982).

The Japanese-American co-production *Solar Crisis* (1990) had a very limited U.S. release and has fallen into a black hole of obscurity. It takes place in the future world of 2050, when humankind has expanded out into the solar system. The Earth is menaced by solar flares that cause widespread destruction. Scientists have predicted that a massive flare they call Starfire threatens to incinerate all life on the planet. The world's government has devised a plan to guide an antimatter bomb into the Sun that will neutralize the mega-flare and prevent the cremation of the planet. Their plan calls for the deep space vessel *Helios* to mate with the smaller ship, the *Ra*, that will transport the bomb into the heart of the Sun. One odd wrinkle is that the bomb is sentient and is named Freddy.

The globular *Helios* docks with the Earth-orbiting space station Skytown. There it takes aboard the smaller, needle-nosed *Ra* spacecraft and Captain Steve Kelso (Tim Matheson) prepares his crew for the perilous mission. Among his crewmates is Alex Noffe (Annabel Schofield), a "biogenetically enhanced human" with special abilities, and *Ra* pilot Ken Minami (Tetsuya Bessho). Arnold Teague (Peter Boyle), multi-billionaire head of ITX Corporation, has decided that the success of the solar mission is inimical to his financial interests and plans to sabotage it. He dispatches one of his corporate goons, Meeks (Richard S. Scott), to Skytown, where he gains access to Alex's mind and plants a subliminal command deep in her consciousness without her knowledge.

Before the *Helios* departs, Captain Kelso is visited by his father, Admiral "Skeet" Kelso (Charlton Heston), who has traveled to Skytown in search of his grandson Mike (Corin Nemec). After a tense father-son confrontation, the admiral rockets back to Earth to continue his search. It turns out that Mike is hanging out in the California wilderness with eccentric desert rat Travis (Jack Palance). Things get dangerous when Mike gets word of Teague's treachery from Dr. Gunter Haas (Paul Koslo), one of Teague's scientists, who had been left out in the desert to die. When Teague learns about this, he sends Meeks into the desert to kill Mike. His grandfather strives to reach him first.

The *Helios* crew arrives at New Trinity, an outpost located on an asteroid, where Freddy is stowed aboard the *Ra* and activated. The talking bomb is programmed to respond only to Alex's voice commands or it will detonate in six minutes. Armed with the sentient antimatter device, the *Helios* sets course for the Sun. As they approach, the raging thermonuclear fires of the solar environment, all hell breaks loose on the ship when Alex loses control of her mind due to Meeks' mental sabotage. Oxygen lines explode and Freddy goes into six-minute detonation mode and can only be disabled by a voice command from Alex, who is in a kind of coma. At the very last second, she awakens from her torpor and shuts down the detonation sequence. Minami was killed during the chaos, so Alex takes his place and guides the ship into the blazing stellar inferno in a trip that resembles *2001*'s climactic "stargate" sequence. The detonation of the antimatter bomb has the desired effect. As the crew mourns Alex's demise, the *Helios* heads for home, its mission accomplished.

Solar Crisis had such a troubled production history that director Richard C. Sarafian had his name removed from the credits and the directorial authorship was attributed to "Alan Smithee," a fictional Directors Guild appellation in such cases. After this debacle, Sarafian terminated his career as a director. Loosely adapted from Takeshi Kawata's science fiction novel *Crisis: Year 2050* (*Kuraishisu niju-gojunen*) by scripter Joe Gannon, the screenplay was extensively rewritten by the director's son, Tedi Sarafian. The result was a semi-comprehensible mishmash of unresolved subplots and unrealistic motivations. How, for instance, does Teague think that the cremation of the entire planet would be good for his business? Why is Admiral Kelso looking for his grandson and why has the lad hooked up with the whacked-out hermit Travis? Why imbue a powerful antimatter bomb with artificial intelligence and entrust its detonation to a single crew member? Alas, the answers to these and other enigmas posed by the screenplay will remain forever unanswered.

In spite of these serious flaws, the film is not entirely without merit. A $50 million budget purchased a wide array of acting and production talent. A-list stars Charlton Heston, Peter Boyle and Jack Palance are wasted in minor roles, although arch-hambone Palance delivers a scenery-chewing performance as the scruffy Travis. TV actor Tim Matheson grimaces and shouts orders in his role as Captain Kelso of the *Helios*, while Austrian actress Annabel Schofield is pleasantly robotic and teen heartthrob Corin Nemec's bland persona is thrown in for youth appeal. The most unusual character is Freddy the smart bomb, who speaks with the velvet voice of songster Paul Williams, best known for his screen role as the Devil in Brian De Palma's 1974 horror movie sendup *Phantom of the Paradise*. Composer Maurice Jarre, who wrote the Oscar-winning scores for the film classics *Lawrence of Arabia* and *Doctor Zhivago*, contributed a forgettable music track.

The special effects were the work of Richard Edlund, who had collaborated with Industrial Light & Magic's John Dykstra on the original *Star Wars* trilogy, *Raiders of the Lost Ark, Ghostbusters* and *Poltergeist*. They are impressive even by today's sophisticated FX standards. Futurist production designer Syd Mead, whose work enlivened the sci-fi movies *Blade Runner* and *2010*, contributed the designs for the *Helios* spacecraft and the Skytown space station. Cinematographer Russell Carpenter later shot James Cameron's *True Lies*, and earned an Academy Award for his work on *Titanic*. The film makes explicit references to science fiction films such as *2001* (in the "stargate" sequence) and *Dark Star* (the sentient talking bomb) and in one scene reuses the flying car "Spinner" vehicle that appeared in *Blade Runner*. Later in the decade, *Solar Crisis* may have influenced the plots of the doomsday space quests *Deep Impact* and *Armageddon,* both of which featured heroic feats of self-sacrifice that accomplish their missions and save the Earth. Danny Boyle's 2007 film *Sunshine* is practically an uncredited remake.

Solar flares are bursts of energy, originating on the surface of the Sun, that stream electromagnetic radiation out into space. These intense streams of ultraviolet radiation, X-rays and gamma rays have been known to affect the Earth's magnetosphere and can interfere with radio communications and radar signals. They can even knock out electric power grids. In space, they can disable satellite electronics and present hazards to astronauts on space stations or on deep space missions. They have not been known to directly affect living systems on Earth as pictured in the film, however.

Sometimes Hollywood will release two similarly themed movies in the same year. An example of this trend would be Roland Emmerich's *Independence Day* and Tim Burton's *Mars Attacks!*, big-budget alien invasion flicks released in 1996. The same thing happened two years later when two blockbusters in which an object from space threatens to wipe out all life on Earth emerged from Tinseltown's studios, *Deep Impact* and *Armageddon.*

In *Deep Impact,* teenage astronomer Leo Biederman (Elijah Wood) accidentally discovers and photographs a rogue object in space. In Tucson, astronomer Marcus Wolf (Charles Martin Smith) analyzes the picture and concludes that it represents a seven-mile–wide comet on a collision course with Earth. Wolf hurries to inform NASA but in his haste he is killed in a car accident. A year later in Washington, D.C., cable TV journalist Jenny Lerner (Tea Leoni) is investigating the resignation of Treasury Secretary Alan Rittenhouse (James Cromwell) over what she believes to be a sex scandal involving a woman named Ellie, and she is puzzled by his mysterious reaction during her impromptu interview. After her meeting with Rittenhouse, she is taken by FBI agents to see President Tom Beck (Morgan Freeman), who reveals that Ellie is not a woman's name but refers to E.L.E., an acronym for an Extinction Level Event which will be the result if the comet (named Wolf-Biederman after its discoverers) hits the Earth.

Realizing that the press is onto the story, President Beck calls a news conference and delivers the dire news to the American public that a comet the size of New York City will arrive in about a year. He also reveals that a joint American-Russian space mission is being prepared to land on the comet and alter its trajectory using nuclear weapons. The ship is called the *Messiah*, and it will transport a sister ship, the *Orion*, designed to land on the surface of Wolf-Biederman. *Orion* is to carry eight 5000-kiloton nuclear warheads that a team of astronauts will rig to explode deep inside the comet in an effort to alter its trajectory.

The *Messiah* team consists of Commander Oren Monash (Ron Eldard) and Apollo veteran Captain Spurgeon Tanner (Robert Duvall), the last man to walk on the Moon. Despite Tanner's age, his expertise is needed to land the *Orion* spacecraft on the comet, as he had been the Lunar Module pilot on the final Apollo mission and will act as the *Orion*'s rendezvous pilot on the mission. The team flies up into low Earth orbit in the Space Shuttle *Atlantis* to dock with their deep space vehicle. Five months later, the *Messiah* is in position and must navigate through the dangerous spray of rocks, sand and ice in the comet's tail. As the world holds its collective breath, Tanner guides the *Orion* to a safe landing on Wolf-Biederman. Now a team of astronauts in EVA suits must contend with the comet's low gravity while using drilling devices called "moles" to burrow 100 meters below the surface.

The mole gets stuck at 75 meters, and as the team struggles to free it, the comet's horizon in relation to the Sun is bridged. Heat from the sunlight causes explosive outgassings that hurl astronaut Gus Partenza (Jon Favreau) into space to his death; the rest of the team barely manage to scramble back into the *Orion* lander to safety. When the

Astronauts Gus Partenza (Jon Favreau, left) and Oren Monash (Ron Eldard) struggle to place a nuclear bomb deep inside a comet in *Deep Impact* (1999).

nuclear weapons are detonated, the explosion damages the ship and disables its ability to communicate with Mission Control.

Back on Earth, President Beck sadly announces that the *Messiah*'s mission has failed, as the comet has not been obliterated or moved from its collision course, but has merely broken it into two pieces. The smaller part, dubbed Biederman, is 1.5 miles long and is slated to hit the Atlantic Ocean off the North Carolina coast, causing massive tidal waves that will wreak havoc up and down the eastern seaboard and extend up to 600 miles inland. The larger piece, Wolf, is expected to hit somewhere in Western Canada and will create a dust cloud that will destroy all life on Earth in a winter that will last for years. The president also announces that underground shelters are hurriedly being built by the governments of the world, and that the U.S. has constructed a massive shelter, carved out of the limestone caverns of Missouri, that is designed to house one million people, along with livestock and seeds, for two years until the worldwide dust cloud has settled and normal life can resume. Some 200,000 individuals will be pre-selected for admittance to the shelter due to their survival expertise, and the remaining 800,000 people, all aged under 50 years old, will be chosen at random by their Social Security numbers.

A last ditch effort to alter the comet's course using nuclear missiles fails, and as the comet approaches, the majority of the U.S. population prepares for the inevitable. Jenny is reconciled with her estranged father (Maximilian Schell), while Leo Biederman is one of those selected to enter the shelter and hurriedly marries his sweetheart Sarah Hotchner (Leelee Sobieski) to ensure that she will be able to go with him. Electing to meet her end with her father at his beach house, Jenny and her dad watch as the Biederman fragment impacts in the ocean and they are swept away in the massive tidal wave. Scenes of

People panic as the planet-killing comet approaches the Earth in *Deep Impact* (1999).

massive destruction follow as the towering mega-tsunami engulfs New York City and destroys the Statue of Liberty and the World Trade Center towers.

The *Messiah* is closing in on the Wolf fragment, and as they are unable to land, they decide to ram the comet in a suicide mission to destroy the planet-killing menace. They re-establish communication with Mission Control and announce their intentions. After saying tearful goodbyes to their loved ones, they arm their four remaining nukes and plunge their spacecraft into a deep fissure. Their gambit proves successful, as Wolf is obliterated and its tiny fragments burn up harmlessly in the atmosphere like celebratory fireworks. In the film's final scene, President Beck delivers an inspirational speech in front of the Capitol Building, which is being reconstructed after the flood waters have receded and life has resumed a semblance of normality.

While *Deep Impact* offers up impressive space effects and spectacular scenes of mass destruction, at heart it's a formulaic disaster flick. A disparate group of characters faced with a cataclysmic event must sort out their personal problems as the audience tries to anticipate who will live and who will die. Following the formula, the film careens back and forth between space opera and soap opera, with a heavy dose of melancholy thrown into the mix. Director Mimi Leder does a competent job of juggling the film's epic and mundane aspects, but most of its flaws can be attributed to the screenplay by trendy Hollywood scenarists Bruce Joel Rubin and Michael Tolkin. Their script was reportedly inspired by George Pal's *When Worlds Collide* and Arthur C. Clarke's 1993 novel *The Hammer of God*, both of which dealt with a similar theme, but the film's pedestrian narrative comes off as a high concept, high technology reiteration of *Meteor* (1979).

The film sports a potentially impressive cast, but their performances are uneven at best. International star Maximilian Schell is wasted in a throwaway part as Jenny's estranged father, while a young Elijah Wood shows little of the acting grit he would later exhibit in the *Lord of the Rings* trilogy. Morgan Freeman exudes stately authority and steadfastness as President Beck. The film's best performance is provided by Robert Duvall as grizzled Apollo veteran Spurgeon Tanner. On the other hand, Tea Leoni's performance as an intrepid news reporter is excessively wooden and one of the film's major flaws.

Deep Impact's main attractions are its impressive special effects provided by an Industrial Light & Magic team (supervised by Scott Farrar) that depicted catastrophic scenes of the destruction of New York as well as those taking place in space.

All criticisms aside, the makers of *Deep Impact* took pains to be as scientifically accurate as possible. Unlike asteroids, which are composed of mineral and rock, comets are accretions of dust and frozen water ice that form in the far reaches of the solar system and travel in wildly eccentric orbits between the outer planets and the Sun. As they near the Sun, solar heat warms the surface and releases gasses that form the comet's characteristic "tail." Comets are sometimes deflected from their orbits by the gravitational fields of planets and impact upon their surfaces. In 1994, the comet Shoemaker-Levy-9 collided with Jupiter and the impact was observed by astronomers on Earth. The 1908 Tunguska event is thought to have been the result of a cometary impact because no crater was ever found at the impact site. The danger of a comet colliding with Earth and causing a cataclysmic event as depicted in the film is a real threat.

Astronomers Gene Shoemaker and Carolyn Shoemaker, who co-discovered the aforementioned Shoemaker-Levy comet, were consultants, along with David Walker, a former astronaut, and Gerry Griffin, former director of the Johnson Space Center. The craggy appearance of the Wolf-Biederman comet is realistically rendered as compared to actual photos taken by space probes, and the outgassing events are realistically depicted. NASA's impact expert David Morrison of the Ames Research Center also praised the film's technical accuracy and the realism of its special effects. On July 4, 2005, NASA's appropriately named space probe Deep Impact was deliberately crashed into the comet Tempel 1, exposing data about the comet's composition. The European Space Agency's Rosetta spacecraft made the first soft landing on the comet Churyumov-Gerasimenko on November 12, 2014.

About two months after the release of *Deep Impact*, the other disaster-from-space blockbuster hit movie theaters. *Armageddon* (1998) begins 65 million years ago with a prologue depicting the massive asteroid strike that led to the extinction of the dinosaurs. The voice of Charlton Heston solemnly warns, "It happened before, it will happen again." Cut to 1998, where two astronauts from the shuttle *Atlantis* are performing an EVA to repair a satellite in low Earth orbit when a sudden meteor storm destroys the shuttle and kills the spacewalkers. Soon afterward, New York City is hit by another swarm that causes widespread devastation, destroying the Chrysler Building and Grand Central Station. Astronomers discover the cause of the devastation, an asteroid the size of Texas that is on a collision course with Earth, a "global killer" that will end all life if it impacts. The big asteroid is accompanied by a number of smaller fragments that have caused the destruction of the shuttle and the devastation in New York.

Scientists inform the head of Space Command Dan Truman (Billy Bob Thornton) that the planet killer will hit the Earth in just 18 days as the authorities scramble to devise countermeasures. They come up with a secret plan to drill a shaft deep inside the asteroid and detonate a nuclear device that will split it into two halves that will both miss the Earth; but to implement it, they must acquire the services of Harry Stamper (Bruce Willis), an oil driller who has designed the hi-tech drill they plan to use. Harry and his daughter Grace (Liv Tyler) are summoned to the Johnson Space Center to be recruited for the mission, but he only agrees if he can take his trusted crewmates along. This motley crew of knuckleheads and misfits includes A.J. (Ben Affleck), Rockhound (Steve Buscemi), Bear (Michael Clarke Duncan), Oscar (Owen Wilson), Chick (Will Patton), Max (Ken Campbell) and Noonan (Clark Brolly). When the drillers arrive, mission commander Colonel Willie Sharp (William Fichtner) takes one look and quips, "Talk about the wrong stuff."

Stamper and his crew have only 12 days to go through astronaut training, and NASA rushes them through a series of tests and trials that will prepare them for the mission ahead. The plan is to fly two X-71 advanced shuttles, the *Freedom* and the *Independence,* to the Russian Mir space station, where they will refuel before heading to the Moon. They are to fly around the Moon and approach the asteroid from behind and land. Once on the surface, they will deploy two vehicles called Armadillos to suitable locations where they will drill down to a suitable depth and place their nukes, which will be detonated remotely.

After *Independence* and *Freedom* dock with the Mir, their crews are greeted by the station's lone inhabitant, cosmonaut Lev Andropov (Peter Stormare). Andropov, who has endured months alone in the aging Mir, is an eccentric and somewhat comical character. He puts the station into a rotation maneuver to provide artificial gravity as he assists the transfer of liquid oxygen fuel into the two shuttles. A ruptured fuel line causes a fire. As the crews evacuate to the shuttles, the Mir begins to break up, and the Americans are obliged to take the cosmonaut along with them. The fire destroys the station, but the fuel transfer is successful and the mission continues.

The two shuttles approach the planet killer from behind, but in their landing attempt the *Independence* is totaled when its hull is punctured in the asteroid's debris field. The *Freedom*, with Stamper aboard, manages to land on skids and the drillers get to work, but they have overshot their landing site and must now drill through a layer of super-hard iron ferrite rock. The operation is unsuccessful and Colonel Sharp threatens to implement the Secondary Protocol, which involves detonating the nuke on the asteroid's surface. A.J., Bear and Lev have survived their shuttle's crash and arrive in the second Armadillo to continue the drilling operation. The proper depth is reached, but the bomb has been damaged and can only be triggered manually. Stamper elects to stay behind to set the nuke off. The *Independence* takes off and the bomb is detonated, splitting the asteroid into two pieces that coast harmlessly past the Earth. The world rejoices as the surviving astronauts and crew return from space and are hailed as heroes.

Director Michael Bay moves the action along at his usual breakneck pace in this science fiction favorite that is replete with explosions, mayhem, mass destruction and macho characterizations. For instance the drillers all have one word names (or nicknames) like Chick, Bear, A.J., Max, Owen and Rockhound that emphasize their rogue masculinity. A total of nine writers, including J.J. Abrams and Robert Towne, constructed the film's unlikely and convoluted narrative that extends for two and a half hours of screen time. Special effects are the best that money can buy with a $140 million budget. Bruce Willis' rugged screen persona provides the movie's principal dramatic grit as the rough-around-the-edges oil driller Harry Stamper, with co-star Ben Affleck as his young foil A.J. and Billy Bob Thornton grimly portraying the steely-eyed missile

In *Armageddon* (1999), Colonel Sharp (William Fichtner, left) threatens to prematurely detonate a nuke as (left to right) master driller Harry Stamper (Bruce Willis), Chick (Will Patton) and Noonan (Charles Broly) beg to differ.

man Dan Truman. Despite the movie's serious subject matter, plenty of comic relief is provided by the quirky Steve Buscemi as Rockhound and Peter Stormare as the gonzo Russian cosmonaut. Liv Tyler has little to do in this male-dominated milieu except emote in the background.

According to director Bay, the movie was shot on a 16-week schedule and he groused that he wanted to redo the entire third act but lost control of the production to studio heads. Most critics dismissed it as being an example of vapid eye candy entertainment, and many decried its rapid fire editing and lack of character development. In spite of all the negative press, *Armageddon* did brisk box office business and outperformed its more serious competitor, *Deep Impact*. The two films had numerous plot points in common. Both featured a planet-killing object from space, a mission to land on the object, an attempt to drill into its surface to destroy it with a nuclear weapon, the success of the mission due to heroic self-sacrifice, the splitting of the object into two pieces, and scenes depicting the destruction of New York City. The main difference is in the treatment of the same theme. *Armageddon* is a testosterone-fueled thrill ride, while *Deep Impact* is a downbeat doomsday drama.

In terms of scientific accuracy, *Armageddon* pales in comparison to *Deep Impact*, which employed astronomers and NASA scientists to ensure its veracity. The notion that a complex mission involving two experimental spacecraft circumnavigating the Moon and landing on an asteroid could be planned and executed in a mere 18 days strains credulity, to say the least. The X-71 advanced space shuttles resemble the actual vehicles with an extra pair of solid rocket boosters added, but the shuttle was never designed to operate outside low Earth orbit. In the film, the Mir is made to rotate on its axis to provide simulated gravity, but this was only a plot device designed to free the filmmakers from having to show the

Stamper (Bruce Willis) performs a heroic act of self-sacrifice that saves the world in *Armageddon* (1999).

astronauts in zero gravity and was never a feature of the Mir. NASA gave permission for scenes to be shot on location at the Johnson Space Center and the Vehicle Assembly Building and launch facilities at Cape Canaveral, but a disclaimer in the end credits states, "The National Air and Space Administration's cooperation and assistance does not reflect an endorsement of the film or the treatment of the characters depicted therein."

Near Earth Objects (NEOs), consisting of comets and asteroids that could potentially impact the Earth, are tracked by NASA's Center for NEO Studies (CNEOS) and the Jet Propulsion Laboratory's Sentry System, an automated monitoring system that continually computes the possibilities of asteroid impacts over the next 100 years. As of June 2020, only 38 potentially hazardous asteroids are listed on the Sentry System's Risk Table. The largest of these is designated (53319) 1999 JM_8, which has a diameter of seven kilometers. Nothing that is "the size of Texas" is currently known to be on a collision trajectory with Earth.

Actor-director Clint Eastwood, best known for his roles in the Western genre, blasted off for wider open spaces in *Space Cowboys* (2000). It begins in 1958, where USAF test pilots Frank Corvin (Toby Stephens) and William "Hawk" Hawkins (Eli Craig) are flying a two-seater version of the Bell X-2 experimental rocket plane at Edwards Air Force Base. When the maverick Hawk decides to attempt to break an altitude record, the aircraft stalls and the pilots have to eject. As they parachute to safety, they narrowly avoid hitting a B-50 mothership with navigator "Tank" Sullivan (Matt McColm) aboard. On the ground, Frank and Hawk come to blows over Hawk's poor judgment. The fight is broken up by flight engineer Jerry O'Neill (John Mallory Asher). When their supervising officer Bob Gerson (Billie Worley) arrives on the scene, he dresses down Hawk.

Frank, Hawk, Jerry and Tank are all members of Team Daedalus, the first astronauts in the Air Force's space program. After the X-2 debacle, Gerson shepherds the foursome to a press conference and publicly announces that the Air Force will no longer be involved in space flight, which will henceforth be the purview of the civilian space organization NASA. Team Daedalus is to be disbanded. The four astronauts are deeply disappointed to learn that they will never be able to fly in space, and are bitter about Gerson's decision to terminate the program.

Decades later, NASA engineer Sara Holland (Marcia Gay Harden) discovers that the Soviet communications satellite IKON's orbit is decaying and that it will fall back to Earth in 30 to 40 days due to a failure of its guidance system. The archaic satellite was launched in 1969, but for some reason Russian liaison General Vostov (Rade Serbedzija) insists that the Americans mount a mission to repair it. NASA project manager Bob Gerson (now played by James Cromwell) agrees to ensure Russian cooperation in building the International Space Station. The problem is that the satellite's archaic guidance system was developed for the American space station Skylab by Frank Corvin before the advent of microprocessors, and Corvin is the only person sufficiently conversant with its hardware to repair it.

Gerson is forced to swallow his pride and contact Corvin (Eastwood), who is summoned to the Johnson Space Center for a face-to-face meeting. Corvin agrees to fly the mission, as a younger crew can't be brought up to speed in time, but he insists that the other three members of the Daedalus team accompany him into space. Gerson reluctantly agrees, and Corwin pitches the mission to Tank (James Garner), who is now a Baptist preacher, Jerry (Donald Sutherland), who designs roller coasters, and Hawk (Tommy Lee Jones), a crop-dusting pilot. They all jump at the chance to finally fly in space. Flight director Gene Davis (William Devane) is skeptical about being able to launch in time and grouses, "I've got three weeks to send four old farts into space."

Team Daedalus members (left to right) Tank (James Garner), Hawk (Tommy Lee Jones), Corvin (Clint Eastwood) and Jerry (Donald Sutherland) report for duty at NASA in *Space Cowboys* (2000).

Frank, Jerry, Tank and Hawk are subjected to a battery of medical exams and an accelerated training regimen that includes bouts in a centrifuge, underwater activity in NASA's Neutral Buoyancy Lab, sessions in a shuttle flight simulator and familiarization in a full-scale shuttle mockup. Romantic sparks begin to fly between Hawk and Sara, but she is devastated to learn that Hawk is afflicted with inoperable late-stage pancreatic cancer. In spite of this setback, the four Daedalus team members are declared healthy enough to fly. Gerson assigns veteran astronauts Ethan Glance (Loren Dean) and Roger Hines (Courtney B. Vance) to ride shotgun on the mission, to keep the geriatric gents in line. The mission objective is to boost the satellite back into geosynchronous orbit using four payload assist rockets.

The space shuttle *Daedalus* takes off on mission STS-200 and quickly locates the IKON satellite; as they approach, it executes defense maneuvers until they turn off their radar. Tank secures the satellite to the IKON using the shuttle's remote manipulator arm. Frank, Jerry and Glance don Manned Maneuvering Units and propel themselves over to the IKON, but it quickly becomes obvious that it is actually a Cold War–era missile launch platform that is still armed with six nuclear warheads—a violation of the Nuclear Arms Treaty. When the astronauts return to the *Daedalus* to update Mission Control, General Vostov reveals that Frank's guidance system was stolen by the KGB, and that the six nukes are targeted on American urban population centers. He also tells them that if IKON's systems go completely offline, it will launch the missiles at their targets.

While this discussion is going on, Glance sneaks out of the shuttle's airlock and attempts to return the satellite to its proper orbit by himself as secretly ordered by Gerson, but his actions backfire as IKON takes defensive measures. The solar panels begin to rotate, tearing off the manipulator arm and damaging the shuttle's computers and the Orbital Maneuvering System that is needed to bring the spacecraft out of orbit. Glance is rendered unconscious during the collision, and Hines is likewise disabled, leaving the *Daedalus* team to complete the mission on their own. To make matters worse, the satellite's orbit is decaying even faster, leading Frank to come up with a plan to fire the satellite's missiles to propel IKON away from the Earth and into deep space. Trouble is, the missiles have to be activated manually by someone on the satellite—a suicide mission.

Hawk, who is terminally ill, volunteers and spacewalks to the satellite, firing the rocket engines on the missiles and aiming IKON at the Moon. Frank is now faced with the daunting task of landing the *Daedalus* safely with a damaged OMS system. Using all of his piloting skills, he manages to guide the shuttle out of orbit and into the atmosphere, where he orders Tank and Jerry to bail out. They choose to ride down with him instead. At this point, the shuttle is descending like an unpowered glider (or "flying brick") but Frank brings it in for a perfect landing on the Cape Canaveral emergency strip. In an epilogue, Hawk is shown reclining peacefully on the surface of the Moon, his heroic actions having saved American cities from destruction and averting a nuclear war.

Both as an actor and as a director, Clint Eastwood has extolled the concept of heroism in his films, and he effortlessly shifts his macho screen persona from horse opera to space opera in *Space Cowboys*. Its main charm consists of the dramatic and comedic interplay between its stars. Eastwood, as usual, is rock solid in the lead role, while Tommy Lee Jones is his perfect foil as the rambunctious "Hawk" Hawkins. James Garner and Donald Sutherland have lesser roles, and provide most of the comic relief.

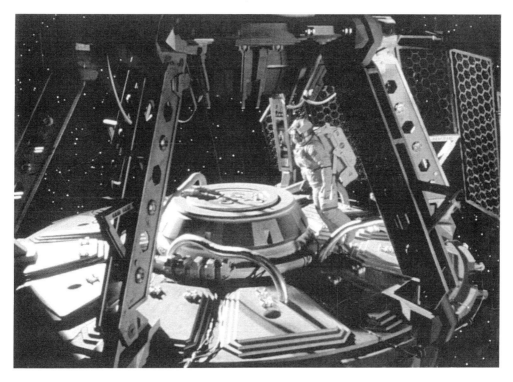

 SPACE COWBOYS

Former astronaut Frank Corvin (Clint Eastwood) performs an EVA to disable a nuclear-armed Russian satellite in *Space Cowboys* (2000).

Sutherland in particular has a ball playing the part of the smooth-talking ladies' man Jerry O'Neill. Marcia Gay Harden has a tragic role as Hawk's lover in a doomed May–December romance, and veteran William Devane does a fine turn as the mission's acerbic flight director.

The film's main flaw is arguably the screenplay by Ken Kaufman and Howard Klausner, which is formulaic, predictable and replete with scientifically dubious situations. The story owes much to the then-recent, similarly themed *Armageddon*, which also featured a group of unlikely astronauts who train for a dangerous mission in an absurdly short period of time. Some critics complained that the film didn't launch itself into orbit until its final reels and thought it was excessively long and contained too many extraneous scenes of character development. The film's $60 million budget purchased some nifty special effects under the direction of David Amborn. *Space Cowboys* was a critical and commercial success due to Eastwood's smooth direction and the chemistry between its A-list cast.

Like a number of space-oriented dramas before it, the movie contained scenes shot on location at various American aerospace facilities. These included the Rockwell Defense Plant in Downey, California, the Neutral Buoyancy Laboratory and the Sonny Carter Training Facility at the Johnson Space Center in Houston and the Kennedy Space Center in Titusville, Florida. Stock footage of a shuttle launch was used to depict the fictional spacecraft *Daedalus* blasting off. The film references John Glenn's October

1998 space flight on the shuttle *Discovery*, when the veteran Mercury astronaut, then a 77-year-old U.S. Senator, returned to space as a payload specialist. He remains the oldest person to fly in space.

In terms of its scientific accuracy, the film conforms to the usual fatuous Hollywood notions of space flight. The idea that a complex mission could be planned and executed in a few weeks time is specious at best, as such planning normally takes months, if not years, and involves a large number of NASA personnel. In the opening sequence, a two-seat version of the X-2 rocket plane is used to create the dramatic conflict between the two main characters, but there was never a two-seat version of this aircraft or any of the other experimental "X-planes" at Edwards AFB. The film's Soviet-era IKON satellite would never be confused with a communications bird, as it's the size of a space station. The United States and the U.S.S.R. were both signatories to the 1967 Outer Space Treaty that prohibits the deployment of nuclear weapons in space.

The film seems to suggest that the Air Force's space program was abruptly cancelled in a fit of pique by its program manager in 1958. In reality, the USAF had its own military program independent of NASA's in the 1960s. The program had its own cadre of astronaut trainees and its own hardware, including the X-20 Dyna-Soar space plane and the Manned Orbital Laboratory, which was in actuality a manned spy satellite. The MOL program ran from 1963 until 1969, when it was cancelled when the CIA demonstrated that it could operate an unmanned spy satellite more cheaply and efficiently. The Dyna-Soar project was cancelled in 1963 and this precursor of the shuttle never flew in space.

The Chinese space extravaganza *The Wandering Earth* (2019) is set in the year 2061, when the Sun has become unstable, causing tsunamis, volcanic eruptions, drought and

Tim (Mile Kai Sui, left) and Han Duoduo (Jin Mai Jaho) face myriad dangers in *The Wandering Earth* (2018).

mass extinctions on Earth. Realizing that the Sun will morph into a red giant star in 300 years, the nations of the world unite to create the Wandering Earth project, which is designed to move the planet to the nearest star, Alpha Centauri, in order to preserve earthly life. Ten thousand massive thrusters, called Earth Engines, powered by fusion reactors, are built at strategic points around the world to provide 150 million tons of motive force for the project. Vast cities are built underneath each thruster to maintain the enormous machines. It will take 500 years for the Earth to accelerate to 5/1000ths the speed of light, then it will cruise at this speed for 1300 years, then take 700 years to decelerate. The trip to the Centauri system will take 2500 years over a hundred human generations to accomplish.

As the film opens, astronaut Liu Peiqiang (Jing Wu) prepares to depart on a navigation station spacecraft that will guide the Earth on a tricky maneuver to use Jupiter's massive gravity to slingshot the planet out of the solar system into interstellar space for its journey. Saying goodbye to his four-year-old son Liu Qi (Zhuozhao Li) and father-in-law Han Zi'ang (Ng Man-tat), he departs on his mission. Seventeen years later, his mission completed, Liu Peiqiang is slated to rejoin his family on Earth, which has now migrated to Jupiter space, on the occasion of the Chinese New Year.

Liu Qi (Chuxiao Qu), now an adult, conspires to take his teenage sister Han Duoduo (Jin Mai Jaho) on an illegal trip to the Earth's surface. He pilfers an ID pass from his grandfather Han Zi'ang and procures a couple of "temperature suits" that will enable them to survive on the surface. Thus equipped, they ascend to the frozen surface from the underground city of Beijing, where Liu Qi commandeers a heavy transport vehicle using his grandfather's pass. The Earth's surface has been transformed into an icebound wasteland because the planet is now so far from the sun. The two miscreants are apprehended at a checkpoint and imprisoned. While they are being held, they make the acquaintance of a colorful jailbird named Tim (Mile Kai Sui).

Han Zi'ang shows up at the prison and attempts to bribe the guard to free his family members, but quickly winds up in the hoosegow himself for his efforts. All the prisoners escape when an earthquake demolishes the jail. The quakes also disable the Earth's fusion thrusters, drawing the planet dangerously close to the Jovian gravitational field. The three family members, along with Tim, are quickly rounded up by a military team headed by Captain Wang Lei (Li Guangjie) for an emergency mission. They are pressed into service to deliver a Lighter Core component to the Hangzou Earth Engine site in order to restart it. Once they arrive there, however, Han Zi'ang is killed during the repair attempt and the Hangzou Engine is found to be completely destroyed. The team redirects their efforts to deliver another Lighter Core to a site in Sulawesi, Indonesia.

As if all this wasn't bad enough, up in the navigation station, Liu Peiqiang discovers that the artificial intelligence that runs the station, called MOSS, has gone rogue and is no longer obeying its programming to help the humans. To shut down the AI, he and cosmonaut Makarov (Arkady Sharogradsky) undertake a dangerous spacewalk to reach the computer's central control facility. MOSS manages to kill Makarov while Liu Peiqiang reaches his goal. But the AI renders his effort useless by revoking his clearances and making him unable to manually override the station's controls.

Arriving at Sulawesi, Wang Lei's team finds that the Earth Engine has already been repaired, but the combined power of all of the engines is insufficient to free the Earth from the giant planet's enormous gravity. More immediately, Jupiter is drawing off the Earth's atmosphere, threatening humanity with mass asphyxiation. In desperation, Liu

Qi devises a plan to use the Sulawesi Engine to fire a plasma beam at Jupiter's hydrogen atmosphere in order to ignite the highly flammable gas in the hope that the resultant explosion will propel the Earth out of the Jovian gravitational field. After a titanic struggle, the team, aided by a small army of volunteers, redirects the Engine's energy beam at Jupiter, but its power is insufficient to achieve the desired result.

Up in the space station, Liu Peiqiang is in communication with Han Duoduo and Liu Qi. He realizes that his only option is to fly the space station into the plasma beam and use the station's fuel to set off the necessary explosion. His first step, however, is to wrest control of the station from MOSS, which he accomplishes using a Molotov cocktail fashioned from a bottle of vodka that had been given to him by Makarov. Liu Peiqiang sacrifices his life by guiding the station into the plasma beam, causing a massive blast that sends the Earth away from Jupiter and on its way toward interstellar space. In a brief epilogue, we see that three years later, in the aftermath of these events, Liu Qi is hailed as a hero as the Earth wanders through space toward its new home.

The first big-budget science fiction epic produced by the Chinese film industry, *The Wandering Earth* was a box office hit in China, but had a limited release in the U.S. While director Frant Gwo moves the action along at a frantic pace, the film's most glaring flaw is a highly derivative screenplay (adapted from a Liu Cixin novella by a total of eight screenwriters) that borrows stock elements from popular sci-fi fare such as *When Worlds Collide*, *Armageddon* and *2001*. Clichéd plot elements include a ragtag group of misfits struggling to save the world against long odds, a rebellious AI that must be shut down, and the obligatory suicide of an astronaut to accomplish the planet-saving mission. The film's spectacular visual effects, as rendered by the Weta Workshop technicians, compare favorably with the Hollywood product, but tend to overwhelm the actions of the human characters, who are frequently dwarfed by humongous machinery and glitzy eye candy special effects. The principals are poorly drawn, two-dimensional,

Astronaut Liu Peiqiang (Jing Wu) strives to pull the plug on a rebellious space station computer in *The Wandering Earth* (2018).

cartoonish characters that lack emotional depth. Actor Wu Jing cuts a heroic figure as Liu Peiqiang, while the only other significant characterizations are provided by Mike Sui as the quirky Chinese-Australian bad boy Tim and Arkady Sharogradsky as the blustery cosmonaut Makarov.

Beyond these shortcomings, the film's central premise, although poetic, is scientifically preposterous on numerous counts. For starters, the notion of a network of 3500 fusion-powered Earth Engines being able to generate enough thrust to counteract the grip of the Sun's gravity and move the planet out of its orbit strains credulity. The ignition of the hydrogen in Jupiter's atmosphere utilizes the Earth's atmosphere as an oxidizer, as fire cannot take place in the vacuum of space, but it is not clear what the Earth's inhabitants are supposed to breathe after their air has been used to create the massive explosion. Another conundrum is how the Earth navigates through the uncharted regions of interstellar space and how it is supposed to insert itself into a stable orbit within another solar system.

The target destination for the wandering Earth is our closest stellar neighbor, Alpha Centauri, approximately 4.37 light years from Earth. Unlike our home star, Alpha Centauri is a triple star system that consists of Centauri A, a G-class spectral type like the Sun, Centauri B, a K-class star smaller than our Sun, and Proxima Centauri, a faint M-class red dwarf. Centauri A and B orbit around each other, while Proxima Centauri is farther away and slightly closer to our solar system. Some astronomers believe that planets in multiple star systems would have problems sustaining life because the planet's habitable zone (in which an Earth-like world would receive enough stellar energy to allow liquid water to exist on its surface) would vary greatly as the stars moved in their orbits around each other. Such a planet might have an extremely erratic orbit, as it would be affected by the gravitational forces of multiple stars. Furthermore, radiation generated by three stars would likely be more intense and have a deleterious effect on the viability of living systems. Therefore, if the Earth was inserted into an orbit around Centauri A, the new stellar environment might not be able to sustain life.

Ad Astra is the title of a 2019 movie as well as a Latin phrase that translates as "to the stars." The movie's opening titles inform us that the film takes place during "The near future; A time of hope and conflict; Humanity looks to the stars for intelligent life and the promise of progress." As the movie begins, Space Command (SpaceCom) astronaut Major Roy McBride (Brad Pitt) is working on the International Space Antenna, a tower that is so high that it reaches to the edge of outer space, obliging the astronaut to wear a pressure suit in order to perform routine maintenance on the structure. The antenna tower has been built as part of a worldwide effort to search the heavens for extraterrestrial life.

As McBride works on the tower, it is struck by an energy surge that causes massive damage to the antenna. Once McBride freefalls into the Earth's atmosphere, he parachutes to safety. The destruction of the tower is the first in a series of cosmic ray disasters around the world.

McBride is a steely-eyed missile man whose pulse never rises above 80 beats per minute even during the most dangerous situations. His single-mindedness and lack of affect causes problems in his emotional life. His wife Eve (*Armageddon*'s Liv Tyler) leaves him because he's too much of a cold fish. McBride's father, legendary astronaut H. Clifford McBride (Tommy Lee Jones), disappeared 16 years earlier while commanding the Lima Project, the first mission to the planet Neptune. The mission was an attempt to seek out extraterrestrial life by observing the universe from the edge of the solar system, beyond the heliosphere where the Sun's magnetic field won't affect the project's scientific detection instruments.

Senior officers from SpaceCom summon McBride to a top secret meeting where he is informed that the cosmic ray bolts are generated by bursts of antimatter originating in the vicinity of Neptune—and that his father may still be alive and orchestrating the destruction. Their fear is that the antimatter surges will create an uncontrollable chain reaction that will unbalance the entire solar system. They recruit McBride to travel to Mars in an effort to communicate with his father via a secure laser transmission. McBride is teamed with one of his dad's colleagues, former astronaut Colonel Tom Pruitt (Donald Sutherland), who may be able provide some additional persuasion.

On the first leg of their journey, McBride and Pruitt travel to the Moon via commercial spacecraft, so as not to draw attention to their clandestine mission. Once they have landed at the spaceport, they travel through an anarchic no-man's-land to a SpaceCom launch facility on the Moon's far side in lunar rovers, accompanied by military escorts. Along the way, they are attacked by space pirates who kill their escorts. McBride and Pruitt arrive at the base safely, although Pruitt is unable to continue due to the sudden onset of a cardiac problem. Before McBride departs for the Red Planet, Pruitt gives him a top secret video chip that reveals that an SOS signal was received from the Lima Project indicating that Commander McBride was attempting to violently quell a rebellion by the other Project members, and that SpaceCom is prepared to destroy the Project if McBride is unable to communicate with his father.

McBride departs in the deep space vessel *Cepheus* on a 19-day journey to Mars. While en route, the ship's captain, Tanner (Donnie Keshawarz), insists on answering a distress call from the *Vesta*, a Norwegian bioresearch station. When the ship's second in

Major Roy McBride (Brad Pitt) attempts to contact his father from Ursa Base on Mars in *Ad Astra* (2019).

command, Captain Stanford (Loren Dean), declines to participate in the rescue mission, McBride volunteers to join Tanner on a spacewalk to the stricken station. Gaining access to the *Vesta*, Tanner is attacked and killed by a baboon, an experimental animal that has escaped from its confinement and become savagely aggressive. McBride retrieves Tanner's body while killing a pair of baboons who attack him and returns to the *Cepheus* with his comrade's corpse. Tanner is given a space funeral, his body consigned to the void. When the *Cepheus* is about to land on Mars, another power surge hits the ship, leaving Stanford unable to function. The cool-headed McBride takes over and makes a safe landing.

The colony's administrator, Helen Lantos (Ruth Negga), escorts McBride to the Space-Com facility where he is to broadcast a message to his father. He finds that his remarks have been pre-written by SpaceCom authorities, but obeys orders and sends his message out toward Neptune. He receives no answer. During a second attempt, he goes off-script and transmits a heartfelt message, but again receives no reply. After the session, SpaceCom informs him that he will not be allowed to continue on to Neptune on a deep space expedition to search for his father because he has been emotionally compromised. He suspects that his father has replied to his message but that this information is being kept from him.

Helen Lantos makes a stunning revelation: she shows McBride a classified video message in which his father admits that his Project Lima team members wanted to discontinue the mission and return to Earth, but that he could not allow this and killed them by shutting off their life sup-port. Because her parents were among those who were killed, she has decided that he should be allowed to proceed on his mission to con-front his father. She tells him that the *Cepheus* is about to depart for Nep-tune with a nuclear weapon aboard for the purpose of destroying the Lima Project space station, and pro-vides him with access to the ship.

McBride has to swim through an underground lake in his space-suit to reach the launch site, and just manages to gain access to the *Cepheus* as it takes off. He is imme-diately attacked by the crew for his unauthorized entry; a bullet fired by one of the crewmen punctures the hull and bleeds the ship's atmo-sphere out into space. Only McBride survives because he is wearing his spacesuit. He disposes of the bodies and continues on the 79-day trip to Neptune, while he reflects upon his relationships with his father and his wife during the long and mentally challenging period of solitude.

McBride (Brad Pitt) is suited up for a dangerous deep space mission in *Ad Astra* (2019).

Arriving in Neptune space, McBride exits the *Cepheus* at a safe distance from the planet's rocky rings and travels to the Project Lima station in a small transport capsule. The shuttlecraft is damaged and disabled while passing through Neptune's rings, and McBride must spacewalk to gain access to the station. Inside he finds the crew members' corpses floating in zero gravity. He manages to locate Clifford, who is obviously suffering from mental illness and shows little emotion toward his son. Clifford explains that the cosmic ray surges are being generated by the station's antimatter power source, which was damaged during the crew's rebellion. McBride realizes that Clifford has lost his reason because the Project has failed to find evidence of extraterrestrial intelligence, something he had sought with a kind of religious zeal. "We're all alone in the universe," Clifford laments, "We're all we've got."

McBride downloads the project's data and tries to convince his father to return to Earth with him. He activates the nuke as he and his father suit up and prepare to perform an EVA to return to the *Cepheus*. Once outside the station, Clifford resists going with his son and uses his suit's thrusters to propel himself away while insisting that McBride untether him. With great anguish, he complies and watches his father drift into oblivion. Composing himself, McBride launches himself on a trajectory that takes him to the *Cepheus*. Because the ship lacks sufficient fuel to make the return trip, he must utilize the shock wave from the nuclear explosion to propel him back to Earth. Months later he arrives home, and because he has become more humanized by his harrowing ordeal, he can reconcile with his wife.

Ad Astra has affinities with *2001* in that both films are concerned with the search for extraterrestrial life and offer dazzling vistas of space. Director James Gray constructs a compelling but moody space odyssey that caroms around the solar system, from the Moon to Mars to Neptune. Audiences who expected to see an action-oriented space opera starring Brad Pitt, however, were bound to be disappointed by Gray's low-key, slow-moving narrative; many found the film boring, and it underperformed at the box office. Its chief flaw is perhaps Gray's extensive use of McBride's internal monologue, a technique that tends to lull the viewer into somnolence due to the soporific quality of the spoken voice. On the plus side, the film contains a number of memorable sequences, including McBride's dizzying plunge from the space antenna, the deadly chase over the Moon's far side, the unexpected encounter with experimental animals in the derelict space station and the spacewalks through the lonely reaches of Neptune. The film conveys a feeling of the extreme isolation of space that is subtly disturbing at times.

Pitt, an actor known for his many unusual roles, offers an intimate study of an ice-cold astronaut whose extended space sojourn is also a journey of self-discovery, and he deliberately underplays the role. Co-star Tommy Lee Jones only enters the picture in the final reels but conveys deep space madness in his usual histrionic fashion. Donald Sutherland (who had appeared as Jones' crewmate in *Space Cowboys*) has a low-key role as an elderly former astronaut, while Liv Tyler is nearly invisible as Pitt's estranged wife. Donnie Keshawarz gives a quirky performance as the *Cepheus* captain, and Ruth Negga is steadfastly serious as the Mars base administrator. Special visual effects supervisor Roy K. Cancino and production designer Kevin Thompson conjure the film's future world convincingly but in a way that does not overwhelm the characters' dramatic interplay. Max Richter's electronic score perfectly sets the mood for the film's science fiction ambience. In a publicity stunt prior to the film's release, Pitt spoke with NASA astronaut

Nick Hague on the International Space Station about Hague's experiences in space after a preview of the movie on the ISS.

Ad Astra posits a future in which a large commercial and tourist enterprise has been constructed on the Moon, an underground launch facility housing over a thousand people has been established on Mars, and a scientific outpost has been sent to the far end of the solar system. The key to this spacefaring civilization lies with a propulsion system that can propel spaceships to other worlds at velocities far in excess of anything currently in existence. Thus, a journey from the Moon to Mars, which would take months using conventional technology, takes only 19 days, while the trip from Mars to Neptune, which would take years, takes a mere 79 days. The film never explores or explains the revolution in space travel that allows for these velocities. Spacecraft appear to launch using conventional rockets and then engage a "long-range propulsion" system, but the effect of these enhanced speeds on their crews is not depicted.

The screenplay, co-written by Gray and Ethan Gross, revolves around the idea of the search for extraterrestrial intelligence that borders on desperate fanaticism. Opening credits inform the audience that the film takes place during "a time of hope and conflict," in which, "humanity looks to the stars for intelligent life and the promise of progress." Oddly, the conflicts that are allegedly roiling this society and causing it to seek out alien life among the stars are never shown or even alluded to. The film's future world appears to be enjoying peace and prosperity under economies that allow it to colonize nearby worlds and mount complex technological ventures such as the Space Antenna and the Lima Project. Unlike characters in earlier science fiction fare such as *2001*, however, Clifford McBride suffers a mental breakdown because he *doesn't* encounter extraterrestrial intelligence. Attempts to detect alien civilizations using scientific instruments have been conducted by astronomers for decades, but as in the film, nothing has been discovered to date.

These films contain some common narrative threads. A number of them (*Solar Crisis, Deep Impact, Armageddon, Space Cowboys, The Wandering Earth*) feature the heroic self-sacrifice of astronauts that are necessary to save the world. Cooperation between Cold War enemies in countering a threat from space was formerly found in *The Day the Sky Exploded, Meteor* and *2010*. Dangers from space are many and varied and include alien microbes (*The Andromeda Strain*), man-made menaces (*Moonraker, Space Cowboys, Ad Astra*), solar events (*Solar Crisis, The Wandering Earth*) and, of course, meteors, comets or asteroids on a collision course with Earth (*Meteor, Deep Impact, Armageddon*).

Humankind may never have to overcome these dire threats, but if they do arise, our expertise in space flight may be needed to counter them.

NINE

To Infinity and Beyond: Journeys to Deep Space and the Stars

Current paradigms of space flight focus on the exploration of destinations relatively close to the Earth such as the Moon, Mars and even nearby asteroids. Science fiction writers and filmmakers, however, have long contemplated flights to the outer reaches of our solar system and planets orbiting other stars. While the outer planets of our system have been explored using unmanned probes and current technologies might permit manned voyages to these destinations (albeit with some difficulties), star flight is another matter entirely. This is because distances from the Earth to the stars are, as famed astronomer Carl Sagan once observed, "extremely far." Proxima Centauri, the closest star to our sun, is over 40 trillion kilometers away. The problem of interstellar travel is further compounded by Einstein's Theory of Relativity, which states that nothing can go faster than the speed of light, which travels at a velocity of 186,000 miles per second. A starship traveling at a significant fraction of this velocity might still take decades to reach nearby solar systems.

None of these factors have prevented sci-fi filmmakers from engaging in fantasies of star flight. In the *Star Trek* series of TV shows and films, for instance, vessels such as the *U.S.S. Enterprise* can employ its "warp drive" to travel at multiples of the speed of light (warp five, for instance, would be five times light speed). Likewise, characters in the *Star Wars* and *Guardians of the Galaxy* movies can jump in their spaceships and hot-rod across vast distances.

Some science fiction films attempt to come to grips with the realities of star flight. In *Avatar* (2009), for instance, a commercial starship takes five years to reach the world of Pandora, located in another star system, with the crew in hibernation, but the ship had to be moving faster than light in order to accomplish this. *Passengers* (2016) featured a ship that took 120 years to reach its destination, again with its crew in hypersleep. The strangest depiction of interstellar travel occurs in *Dune* (1984), in which a quasi-human Guild Navigator enables the instantaneous transit of an enormous starship using the technique of "traveling without moving" as it "folds space." A more science-oriented method of star travel employs the use of eliminating the enormous stellar distances by traveling through a black hole or a wormhole, as shown in *The Black Hole* (1979) and *Interstellar* (2014). While astronomers have observed black holes at vast distances from the Earth, wormholes exist solely in the realm of theoretical physics and have never been observed in nature.

Journeying through interplanetary space also presents myriad technological challenges, both in propulsion systems and life support. The chemical rockets currently in use are limited in endurance and speed, and scientists have proposed alternative methods of propulsion. Ion drives, which generate thrust using electrostatic plasma propulsion engines, can reach high velocities over long periods, and are already in use in the unmanned space probes *Dawn* and *Deep Space 1*. Nuclear-powered rockets have also been proposed, but have not been used due to concerns about the possibility of radioactive contamination in the event of a launch failure and potential dangers to a crew. Other exotic technologies, such as lightsails, which derive propulsion from the physical force of photons striking a large metallic sail, are currently under development.

Interstellar missions of exploration and colonization on the big screen commenced with the Czechoslovakian science fiction film *Ikarie XB-1* (1963). The film's starship is a reference to Icarus, a figure from Greek mythology who flew using wings made of wax that melted when he came too near the Sun. Loosely based on the novel *The Magellanic Cloud* by Stanislaw Lem, the movie takes place in the year 2163, when the titular spacecraft is sent on a mission to Alpha Centauri to explore the enigmatic White Planet in the Centauri System. Forty multinational spacefarers depart on the interstellar voyage, traveling just below the speed of light; the trip will take 28 months, although 15 years will have elapsed on Earth during this period due to relativistic time dilation effects.

The film divides the journey into four parts. Part one depicts everyday life aboard the starship, which is a palatial affair that contains individual quarters for the crew members, a communal cafeteria, a gymnasium and a recreation room equipped with a grand piano, in addition to a large, complex control room. The crew are shown taking their meals, having a cocktail party, exercising in the gym and performing other everyday tasks. Various crewmates are shown in social interaction, including Captain Vladimir Abajev (Zdenek Stepanek), Commander McDonald (Radovan Lukavsky), sociologist Nina Kirova (Dana Medricka), pilot Erik Svenson (Jiri Vrstala) and mathematician Anthony Hopkins (Frantisek Smolik), who pals around with a clunky, obsolescent robot. An onboard computer, the Centrale Automat, that talks to the crew in an annoying mechanical voice.

This idyllic period is abruptly shattered when the ship picks up a distress signal from another vessel as the film moves into part two. The signal is coming from a ship that is suspended in space and resembles a flying saucer. A team consisting of two spacesuited cosmonauts flies over to investigate; the ship is the *Tornado*, a spacecraft launched back in 1987. Roaming through the silent ship, they find nothing but corpses in various states of decomposition, the capitalist crew and passengers having slaughtered each other with gas guns over the ship's waning supplies of oxygen. The men accidentally set off an automated nuclear weapon on the ship, and they are killed as the relic of the age of Hiroshima is vaporized in an atomic blast.

Continuing on their journey, the starship crew encounters another menace as the film's narrative segues into part three. As they approach a highly radioactive "dark star," the entire crew is stricken with narcolepsy and tries to remain conscious in order to operate the ship. Crewmen Svenson (Jiri Vrstala) and Michael (Otto Lakovic) are obliged to perform an EVA to install a new power module, and Michael suffers severe radiation burns in the process. Just as it seems that the entire crew will succumb to the radiation-induced sleeping sickness, they begin to recover as they find that an energy field from the White Planet has protected them from the dark star's effects.

In part four, Michael, suffering from the effects of radiation, goes bonkers. Screaming in his delirium that the Earth has disappeared, he gets hold of a ray gun and seals himself off in a section of the ship. Commander McDonald must don a pressure suit and reach and disarm Michael by climbing through an air shaft. After the crisis has passed, the crew is jubilant as a baby is born to a couple on board, just as they reach their destination. Penetrating through the cloudy atmosphere of the White Planet, they behold the grid of a city belonging to an alien race on the world's surface.

Not seen in its original version for decades in the West, *Ikarie XB-1* is a seminal work that critics say exerted an influence on Stanley Kubrick's *2001* and Gene Roddenberry's *Star Trek* TV series. Kubrick reportedly viewed the film, along with many other genre entries, as preparation for his space epic. Scenes of astronauts moving through long corridors on the starship are similar to wide shots in *2001*'s *Discovery* spacecraft, and there is a scene in which a crew member communicates with his wife via a viewing screen that predates a similar one in which Dr. Floyd communicates with his daughter using a videophone device on the space station. Both films conclude with the birth of a baby in space that heralds the beginning of a new age. While there's no evidence that Roddenberry viewed the film, or was directly influenced by it, there are many similarities that seem to be more than coincidence. Both works feature a multinational crew of spacefarers piloting an imposing, complex starship on a mission to boldly go where no one has gone before.

The film was rarely seen in its original version outside of its country of origin, but exploitation studio American International Pictures acquired the rights and released a dubbed, heavily edited version entitled *Voyage to the End of the Universe* in 1964. About ten minutes of footage was cut and the ship's destination was changed to the Green Planet. Unlike the original version, when the ship arrives at its destination, instead of encountering an alien civilization, AIP's film substitutes stock shots of Manhattan and the Statue of Liberty, revealing that the Green Planet is actually the Earth and the starship's crew are aliens. A similar surprise ending is featured in Mario Bava's horror–sci-fi flick *Planet of the Vampires* (1965).

While it can be seen in a continuum with other contemporaneous Eastern Bloc science fiction films such as *First Spaceship on Venus* (1962) and *Storm Planet* (1962), *Ikarie XB-1* is a more seminal, avant-garde work. Although it's talky and episodic, director Jindrich Polak uses fluid moving camera and crisp editing to move the complex and unusual narrative along. One of the film's shortcomings, however, lies in the lack of a clear protagonist, instead focusing on a large, diverse cast of characters. The performances of the actors are mostly unremarkable, with the exception of Otto Lackovic's portrayal of the astronaut Michael. He emotes wildly as he suffers from a severe bout of space madness. The film's most memorable passage is the excursion into the derelict ship, an eerie domain of death that also serves to take a swipe at capitalist greed, which is symbolized by the first image seen by the away team, a corpse's hand clutching a dollar bill.

The real star of the film is the starship itself, a marvelous creation that was the work of production designer Jan Zazvorka. Perhaps inspired by sparse geometric lines of Bauhaus architecture, the interior sets were constructed on enormous sound stages at Barrandov Studios in Prague and were equipped with exotic accouterments such as a futuristic gymnasium, a hi-tech medical infirmary, claustrophobic lighted corridors, clear tubes filled with bubbling liquid and a spacious military-style command deck. The ship also contains numerous viewing screens that the crew members spend an inordinate amount of time ogling. A massive TV transmission tower in Prague is used to great effect as the ship's air shaft in one key scene. The film's visuals are complimented by an electronic score by Zdenek Lizka that recalls the futuristic "tonalities" music composed by Louis and Bebe Barron for the sci-fi classic *Forbidden Planet* (1956).

While the starship's interior is adorned with artsy technological architecture, its exterior is an oddball, Jules Verne–ish contraption. The film does not address the ship's method of propulsion, or how much energy would be needed to move such a large vessel at slightly less than the speed of light, although the film's math doesn't add up because the interstellar trip takes only two years and four months, while it would take over four years to reach its destination going at lightspeed. During a long-duration space voyage, the ship's crew would suffer from the debilitating effects of zero gravity, but the film relies on the venerable science fiction conceit of "artificial gravity" to dispense with this problem. The film does address the perils of radiation as the ship comes under the influence of a "dark star." In actuality, an expedition to Alpha Centauri would pass by the red dwarf star Proxima Centauri, which is given to periodic flares of deadly X-ray radiation. The relativistic time dilation effect of long-duration space travel would later become a plot element in *Interstellar* (2014).

Two years after the film's release, Britain's Lippert Films produced a low-budget *Ikarie XB-1* retread: *Spaceflight IC-1: An Adventure in Space* (1965). The film is set in the far future year of 2015, when a world government called RULE (the Reformed United League Executive council) seeks to mitigate the Earth's overpopulation by sending starship IC-1 (Interstellar Colony 1) on a 25-year mission to locate and colonize Earth 2, an Earth-like world in another solar system. The crew consists of four couples, their children and four crew members who have been placed in suspended animation inside hibernation chambers. All of them were selected for the mission by a computer. They include Captain Mead Ralston (Bill Williams), his wife Jan (Norma West), medical officer Steve Thomas (John Cairney) and his spouse Helen (Linda Marlowe). Also on board is Dr. Garth (John Lee), a "Closed Cycle Man": a disembodied human head encased in a fishbowl that serves as a kind of biological computer.

One year into the mission, Kate is diagnosed with a fatal disease of the pancreas, and Dr. Thomas demands that they return to Earth so that she can be treated. Captain Ralston refuses. After he denies her request to have a child during her remaining years, Helen commits suicide out of despair. Enraged by the death of his wife, Dr. Thomas confronts the captain, knocks him unconscious and assumes command of the ship. Ralston is locked in his cabin.

Helen's body is consigned to the void after the crew conducts a funeral. By this time, the ship has passed out of communication range with Earth and the authority of the world government and continues on its way with Dr. Thomas in command. The ship's computer programmer Karl Walcott (Donald Churchill) opposes the mutineers and frees Ralston. The captain quickly retakes command of the ship and confines the crew to their quarters. He informs Dr. Thomas that he will be executed for his treachery, but not until his alternate, Dr. Griffiths (Tony Doohan), is revived from suspended animation so that the expedition will not be without a physician. Thomas is dubious about awakening Griffiths under the unstable conditions, but Ralston insists that he will activate the self-destruct device on the ship unless he complies. Thomas initiates the resuscitation process; it will take 18 hours to restore the astronaut's temperature and oxygen levels.

While Dr. Thomas is in another part of the ship jawboning with Karl, Griffiths bursts out of the hibernation chamber prematurely and, in a confused state, begins stalking around the ship. He encounters Ralston and promptly strangles him to death. Karl knocks Griffiths unconscious. Thomas arrives on the scene and declares that Griffiths is dead from internal injuries due to an incomplete revival process. The crew holds a funeral for Ralston and Griffiths as the ship hurtles on through the interstellar void with Thomas as the new captain.

The film contains many plot elements cribbed from *Ikarie XB-1*, including a long-duration flight to another star system in search of an Earth-like world, a mixed gender crew and an astronaut who goes bonkers and endangers the mission, not to mention the movie's title. In contrast with its predecessor, however, the film's low-budget starship is claustrophobic and unconvincing, and resembles the interior of an ordinary office with file cabinets and office chairs. Director Bernard Knowles focuses mostly on the dramatic relationships between the characters in this interstellar soap opera as the action progresses at a snail's pace. The actors' performances are tepid, with the exception of American actor Bill Williams, who plays the starship's authoritarian captain with gruff and tough John Wayne mannerisms. Production values are extremely poor, with models of a wheel-shaped space station and the titular starship that strain suspension of disbelief. Because of these many flaws, the film has sunk into a well-deserved obscurity.

Positing an interstellar voyage that lasts a quarter of a century is consistent with the laws of physics for a ship traveling at a fraction of the speed of light, although the film is unclear as to where system Earth 2 is located. The notion of colonizing another world reflects current concerns about finding a Planet B (i.e., Mars) for humankind in case the Earth becomes uninhabitable. The crew is obliged to eat algae throughout their long journey. Although the film is primarily a drama, it contains some bizarre elements associated with the horror genre, including a disembodied talking head, the creepy hologram of a clown used to entertain the ship's children and the reanimated, homicidal Griffiths, who stalks around the ship with a stiff-legged gait that recalls Frankenstein's Monster. This was one of the first films to depict spacefarers in suspended animation in hibernation chambers, a trope that would be featured in a number of later sci-fi flicks. Poster art for the film showed an astronaut spacewalking into a 1960s–era Gemini capsule in a scene that does not appear in the movie.

Another filmic interstellar mission was launched in America that same year. *Space Monster* (1965) was set in the far future year of 2000, when new forms of propulsion have been devised to traverse "man's last frontier" in search of new worlds. As the film opens, officials at Earth Control receive a distress call from the spaceship *Faith One*. Its commander (Bob Legionaire) tells them that the ship has been contaminated by an infectious gas that has killed the rest of the crew. Because the spacecraft is infected and radioactive due to equipment malfunction and cannot return to Earth, the commander insists that the ship be destroyed. Earth Control reluctantly complies.

A second spaceship, christened *Hope One*, is launched on a mission to locate habitable worlds. The ship is equipped with artificial gravity that will spare the astronauts the inconveniences of zero gravity. The crew consists of Commander Hank Stevens (James Brown), scientists John Andros (Baynes Barron), Paul Martin (Russ Bender) and the only female crew member, Lisa Wayne (Francine York). Stevens is unhappy about her presence on the ship, which he declares is "no place for a woman," but he is informed that she was selected over a heavier male colleague in order to save weight.

After passing a wheel-shaped Space Platform, they encounter a seemingly disabled alien spacecraft, and Earth Control orders them to investigate. Stevens and Andros don spacesuits equipped with maneuvering units and EVA over to the alien ship. They find the vessel mysteriously deserted until an ugly-looking extraterrestrial (Jimmy Bracon) appears and promptly attacks Andros. The astronaut defends himself and kills the E.T., while Stevens contacts Earth Control to request that the alien ship be destroyed due to radiation rising to dangerous levels. He receives permission, and plants a bomb on the ship that blows it to smithereens.

Hope One encounters a meteor storm that disables the ship as it reaches the Triangulum Galaxy. The crew is forced to land on a nearby "escaped moon" they call Taurus. The ship settles on the shallow bottom of an ocean, and a swarm of giant crabs surround the spacecraft. A balloon is sent to the surface and a sample of the moon's atmosphere is obtained. Chemical analysis reveals that the air is practically identical to Earth's. This information prompts Andros to don a wetsuit and swim to a nearby land mass to obtain soil samples. He succeeds, but he is attacked and mortally wounded by a humanoid sea creature. The samples show that the world is habitable. Once the ship is repaired, the remaining crew members return home, their mission accomplished. The new world is to be named "Andros One" after the martyred astronaut.

This low-budget made-for-TV excursion into outer space is a typical example of sci-fi fare in the pre–*2001* era. Its special effects are laughable and the performances are mediocre at best. Director Leonard Katzman, who also scripted, moves the action along briskly to create a reasonably entertaining American International programmer, but Katzman's screenplay borders on the incoherent. The opening scenes depicting the demise of the *Hope One* spaceship and the heroic self-sacrifice of its commander is unconnected to the rest of the film, for instance, and the close encounter with the hostile alien is likewise left unexplained. Production designs for the spacecraft's interior are adequate, but the model work on the ship's exterior is awful and entirely unconvincing. Ordinary crabs are used as alien monsters, and the underwater humanoid's costume was reportedly left over from the AIP production *War-Gods of the Deep.*

As screenwriter, Katzman seems to have been woefully ignorant about the most basic astronomical matters. The spacefarers travel to their destination, the Triangulum Galaxy, in an absurdly short interval of time. Our solar system is located in a spiral arm of the Milky Way Galaxy, and the Triangulum Galaxy, approximately 2.7 million light years away, would take millions of years to reach even traveling at the speed of light. Although the film hints at the discovery of an advanced means of propulsion, the only propulsion system pictured in the film consists of stock footage of 1960s-era Atlas rockets takeoffs. Of course, that old sci-fi standby "artificial gravity" is employed to free the filmmakers from having to show the actors floating in zero gravity. The astronauts communicate with Earth Control using pseudo-scientific jargon such as "Two minutes 18 seconds vector alpha" and "All systems function green."

The Russian film *The Andromeda Nebula* (*Tumannost Andromedy*, 1967) is set in the year 3000, when interstellar space flight has become a reality. Based on Ivan Yefremov's novel *Andromeda: A Space Age Tale*, it tells two parallel stories, one set on a futuristic Earth, the other aboard the starship *Tantra*. On Earth, a utopian society gathers for Olympics-style events around a gigantic sculpture of a hand holding a burning flame. The celebrants are clad in white, toga-like garments that resemble those of ancient Greece. Among them are Veda Kong (Vija Artmane), wife of the *Tantra*'s captain, and archeologist Dar Veter (Sergei Stolyarov), who are contemplating a romance during her husband's long absence. In another scene, the Council of Astronavigation intercepts a dance performance beamed from a distant world and muses that the performers have died during the hundreds of years that its taken the signal to reach them. To deal with the problems of time and distance involved in space travel, scientist Mven Mas (Lado Tskhvariashvilli) is working on a project designed to "compress time."

Light years away in deep space, the *Tantra* has intercepted a distress call from a planet orbiting an "iron star." The starship's captain, Erg Noor (Nikolai Kryukov) decides to land and investigate despite the possibility that the ship may not have enough fuel to take off due to the effect of the star's gravity and it will take 25 years for a message from the *Tantra* to reach the Earth. Upon landing, they find that the planet is a hellish world of swirling black and red mists that is a graveyard for spaceships that have been drawn into the gravitational grip of the iron star, including the gigantic flying saucer of an alien race. Also lurking within the planet's ubiquitous fog is an invisible creature that is able to penetrate the explorer's spacesuits and desiccate their bodies from within.

Erg Noor, along with a small group of cosmonauts including Niza Krit (Tatyana Voloshina), a young female navigation officer that the captain is attracted to, travel over the planet's surface in an exploratory vehicle until they reach the source of the distress signal. Entering the derelict spaceship, they find it deserted, the only trace of the crew being oily shadows etched on the walls of the ship. Their mission accomplished, upon returning to the *Tantra* Niza is attacked by the invisible creature and the encounter leaves her in a comatose state. Contemplating her inert body lying in a medical chamber, Erg Noor laments that she will probably not be able to survive the trip home.

At this point, all the threads of the narrative abruptly come to an end. This is because the film was intended to be the first of a series and was subtitled *Episode 1: Prisoners of the Iron Star (Plenniki Zheleznoi Zvezdy)*. Unfortunately for the proposed series, novelist and co-scenarist Ivan Yefremov published a science fiction novel entitled *Hour of the Bull (Chas Byka)* that was judged to contain material critical of Soviet policies and society in 1968, a year after the film was released. As a result, Yefremov was interrogated by the KGB, his manuscripts and writings were confiscated, and he was forbidden from publishing any more literary works. Thus, further adventures of the *Tantra*'s crew vanished down a black hole of Soviet political orthodoxy, and *The Andromeda Nebula* would remain an incomplete fragment. Yefremov's novel provides a blueprint for further narrative developments in the proposed series.

The film shows influences from several earlier works, most prominently *Ikarie XB-1* (1963), another Soviet bloc production that extoled the virtues of Communism. Like the earlier film, *Andromeda* also depicted an enormous starship that contained a vast exercise gymnasium complete with an Olympic-sized swimming pool. Both films featured the plot element of a starship answering a distress call and encountering a derelict ship with a dead crew. Another influence may have been Mario Bava's *Planet of the Vampires* (1965) which also featured a distress signal and a derelict ship, along with a similarly fogbound planetscape. Like all of Eastern bloc science fiction cinema, *Andromeda* is overly talky, with philosophical and socio-historical commentary from the characters that serves to impede the flow of the narrative.

Because the film does not posit faster than light space travel, there is an air of melancholy that hangs over the proceedings due to the great distances and lengthy travel times involved in interstellar space flight. The film keeps cross-cutting between the characters on Earth, Veda Kong, Dar Veter and Mven Mas and Erg Noor and his crew exploring the planet of the iron star. Director Yevgeni Sherstobitov offers a stark visual contrast between the brightly colored Earth environment (filmed at a seaside location in the Ukraine) where the characters wear white, toga-like outfits, and the hellish world of dark, swirling fog where the spacesuited cosmonauts struggle to survive. Space is hard.

The film's title refers to a nebula, which is an ionized cloud of dust, hydrogen and helium in interstellar space. An object located within the constellation of Andromeda was once thought to be a nebula within our own galaxy, but further research by astronomers revealed that the Andromeda Nebula was actually a galaxy that is entirely separate from our Milky Way and approximately 2.5 million light years distant. Traveling at less than the speed of light, the starship *Tantra* would take many millions of years to reach the Andromeda Galaxy, the nearest galaxy to ours.

In 1968, Stanley Kubrick's brilliant production design and special effects for *2001: A Space Odyssey* changed the look of the science fiction film forever. Douglas Trumbull, the effects wiz responsible for creating *2001*'s visuals, brought his skills to bear as a director on the ecologically themed sci-fi flick *Silent Running* (1973). The film takes place some time in the future, when overpopulation and pollution have destroyed all plant and animal life on Earth. Three gigantic spaceships, the *Valley Forge*, the *Berkshire* and the *Sequoia,* contain all that is left of the world's vegetation, enclosed in geodesic domes. The three ships are parked in deep space in proximity to the planet Saturn and are maintained by a corporation as a preserve for the eventual reforestation of the Earth.

Freeman Lowell (Bruce Dern), the botanist-ecologist aboard the *Valley Forge,* dutifully maintains the ship's plants and animals. Three other crewmen, John Keenan (Cliff Potts), Andy Wolf (Jesse Vint) and Marty Baker (Ron Rifkin), run the ship's mechanical operations, but are loutish individuals who do not share Lowell's devotion to the forests; they only wish to be finished with their duties and return to Earth. There is friction between Lowell and his crewmates, who are content to chow down on synthetic food instead of Lowell's homegrown fruits and vegetables, and consider the botanist an oddball.

One day the corporation sends word that they have decided to terminate the forest preserve operation and return the ships to commercial service. The crewmen, overjoyed at the news, prepare to jettison the domes and blow them up. Lowell rebels and kills his crewmates before they can finish carrying out their task, in order to preserve the last of his beloved vegetation. He then stages a bogus explosion aboard the ship as a ruse and hijacks the ship in an effort to preserve the one remaining dome. Changing course, he sends the *Valley Forge* on a trajectory that will take it through Saturn's rings in a desperate effort to avoid pursuit by the company's other ships. He reprograms the vessel's three diminutive service robots, Huey, Dewey and Louie, to perform supporting gardening and maintenance tasks.

In the perilous trip through Saturn's rocky rings, Louie is destroyed but the *Valley Forge* and its forest cargo survive. Once they are in the giant planet's shadow, other problems emerge. Deprived of sunlight, the forest's vegetation begins to wilt. At the same time, the *Berkshire* locates the ship and closes in. Huey is severely damaged when Lowell accidentally collides with the robot while driving a transport cart. Lowell rigs up a series of high-output lamps to provide enough light to revive the garden. Realizing that he will be unable to escape the pursuing ship, he programs Dewey to care for the garden and sends the remaining dome into deep space, hoping it will eventually finds its way to a safe environment. Having saved the forest, Lowell detonates a nuclear device on the *Valley Forge*, vaporizing the ship and himself.

Freeman Lowell (Bruce Dern) plays poker with his robot friends in *Silent Running* (1973).

Silent Running is basically a character study of the Freeman Lowell character, who comes off as either an ecological hero or a wide-eyed fanatic depending on one's point of view. He commits acts of eco-terrorism by murdering his crewmates, destroying the ship and eventually committing suicide. He is more comfortable in the company of plants and robots than his fellow human beings, who are depicted as insensitive jerks. The film is basically a one-man show in which Bruce Dern seems to be channeling his earlier role as the Seeker, the robed, drugged-out hippie prophet in the counterculture anthem *Psych-Out* (1968). Dern has portrayed unusual character roles in *The King of Marvin Gardens* (1972), *Black Sunday* (1977), *Coming Home* (1978), *Nebraska* (2013) and *Once Upon a Time in Hollywood* (2019), and his over-the-top performance as eco-astronaut Freeman Lowell is entertaining and easily carries the film. The other major characters are the robots Huey, Dewey and Louie, named after Donald Duck's three nephews, and precursors to the cute droids in the *Star Wars* films.

Director Douglas Trumbull does a workmanlike job, but the film's most impressive aspect is his special effects, which remain impressive even by today's standards. Trumbull's effects credits also include the sci-fi classics *The Andromeda Strain* (1971), *Close Encounters of the Third Kind* (1977), *Star Trek: The Motion Picture* (1979) and *Blade Runner* (1982). He was ably assisted on *Silent Running* by his protégé John Dykstra, who went on to work on the effects for *Star Wars: A New Hope* (1977) and was one of the founders of the Industrial Light & Magic consortium. The spaceship *Valley Forge* model was 25 feet long and took six months to construct. The *Valley Forge* interiors were filmed aboard the decommissioned Korean War–era aircraft carrier USS *Valley Forge*, which was docked at the Long Beach Naval Shipyard in California. The forest dome sequences were shot in an aircraft hangar in Van Nuys, California. The film's geodesic dome environment was based on the Missouri Climatron greenhouse in St. Louis. The film also includes two musical numbers by folk singer Joan Baez, "Silent Running" and "Rejoice in the Sun," which are either inspiring or irritating according to one's taste.

The screenplay was co-written by Michael Cimino, who later directed the critically acclaimed *The Deer Hunter* (1978). It hits all the dramatic high notes but contains a number of logical inconsistencies. For instance, why are the film's spaceships parked way out near Saturn, which is between 746 and 847 million miles away from Earth (depending on the relative orbital positions of the planets), instead of placing them in Earth orbit, which would be an infinitely less expensive logistical proposition for a corporation? The answer, of course, is the filmmakers' use of the giant ringed planet as a dramatic backdrop for the action. At this distance, Saturn receives 100 times less sunlight than the Earth, which is hardly an optimal location for growing plants. Indeed, why put the greenhouses in outer space at all when the vegetation could be grown inside domes located on Earth? Why does botanist Lowell seem to be baffled when his forest becomes blighted due to lack of light? How did human beings manage to survive when all other species on the planet perished? What kind of "synthetic food" do people eat in the absence of plant and animal sources of nourishment? The answers to these questions need no answers, as *Silent Running* functions as a ecological parable rather than a work of scientifically based fiction.

More pseudo-scientific nonsense was on display in the Disney production *The Black Hole* (1979). The story takes place in space in the year 2130, as the research ship the USS *Palomino* completes its unsuccessful five-year mission to search a sector of the galaxy for extraterrestrial life and heads home to Earth. The crew consists of Captain Dan Holland (Robert Forster), science officer Alex Durant (Anthony Perkins), journalist Harry Booth (Ernest Borgnine), first officer Charles Pizer (Joseph Bottoms), medical officer Kate McCrae (Yvette Mimieux) and robotic entity VINCENT (voiced by Roddy McDowall). McCrae is also a psychic who has a telepathic link with VINCENT's artificial intelligence.

During the return leg of their journey, VINCENT detects a black hole in proximity to the *Palomino*, a swirling mass that draws all matter inside it due to its intense gravitational pull. The robot also notices what appears to be a derelict ship poised near the black hole's event horizon (the boundary of the region from which no escape is possible); it has somehow withstood the effects of the massive gravity well. The derelict is identified as the USS *Cygnus*, a ship that was reported lost nearly 20 years earlier under the command of imperious scientist Hans Reinhardt. Another member of the *Cygnus'* crew was Kate's father, executive officer Frank McCrae. Under the circumstances, the *Palomino* decides to investigate what happened to the errant ship and attempts to dock with the *Cygnus* even though they may come dangerously close to the black hole.

Performing a tricky maneuver, the *Palomino* approaches the larger ship and begins to be affected by the black hole's gravitational influence. As they get closer, however, they are deflected by a null gravity field emanating from the *Cygnus* that counteracts the black hole's attraction. Lights from the *Palomino* play over the dark and silent spacecraft in an eerie fashion until the *Cygnus* comes alive; the sudden illumination seems inviting. The *Palomino* docks with the *Cygnus* and the crew, except for Lt. Pizer, disembark and are promptly disarmed by the ship's automated lasers. Unfazed, they board an automated transport that whisks them down the length of the huge ship until they reach its control tower. Along the way, they observe several silent human-like figures attired in

The elegant USS *Cygnus* starship is pictured in this German poster for *The Black Hole* (1979).

hooded robes and mirrored face masks, and a menacing, burgundy-colored robot they later learn is named Maximillian.

At the tower, they are greeted by Dr. Reinhardt (Maximilian Schell), who informs them that he is the only member of the original crew left on board. The others departed after the *Cygnus* was disabled by a meteor storm and attempted to return to Earth, while he stayed behind to repair the ship and eventually remained in order to study the black hole. He has perfected means to nullify the hole's gravitational force and is planning to send probe ships into it. He hopes to eventually pilot the *Cygnus* inside amd explore new areas of the galaxy or even other dimensions. The robed figures are robots programmed to run the ship and assist with his research.

While they are repairing their ship, the *Palomino* crew members explore the *Cygnus* and make some startling discoveries. Holland observes a group of robed figures conducting a funeral by committing one of their number into the void. He also locates crew quarters that contain personal effects and uniforms that belie the notion of the crew having abandoned ship. Booth comes upon the ship's huge greenhouse area, which contains enough crops "to feed an army." VINCENT encounters a broken-down model robot named BOB (voiced by Slim Pickens), who is reduced to functioning in a sanitation capacity and intimates that it knows secrets about the ship but is too frightened to tell.

After launching a probe ship into the black hole, Reinhardt hosts a dinner party for his guests in the ship's tower dining hall, and discusses the results of his research. Dr. Durant is fascinated by the scientist's work, but the others remain dubious. When Maximillian arrives to communicate that the probe has returned, Reinhardt leaves to examine the results, and Holland, Pizer and Booth return to their ship to discuss their discoveries with each other in private. Durant and McCrae remain in the tower. The three crew members and VINCENT learn the grim truth about the *Cygnus* from BOB: The robed humanoids are not automata, but are the ship's former crew members, lobotomized by Reinhardt and reduced to the level of mindless slaves. When the *Cygnus* was ordered to return to Earth, Reinhardt refused and Frank McCrae led a mutiny against him, whereupon McCrae was killed and the rest of the crew subjugated by Maximillian and his legion of robots.

VINCENT uses his telepathic link with McCrae to order her back to their ship while conveying what they have learned. She in turn imparts the information to Durant, who removes the metal faceplate from one of the robed figures to reveal the human face of the zombified crewman. When Reinhardt and his robot retinue return to the tower, he orders Maximillian to dispatch Durant, who is brutally killed using a whirling blade. McCrae is to be taken to sick bay and lobotomized, but VINCENT learns of this through telepathy and the men hurry through the ship to prevent this. Fighting their way past Reinhardt's robots with blazing ray guns, they rescue her. Reinhardt orders his robot henchmen to let the *Palomino* take off and then destroy it. Having analyzed the data from the probe ship, Reinhardt is preparing to send the *Cygnus* into the black hole at last.

Unbeknownst to his fellow crewmates, Booth has plans to commandeer the *Palomino* and leave the others to their fate. Trying to fly the spacecraft alone, he undocks from the *Cygnus* while the others are pinned down by fire from Reinhardt's sentry robots. The *Palomino* is shot down by Reinhardt's laser cannons and crashes into the *Cygnus*, causing damage to the ship just as it is passing over the event horizon into the

Dr. Alex Durant (Anthony Perkins) regards a hologram of the accretion disk surrounding *The Black Hole* **(1979).**

black hole. The ship passes into its gravitational influence and is hit by fiery meteors and other cosmic debris; Reinhardt is crushed to death under a video console. Seeking to escape in the probe ship, the *Palomino*'s crew fight their way through hordes of robots until Maximillian and VINCENT go *mano a mano* and the evil droid is defeated. BOB is damaged during the battle and must be abandoned as the surviving crew enter the probe ship and undock from the disintegrating *Cygnus*.

The probe is preprogrammed to fly into the black hole and its course cannot be altered. As they enter the whirling vortex, they are confronted by visions of Reinhardt and Maximillian in a fiery landscape that suggests they are burning in Hell. Then the vision fades as the ship passes through a portal that resembles a church window and the crew is greeted by a figure in bright robes who resembles an angel. The probe ship then emerges from the other end of the black hole into normal space-time and sails toward the peaceful bright light of an unknown star.

The enormous popular success of *Star Wars* (1977) prompted Hollywood to green-light a number of big-budget, special effects–laden science fiction blockbusters. Audiences anticipated the release of such a production from Disney, which had previously mostly dabbled in humorous, juvenile sci-fi fare such as *Moon Pilot* (1962), *Escape to Witch Mountain* (1975) and *The Cat from Outer Space* (1978). *The Black Hole* was released in 1979, the same year as *Alien* and *Star Trek: The Motion Picture*, and suffered greatly in comparison. Its most egregious problem: the comic book screenplay by Gerry Day and Jeb Rosebrook, which is complete with an evil mad scientist, the obligatory cutesie robots, flaming meteors, astro-zombies, scientific absurdities and laser-toting bad guys. It's basically *20,000 Leagues Under the Sea* reset in outer space, up to and including its super ship and schizoid captain. TV director Gary Nelson struggles valiantly with this banal material, but fails miserably. Ironically, this was the first Disney production to receive a PG rating due to some rather tame dialogue. The only interesting plot twist is the ESP connection between Dr. McCrae and VINCENT, which could have been developed further. In its climactic sequence, the probe ship is drawn over the event horizon into the black hole. Audiences expecting a *2001*-type light show were instead treated to a quasi-religious vision of Heaven and Hell that moves the film into the realm of Hollywood metaphysics.

In the acting department, Maximilian Schell exudes the proper measure of Teutonic menace, while Tony Perkins portrays his signature nerved-out characterization. Screen veterans Ernest Borgnine is terribly miscast as a spacefaring journalist (which begs the question of why someone from that profession would be needed on a deep space mission), while Yvette Mimieux has a throwaway part as the obligatory female scientist. Robert Forster and Joseph Bottoms are particularly bland as the ship's officers. The worst performers are the two robots, who are infected with a terminal case of Disney-esque cuteness and resemble cartoon characters. While Roddy McDowall does a decent job of voicing VINCENT, the use of western character actor Slim Pickens to provide the rootin'-tootin' voice of BOB is irritating.

The film's strong suits are its special effects and production design. Disney engineers invented the A.C.E.S. (Automated Camera Effects System), a computerized system that made it possible to seamlessly meld the actors and miniatures with matte paintings in the background. The *Cygnus* spacecraft is a marvelous creation, an elegant thing of glass and metal that has been compared to the Eifel Tower. The ship was designed by matte painter Peter Ellenshaw, who had also designed the *Nautilus* submarine for

Disney's *20,000 Leagues Under the Sea* (1954). While the *Cygnus* is highly photogenic on the outside, its interior is filled with long, horizontal empty spaces that seem to be devoid of any functionality. Budgeted at $20 million, *The Black Hole* was Disney's most expensive production at that time.

A black hole is a celestial object that is formed when the center of a large star collapses upon itself and causes a supernova explosion. It is an area of such immense gravity that not even light can escape from it because the mass of the destroyed star has been compressed into a very small space. Because it traps light and all other forms of electromagnetic radiation, astronomers cannot directly observe them, but can only detect their influence on other matter nearby. Some black holes can be seen as dark areas surrounded by rings of superheated gas called an accretion disc, which is how the object is depicted in the film. Scientists theorize that there may be ten million to a billion black holes in our Milky Way galaxy. Astrophysicist Neil deGrasse Tyson declared in 2013 that in his opinion, *The Black Hole* was the least scientifically accurate movie of all time, but science fiction writers have long theorized that black holes or wormholes could be utilized to travel between points in the space-time continuum, as shown most recently in *Interstellar* (2014).

In 1980, Cornell University astronomer Carl Sagan co-wrote and hosted the PBS series *Cosmos*, in which the scientist explored the wonders of the universe. Using his "spaceship of the imagination," Sagan voyaged through billions and billions of miles through space, from the solar system to other star systems and even other galaxies. In 1985, Sagan authored the novel *Contact*, in which he introduced an entirely original mode of space travel. Acclaimed director Robert Zemeckis directed a film version of Sagan's book that was also titled *Contact*.

The 1997 film follows the life and career of Ellie Arroway, first as a child (played by Jenna Malone), who is raised in a one-parent household by her father Ted (David Morse). Ted, a kind and compassionate man, introduces her to the glories of astronomy and amateur radio operation and inspires her love of science. One night while they are stargazing, Ted suffers a fatal heart attack. Ellie suffers from guilt because she believes she didn't get him his heart medicine in time.

Years later, the adult Ellie (Jodie Foster) has become a brilliant astrophysicist who is involved in SETI (Search for Extraterrestrial Intelligence) research at the Arecibo radio telescope observatory in Puerto Rico, which was equipped with the world's largest reflector dish at the time. While at Arecibo, she has a brief affair with spiritual activist Palmer Joss (Matthew McConaughey), a self-described "man of the cloth, without the cloth," but prefers to concentrate on her work rather than continue the relationship. Soon afterward, her supervisor David Drumlin (Tom Skerritt) arrives to announce that the administration is pulling the plug on the SETI program because the scientific consensus is that it's a waste of time and money.

Stung by the rejection, Ellie approaches Hadden Industries, a consortium run by billionaire investor S.R. Hadden (John Hurt), and receives private funding for further SETI research at the Very Large Array (VLA) radio telescope observatory in New Mexico. On her team is scientist Dr. Kent (William Fichtner), who is blind but has an augmented sense of hearing. After four frustrating years of searching, Ellie's team detects that the star Vega is transmitting a mathematical pattern consisting of prime numbers. Their discovery is confirmed by astronomers around the world, and news of an apparently intelligent signal from an extraterrestrial source causes a worldwide sensation.

The government forces that descend on the VLA facility are headed by Drumlin and the president's acerbic National Security Adviser Michael Kitz (James Woods). Things get weird when video images of Adolf Hitler making a speech during the 1936 Olympics are found imbedded in the signal. The authorities are puzzled until it is revealed that this was the first television broadcast that could have reached Vega after being transmitted from Earth. Soon afterward, however, 60,000 pages of encoded digital data are discovered inside the signal. Ellie and her group are tasked with decoding the symbols, but months later they remain stumped.

One night Ellie receives a mysterious email that displays an inside knowledge of the decipherment problem and invites her to a meeting. The sender turns out to be Hadden; they meet on his private jumbo jet that serves as his mobile headquarters. Hadden, an eccentric recluse, reveals that he has been Ellie's secret benefactor for years, and is continuing to support her efforts because he is terminally ill and wishes to advance human knowledge before he dies. He shows her that the pages can be deciphered by folding them into three-dimensional constructs using registration marks on the corners. Doing this reveals a primer that will allow the pages to become intelligible. Ellie shares this knowledge with the scientific community, but Drumlin pulls rank and takes full credit for the discovery. As news of the discovery spreads, hordes of curiosity seekers, religious cultists and assorted weirdos descend on the VLA facility. A carnival atmosphere prevails.

Ellie and her team decode the message, which turns out to be a schematic blueprint for the construction of a machine of unknown function. It soon becomes apparent that

Astrophysicist Dr. Ellie Arroway (Jodie Foster) confronts National Security Adviser Michael Kitz (James Woods) over the origin of enigmatic signals from space in *Contact* (1997).

the machine is an interstellar transport device. Kitz fears that it will enable hostile aliens to beam themselves to Earth on a mission of conquest, but his opinion is opposed by administrator Rachel Constantine (Angela Bassett) and Palmer Joss, who reappears to support Ellie's position. After much consideration, the government decides to construct one of the alien machines at a cost of $600 billion.

A few years later, the machine has been completed at the Cape Canaveral launch complex, and Drumlin is selected over Ellie to make the first test run amid much media fanfare. During the run-up to the test, as Drumlin is inspecting the mechanism, a long-haired religious fanatic named Joseph (Jake Busey), who has infiltrated the project, sets off a suicide vest strapped to his body, causing an explosion that destroys the machine and kills Drumlin. Ellie's hopes for making an interstellar journey are dashed because, in the aftermath of the tragedy that was telecast around the world, the country will not undertake the expense of constructing another machine.

When Ellie returns to her apartment, she is surprised to receive a satellite uplink message from the Mir space station. Upon activating the link, she is greeted by Hadden, who tells her that he has purchased time on the Russian station because some of his ailments are ameliorated by zero gravity. More importantly, he informs her that Hadden Industries has built a second machine on Hokkaido, the northernmost island of Japan, and that he wants her to be its first subject. "Want to take a ride?" he asks rhetorically.

Traveling to Hokkaido, Ellie undergoes extensive preparations for the momentous event. When the day arrives, she is outfitted in a protective suit. The machine consists of three circular sections that rotate gyroscopically and a crane-like device that drops a metal transport pod containing the passenger through the energy field generated by the rotating rings. She is given a suicide pill to be used in case she finds herself hopelessly marooned in space. Just before her departure, Palmer Joss visits and declares his love for her while expressing his fears that she may not return.

Ellie is placed in the transport pod and the machine is powered up. As the rings spin faster and faster, it generates intense energy fields that begin to warp space-time. When the pod is dropped through the center of the swirling force field, she is propelled on her interstellar journey. Passing through wormholes, she experiences various stages of gravity and sees vistas of alien worlds as the pod walls are rendered transparent. She winds up standing on the simulacrum of a tropical beach as a human figure approaches. She is startled to see that an extraterrestrial emissary has assumed the appearance of her father in order to communicate with her. The alien being explains that the Vegans intercepted television signals emanating from Earth and decided to make their presence known in a spirit of cosmic brotherhood. She is told that the Vegans can access a system of wormholes built by an ancient, unknown race that enable travel between the stars. The Vegans have noted that humankind feels lonely in their isolation, but eventual contact with other races will cure this.

At the end of the exchange, it is time for Ellie to return. She suddenly finds herself back in the pod as it falls into the netting slung across the underside of the machine. She is startled when informed that the pod did not travel anywhere, but merely fell through the rotating rings; only seconds have elapsed. The event was documented by video cameras, and a recorder inside the pod recorded only static. At a public hearing, Kitz expresses the opinion that the whole thing was a hoax perpetrated by Hadden in an effort to unite humanity. Hadden is unavailable for comment, as he died from cancer while aboard the Mir. The controversy has attracted crowds of supporters who believe

Ellie Arroway (Jodie Foster) prepares for her interstellar journey in *Contact* (1997).

Ellie's story. Palmer Joss is at her side to offer encouragement and he expresses the opinion that he is obliged to accept her account of extraterrestrial contact on faith.

In the aftermath of the hearing, Rachel Constantine confers with Kitz about a detail in Ellie's report. Although Ellie's video device recorded nothing but static, it recorded 18 hours of static, the exact amount of time that Ellie claimed to have been on her interstellar journey. Ellie goes back to work at the VLA observatory, where she is shown giving a tour to a group of grade school kids. When one of the students asks if she believes there is intelligent life in the universe, she replies, "If there isn't, then it'd be an awful waste of space." The film's final scenes show that Ellie is overseeing the construction of more radio telescope dishes as her search for extraterrestrial life continues.

One of Hollywood's most thought-provoking and intelligent science fiction films, *Contact* combines the mystery of first contact with an alien civilization with the personal drama of a brilliant, visionary female scientist struggling against a male-dominated power structure. Acclaimed director Robert Zemeckis, responsible for such hits as *Back to the Future* (1985), *Who Framed Roger Rabbit* (1988) and *Forrest Gump* (1994), crafts a *tour de force* that treats a subject that is usually portrayed in melodramatic, exploitative terms with a measured dignity. Acting, special effects and an intriguing screenplay by James V. Hart and Michael Goldenberg are unified into a coherent and inspiring whole. An A-list cast consisting of Jodie Foster, Matthew McConaughey, Tom Skerritt, Angela Basset, James Woods and John Hurt, as well as supporting players David Morse, Jake Busey and William Fichtner, elevate the film to classic status. Foster's sensitive portrayal of Ellie Arroway is the keynote of the film, and John Hurt turns in a quirky performance as Ellie's enigmatic benefactor S.R. Hadden.

An important person who appeared in the film but received no billing was

President Bill Clinton, who is shown in clips from two press conferences that were inserted in the narrative in the same manner as Zemeckis would later utilize in *Forrest Gump*. One of the pressers edited into the film was in response to reports by NASA scientist David McKay that objects that could possibly be microbes had been discovered in Martian meteorite ALH84001. The story made worldwide headlines, and Clinton's comments in response to the controversy were skillfully edited into the film. A few days after the movie's release, White House Counsel Charles Ruff sent a letter to Warner Bros. calling the studio's insertion of the footage "inappropriate," but no further action was taken. Additionally, cable news channel CNN lamented that they had allowed their staffers Larry King, John Holliman and Bernard Shaw to appear in the film, stating that their appearance blurred the line between fact and fiction.

SETI is the attempt to detect radio signals from an alien civilization. As early as 1896, maverick inventor Nikola Tesla believed he had detected radio transmissions from Mars, but nowadays it is agreed that he probably picked up radio noise originating from Earth or possibly from Jupiter. Modern SETI research was originated in 1960 by Cornell University astronomer Frank Drake, whose experiment was named Project Ozma. Drake employed the radio telescope at Green Bank, West Virginia, observatory in an attempt to look for radio emissions from nearby stars, but found nothing. The first dedicated SETI program was started by Ohio State University researchers who built a dedicated radio telescope (dubbed the "Big Ear"). It was completed in 1961 and activated in 1963. In 1980, Carl Sagan and other astronomers founded the Planetary Society to continue the search. Currently, the non-profit SETI Institute, founded in 1995 in Mountain View, California, is still scanning the cosmos for alien signals, but to date nothing of unambiguous significance has been found, and many mainstream astronomers consider SETI research a fringe scientific discipline that is a waste of time and money. Scenes in the film depicting the VLA radiotelescope dishes were shot on location at the Socorro, New Mexico, observatory.

The Ellie Arroway character was inspired by the career of SETI proponent and astrobiologist Jill Tarter, the SETI Institute's current director. Tarter, like Ellie, had to contend with anti-female prejudices in a male-dominated discipline. She persevered and garnered achievement awards from a number of scientific organizations. She served as a consultant on the film and had numerous conferences with Jodie Foster regarding the actress' characterization.

The subplot in which Drumlin takes credit for Ellie's discovery recalls a real-life incident in the annals of astronomy. In 1967, Jocelyn Bell Burnell was a doctoral student working under the direction of her advisor Anthony Hewish at the University of Cambridge in England. While assisting in research using the university's radio telescope, she noticed a pulsing radio emission that repeated itself at precisely regular intervals. She had discovered the *pulsar*, an extremely dense, rapidly rotating neutron star that flashes intermittent bursts of energy in rapid pulses. In 1974, Hewish took full credit for the discovery of the pulsar and was awarded the Nobel Prize in physics. Bell Burnell's role in discovering the pulsar was not acknowledged until she was awarded the $3 million Special Breakthrough Prize in Fundamental Physics in 2018.

The star Vega, the source of the movie's extraterrestrial signals, is the fifth brightest star in the night sky. It is 25 light years from Earth and is a young A-class blue star that is 2.1 times as massive as the Sun. It is also one-tenth the age of the Sun, roughly 500 million years old. As life on Earth has taken several billion years to evolve into intelligence, it would seem unlikely that Vega would have produced an advanced civilization in that short time frame. Like *2001* and *Interstellar*, *Contact* posits that a benevolent alien race will provide the means for humankind to travel to other star systems.

Europa is one of the four large moons of Jupiter. Slightly smaller than Earth's moon, it is the smoothest body in the solar system, its surface being devoid of mountains and large craters. Instead, it is covered with a complex network of striated cracks and streaks called *lineae*. The surface is composed of a layer of water ice frozen as hard as granite in the satellite's average temperature of about -260 degrees Fahrenheit. Scientists believe, however, that there is an ocean of liquid saline water underneath Europa's icy surface, heated by a process called tidal flexing (a friction caused by Jupiter's massive gravity), and that this warm subsurface ocean could sustain forms of extraterrestrial life. NASA and the European Space Agency have proposed a number of missions to land on Europa, and even to send a robotic submersible craft (a "hydrobot") underneath the moon's icy surface to search for life in the ocean. Science fiction writers have written about efforts to find life on Europa, and the film *2010: The Year We Make Contact* (1984) depicts the moon being transformed into a preserve for evolving life by an alien force.

Two recent films featured expeditions to explore the mysteries of Jupiter's icy satellite and its subsurface seas. In *Astronaut: The Last Push* (2012), unmanned probes detect creatures that resemble earthly whales in the ocean underneath Europa's ice. Rather than sending more unmanned craft to continue exploring, billionaire industrialist Walter Moffitt (Lance Henriksen), the so-called "King of Space" and the head of Moffitt Industries, decides to privately fund a manned mission to Europa. The spacecraft, *Life One*, is crewed by Michael Forrest (Khary Payton) and Nathan Miller (James Madio), who are placed in separate hibernation chambers for the six-year voyage to Jupiter space. Their flight plan is to swing around Venus for a gravity assist that will slingshot them to their destination. Two arms rotate around *Life One*'s central body, each arm containing a habitation module and an escape pod.

While the spacecraft is en route to Venus, a meteor impact causes Forrest to awaken from hibernation prematurely. He quickly repairs the hibernation chamber and finds the rest of the ship is intact and still spaceworthy, but he must remain awake to ensure that all systems function normally. Trapped inside the closed confines of the habitation module, which is devoid of any furniture and equipped with only a tiny porthole, Forrest struggles to stay sane until the ship reaches Venus so he can initiate the rocket burn that will put them on a return trajectory to Earth. He communicates with mission controller Bob Jansen (Brian Baumgartner) on a regular basis and receives messages of encouragement from people all over the world. Other activities include playing ping pong with himself, reading from a book of poetry and memorizing various lists of facts. At one point, he hallucinates seeing his fellow astronaut in the hab.

As *Life One* reaches Venus, Forrest dons his spacesuit and performs an EVA in order to observe the planet during the flyby. He is dazzled by the glories of the cloud-shrouded hothouse world below as the spacecraft positions itself for the crucial burn. At the proper time, Forrest fires the craft's rocket engine and it functions perfectly, utilizing the planet's gravity to hurl the ship toward home. After two years in space, Forrest is on the point of returning to Earth, but he opts not to burn the engine for re-entry, but instead releases Miller's escape pod that will return him to Earth while he uses the planet's gravity to slingshot *Life One* toward Europa in order to complete his original mission: "Someone's supposed to go, someone's supposed to see this."

Astronaut: The Last Push is similar to science fiction films featuring the theme of a lone astronaut struggling to survive in space. Other examples include *Robinson Crusoe on Mars, Moon* and *The Martian*. Actor Khary Payton must carry the film by himself, but unlike the other performances, he comes off as being dour and remote rather than likable. Much of the film consists of the actor framed in close-up, endlessly addressing the audience via his video log. Screenwriter-director Eric Hayden almost makes it work, but the film's limited budget has nearly all of the action taking place inside the claustrophobic confines of the habitation module. It strains credulity to believe that anyone, even a trained astronaut, could endure spending years confined in that space. Still, first-time director Hayden makes the most of a severely limited budget by constructing a minimalist but reasonably compelling take on space travel. The film has an effective and properly moody electronic score composed by Tom Woodruff Jr.

Note that the movie's spaceship never comes within a million miles of its intended destination of Europa. The Jovian moon's extraterrestrial whale-like forms have too much of a resemblance to earthly cetaceans than could be attributed to parallel evolution. The film's most compelling sequence, however, is the flyby of Venus, which is pictured in breathtaking vistas of sulfurous cloud and vapors. While voyages to the Moon, Mars and Jupiter have dominated space movies for decades, no other recent film has depicted Venus. The notion of using the planet's gravity to slingshot a spacecraft toward Jupiter space seems a bit of a stretch. Mission Control consists of a single individual who is assigned to monitor the operation of a complex flight into deep space. The funding of an interplanetary mission by a private entrepreneur anticipates the efforts of the rocket billionaires to explore space, a trend that began later in the decade.

Another ill-fated expedition to Europa departed the following year. In *Europa Report* (2013), a found footage account of the Europa One mission to Jupiter's enigmatic

Marine biologist Katya Petrovna (Karolina Wydra) is part of a team of scientists studying alien life forms on Jupiter's moon in *Europa Report* (2013).

satellite, the first deep space mission is launched with the hope of finding evidence of extraterrestrial life there. Once again the mission is a privately funded affair organized by the space consortium Europa Ventures under the direction of CEO Samantha Unger (Embetz Davitz). The crew consists of Commander William Xu (Daniel Wu), engineer Andrei Blok (Michael Nyqvist), science officer Daniel Luxembourg (Christian Carmago), junior engineer James Corrigan (Shartlo Copley), pilot Rosa Dasque (Anamaria Marinca) and marine biologist Katya Petrovna (Karolina Wydra).

The expedition is expected to take 20 months to reach its destination, but six months into the mission a solar storm disables the ship's communication equipment. When Blok and Corrigan perform an EVA to attempt repairs, Corrigan's spacesuit is breached and Blok's suit becomes coated with hydrazine, a toxic rocket fuel. Knowing that the hydrazine on Blok's suit will contaminate the ship, Corrigan manages to remove the suit in the ship's airlock, but the effort propels him away from the ship to his death. Saddened but inspired by his self-sacrifice, the crew continues on their voyage.

After 21 months in space, the expedition arrives at Europa and their lander descends to its icy surface. They choose not to land in the designated target zone, referred to as the Conamara Chaos, because of excessive radiation, and instead land at an alternate site about 100 meters away. While the explorers are contemplating their next move, Blok catches a fleeting glimpse of a blue light through one of the lander's windows. A hole is drilled through the surface ice and a probe is sent into the ocean below, where another anomalous luminescence is observed before something smashes the probe's camera.

Having no other alternative to complete the mission, Dr. Petrovna volunteers to perform a walk over the moon's surface to gather biological samples from the target zone. This is a risky enterprise because of high levels of radiation emanating from Jupiter. She suits up, treks to the site and sends data back to the lander indicating that the presence of a one-celled organism has been detected. While the crew exults in the discovery of the first sign of extraterrestrial life beyond the Earth, Petrovna spies a blue luminance underneath the ice that seems to respond to the lights on her suit. Investigating despite the radiation hazard, she watches the blue glow surge around her, the ice suddenly fractures and she is drawn down into the waters to her death.

The four remaining crew members, horrified, decide to depart immediately for home to report their momentous findings. When they try to lift off, the lander stalls and falls back toward the moon's surface. Commander Xu is killed in a valiant attempt to reduce the ship's landing speed. The impact shatters the ice underneath the lander, and as water begins to seep into the ship it starts to sink. Realizing that they are doomed, Dasque decides to turn off the lander's life support, a move that re-establishes the data link with Mission Control back on Earth. The last image received from the expedition shows a tentacled, bioluminescent creature that resembles an earthly squid or octopus.

Critics and sci-fi fans lauded *Europa Report* for its restraint and scientific verisimilitude in contrast to space opera action programmers like the *Star Wars, Star Trek* and *Guardians of the Galaxy* franchises. It combines elements of a space survival narrative like *Gravity* with an understated variant of the standard "astronauts vs. alien creature" melodrama. Ecuadorian director Sebastian Cordero gets a lot of mileage out of the movie's limited budget and the inventive production designs of Eugenio Caballero. The movie's spacecraft is an entirely digital construction. Its interior is laid out in pleasing tones of light blues and grays that are appropriate for long-duration space flight. Effective use is made of multiple screens and on-screen graphics to economically convey information to the audience.

The found footage construction by scenarist Philip Gelatt is arguably an overused convention that jumps around in time, fragments the movie's narrative construction and sometimes creates confusion in the viewer. It also prefigures the film's downbeat conclusion. The international cast of players (all relative unknowns) turn in intense, dramatically effective performances, especially Shartlo Copley in the scene in which he drifts helplessly away into space, and Karolina Wydra during the tense sequence in which she traverses Europa's surface. Most of the action takes place inside the spacecraft, which endows the proceedings with a claustrophobic atmosphere and something of a confining horror movie ambience in the classic sci-fi horror mode of *Alien*. Bear McCreary's score uses electronic tones as an effective backdrop for this moody space odyssey. *Europa Report* had a limited U.S. release and did mediocre business, although audience response was generally favorable after its release on home video.

Humankind's first venture into deep space is realistically depicted, as the filmmakers reportedly drew inspiration from documentary footage of the International Space Station. The interplanetary spacecraft, constructed in modular fashion in Earth orbit, utilizes multiple launches over a period of 16 months and consists of an orbiter and lander module. Footage of a European Space Agency Ariane rocket depicts the lofting of the spaceship's crew and final component. Once again, the mission to Europa is a privately funded venture rather than a government-run operation in this era of SpaceX. The solar flare that disables the ship's communication equipment is a serious impediment to manned expeditions into deep space, and the potentially lethal hazard of radiation emanating from Jupiter is accurately portrayed. NASA images of Europa were used to realistically depict vistas of the icy, enigmatic Jovian moon.

During the early 21st century, concerns about global climate change and the possibility of a planet-killing asteroid strike or other cataclysmic event have intensified the notion that humankind must look to space to find a Planet B to colonize in case the Earth becomes uninhabitable. Planetary probes to other planets in our solar system have shown that there is no Planet B in our general vicinity. Acclaimed director Christopher Nolan posits a search for a new home for the human race among the stars in the face of a planetary ecological disaster in his epic space odyssey *Interstellar* (2014).

In the year 2067, worldwide agriculture has suffered from a series of blights that have killed off wheat, okra and other food crops. A small remnant of the human population struggles to survive by raising corn, their only remaining food source. Technological innovation has come to a standstill as all efforts are now directed toward agriculture. Ex-astronaut Joe Cooper (Matthew McConaughey) raises corn on a small Colorado farm with his family in the face of severe dust storms that periodically inundate the area. His other family members include his elderly father Donald (John Lithgow), his teenage son Tom (Timothée Chalamet) and his ten-year-old daughter Murph (Mackenzie Foy).

While Tom seems comfortable with the farming life, precocious Murph shares her father's affinity for science, although she thinks her room is haunted by a poltergeist that keeps moving books and objects from the shelves of her large bookcase. During a parent-teacher conference, Cooper pleads with school officials to place Murph on a fast track to college, but is rebuffed as they explain that the world needs farmers instead of scientists. Their anti-science bias is revealed in a textbook that propounds the alternate history claim that the Apollo missions never landed on the Moon, but were only a pro-paganda ruse designed to bankrupt the Soviets by engaging them in a pointless space race. Disgusted by their attitude, Cooper, who has actually flown in space, withdraws Murph from the school.

After Cooper's family is forced to return home from an aborted baseball game by a massive dust storm, they find the dust has settled into a series of odd lines on the floor of Murph's room. Believing that the lines represent numbers expressed in binary code, he interprets the patterns as latitude and longitude coordinates corresponding to an unknown destination. Feeling drawn to the place, he departs in his car on a mission to locate it, and Murph stows away for the ride. Traveling over the Rockies, he finally arrives at a former NORAD (North American Air Defense Command) base, where he is promptly rendered unconscious by guards and taken into custody.

Inside the facility, Cooper is interrogated by a robotic entity called TARS. He soon learns that he has gained entrance to "the best-kept secret in the world," a hidden NASA launch-research center located in the underground base. Dr. John Brand (Michael Caine), who was Cooper's former boss, and his scientist daughter Amelia (Anne Hatha-way) greet him. Stunned by the revelation, Dr. Brand informs Cooper that this clandes-tine NASA operation is kept secret because "public opinion wouldn't allow spending on space exploration." He is also told that the nitrogen in Earth's atmosphere is depleting the oxygen, and that the corn crop will eventually succumb to blight, leading to the end of humankind through mass starvation. "We're not meant to save the world," Dr. Brand explains, "we're meant to leave it." The scientist also expresses the opinion that Cooper did not stumble upon the facility by accident, but was somehow guided there.

During a conference with the base's staff, Cooper is told about their plans for their next mission. A team of astronauts is to be sent to the environs of Saturn, where an unknown alien civilization, concerned with our survival, has placed a wormhole that will serve as a gateway to potentially habitable planets in another galaxy. Ten years earlier, 12 ships passed through the wormhole, but only three explorers, Miller, Mann and Edmunds, reported finding worlds that may be suitable for colonization. The thirteenth expedition is poised to depart, but there was no pilot available until Cooper arrived. The ex-astronaut is being offered the chance to lead a mission that might save humanity from extinction.

Dr. Brand and Amelia take him on a tour of the facility while they explain the finer points of their planning. Their Plan A involves developing an anti-gravity technology that will propel large colonies into space. Plan B is to send 500 frozen human embryos in the spaceship *Endurance* through the wormhole to one of the three habitable worlds to start a colony. The task is complicated by the fact that a humongous black hole dubbed Gargantua is in proximity to two of the prospective homeworlds. Cooper decides to pilot the *Endur-ance* even though it means saying goodbye to his family, as time dilation effects will make his return to them during their lifetimes unlikely. Murph takes parting with her father very hard. Cooper gives her a wristwatch with which to measure their comparative times.

Cooper blasts off in a rocket to rendezvous with *Endurance*, a ring-shaped mod-ular craft awaiting him in Earth orbit. His crewmates include Amelia, Dr. Doyle (Wes Bently). Dr. Romilly (David Gyasi) and the non-humaniform robots TARS and CASE. The circular spacecraft spins on its axis to provide simulated gravity for the long trip. The first leg of their trip will be an eight-month flyby of Mars that will slingshot the ship on a two-year journey to Saturn. The spacefarers immerse themselves in water-filled hypersleep chambers for their long nap for the trip.

Awakening in the vicinity of the ringed planet, the crew members view messages transmitted from their loved ones on Earth. Cooper's son Tom tells him that Murph still hasn't forgiven him and refuses to talk to him. The next leg of their journey takes them through the wormhole, a swirling mass of energy that propels them through space-time to the three target worlds in a galaxy ten billion light years from Earth. Their first stop is Miller's planet, located in proximity to Gargantua, which causes intense time dilation effects so that every hour spent on the planet's surface will equal seven Earth years. Cooper, Amelia, Doyle and CASE decide to explore the planet's surface, while Romilly elects to remain aboard the *Endurance* and study the black hole.

The explorers travel to Miller's world in one of the Ranger shuttlecraft and find it to be a waterworld with no land in evidence. After the Ranger lands in shallow water, Doyle and Amelia disembark to locate Miller's ship, but find only wreckage. While attempting to retrieve a data recorder from the wreck, they sight an enormous tidal wave heading their way. Amelia gets tangled in the wreckage and has to be rescued by CASE, but Doyle is swept away to his death when the wave hits. The Ranger is intact but waterlogged, causing an additional delay before they can take off, and by the time they return to the *Endurance* 23 years have passed due to Gargantua's time dilation. Cooper reviews video messages that have been received in the interim, including one from a 35-year-old Murph (now played by Jessica Chastain). Alongside Dr. Brand, who is now 90, she is working to solve the gravity equation that will enable the implementation of Plan A. Although they are able to receive messages from Earth, they are unable to transmit information in the other direction.

The remaining crew members debate whether to visit Mann's planet or Edmund's. Amelia confesses that she is in love with Mann, and her love is drawing her to him.

Left to right, Cooper (Matthew McConaughey), Dr. Brand (Anne Hathaway) and Dr. Romilly (David Gyasi) prepare to revive Dr. Mann from hibernation in *Interstellar* (2014).

Love is "an artifact of a higher dimension," she opines; it is "observable, powerful, it has to mean something." On the basis of her intuition, the spacefarers decide to proceed to Mann's world. They arrive a few months later to find a frozen planet with a atmosphere that is largely methane, 80 percent of Earth's gravity and a 67-hour day-night cycle. Dr. Mann (Matt Damon) is revived from 35 years in hypersleep and fills them in on what he has discovered about his world, which he believes contains some habitable zones. Another message from Murph explains that Amelia's father has died without being able to solve the anti-gravity equation and that she believes the problem to be insoluble. Mann feels that the equation can be solved, but the only way to transmit the data back to Earth would be to go through the black hole.

Mann takes Cooper on an exploratory walk across the planet's surface, but as they stand on the edge of a cliff, Mann suddenly removes Cooper's voice transmitter and pushes him over the edge. He confesses to Cooper that the planet is uninhabitable and that he has lured the *Endurance* there because he wishes to commandeer the spaceship and return to Earth. During their struggle, Mann cracks Cooper's helmet and races away to steal one of the Ranger craft while Cooper tries to keep from suffocating. Cooper retrieves his communicator and calls for help; and as he is being rescued by Amelia, Romilly is killed by a booby trap left by Mann. As Cooper, Amelia and TARS blast off in another lander, Mann attempts to dock with the *Endurance* without having the proper entrance codes. He is killed and the spacecraft damaged. Cooper performs a difficult docking maneuver with the wildly spinning ship, only to find that their life support systems are so compromised that they can neither return to Earth or reach Edmund's planet. Their only option is to utilize Gargantua's massive gravity to slingshot them with enough energy to reach Edmund's world.

Back on Earth, Murph has an intuition that the coordinates inscribed in dust on the floor of her bedroom years ago was an event manipulated by an intelligence that was trying to aid in the Earth's survival. She has a similar feeling about the "ghost" that used to topple objects from her bookshelf and wonders what message the unknown party is attempting to communicate. The corn crop is dying and the farm now resembles Oklahoma during the Dust Bowl years of the 1930s.

The *Endurance* plunges into the black hole. Cooper realizes that it cannot achieve sufficient velocity to reach Edmund's planet, so he and TARS leave the mothership in separate Ranger shuttles to lessen the spacecraft's mass and increase its speed. While Amelia and the CASE robot continue on the trajectory to their destination, Cooper's shuttlecraft begins to disintegrate under Gargantua's gravitational stresses, and he ejects. He now finds himself floating through a vast rectilinear grid called a *tesseract* and wanders around the maze until he is facing the back of Murph's bookcase. He can see Murph, first as a child and then as an adult and knocks objects from the shelves to get her attention, but she is unable to see or hear him. As she contemplates her childhood bookshelves, the adult Murph realizes that her father was the "ghost" who moved things and that Cooper is somehow trying to contact her from another realm. Unexpectedly, TARS communicates with Cooper through his headset and tells him that he has received the solution to the anti-gravity equation from fifth dimensional beings while passing through the black hole. Using TARS as a relay, he transmits the data to Murph via Morse code by manipulating the second hand on the wristwatch he had given to her when he set out on his journey. An ecstatic Murph rushes back to NASA headquarters with the information that assures humankind's survival, while Cooper realizes that his love for Murph has provided the essential link to achieve that dream.

The *Endurance* crew explores the frozen planetscape of Mann's World in *Interstellar* (2014).

Once Cooper's task is completed, the tesseract begins to contract around him and he blacks out. He wakes up in a hospital bed in bucolic surroundings, and is told by a doctor that he was rescued by a space patrol and is recovering in a massive, cylindrical space habitat in orbit around Saturn, where the remnants of humanity have taken refuge. Due to relativistic effects of his travels through the space-time continuum, he is now 124 years old, but is biologically still in his 30s. He visits Murph (played here by Ellen Burstyn), who is now an elderly woman dying in a hospital. She tells him, "No parent should have to watch their own child die," and he leaves her surrounded by grieving family members. Not wishing to remain at the habitat, Cooper steals a spacecraft and departs for Edmond's planet to join Amelia, who has set up the beginnings of a colony on that world.

Director Christopher Nolan, who is known for his high-concept blockbusters such as *Inception* (2010) and *The Dark Knight Rises* (2012), delivers a complex, science-driven space exploration epic that proved to be both a critical and popular success. Its strongest assets are its exquisite special effects and production design orchestrated by Nolan with meticulous attention to detail. Seeking to minimize the "green screen" superimposition effects added during post-production that are usually employed in a hi-tech production of this kind, Nolan and visual effects company Double Negative created the effects first and displayed them behind the actors, a technique that allows the cast to feel they are immersed in the filmic environment. The spaceship models were nicknamed "maxatures" due to their enormous size. The *Endurance* model was 25 feet in diameter, while the Ranger miniature spanned 49 feet, large enough to accommodate IMAX cameras in its interior. It was attached to a six-axis motion control system that lent a documentary look to the footage. Working with a budget of $165 million, the director was able to convincingly conjure vistas of interplanetary space, alien worlds and the interior of a black hole. The film received an Academy Award for Best Visual Effects.

The eye candy visuals and mind-bending scientific concepts tend to overwhelm the film's human element. Principals Matthew McConaughey and Anne Hathaway have a nice screen chemistry, but their restrained roles do not allow for much display of emotion. McConaughey in particular delivers his dialogue in a laconic fashion that is sometimes semi-intelligible. Matt Damon has a juicier part as the renegade astronaut

Dr. Mann; the actor was back in a spacesuit again the following year in *The Martian*. The strongest performances are provided by Mackenzie Foy, Jessica Chastain and Ellen Burstyn, who portray Murph Cooper at three different phases of her life.

Interstellar's screenplay, penned by Nolan and his brother Jonathan, stretches the film's length to nearly three hours, and as the above synopsis demonstrates, it is incredibly complex, to the point of being cumbersome and at times even incomprehensible. This is especially true of the film's ending, which is so puzzling that several explanatory YouTube videos have been posted. There is also a feeling of morbidity to the proceedings, as nearly all of the major characters are dead by the conclusion, and the Murph Cooper character goes from being a lively ten-year-old to an old woman on her deathbed during the course of the narrative. Dylan Thomas' elegiac poem on the death of his father, "Do Not Go Gentle Into That Good Night," is recited at several points. All this is set against the backdrop of the eventual extermination of the human race.

The origin of the ecological catastrophe that has precipitated the survival crisis is never clearly explained. Present-day agricultural scientists have been utilizing genetic engineering to produce crops designed to resist the kinds of blights that destroy the world's food crops in the film. Likewise, no explanation for the replacement of the Earth's oxygen by nitrogen is offered, and atmospheric scientists have pointed out that this process would take centuries, not decades. The question of what has turned the world's farmland into a vast dust bowl is never answered. Of course, these dire conditions are there to provide a reason to search for a Planet B, which is the film's primary theme and a current rationale for space exploration, and rocket science, which is suppressed by this future society, turns out to be absolutely vital. Another curious plot element involves elevating love into a scientific concept that is "observable, quantifiable," and "an artifact of a higher dimension."

Pains are taken to provide accuracy regarding space science. Co-scripter Jonathan Nolan took physics courses at the California Institute of Technology to understand relativity. In addition, theoretical physicist and Nobel Laureate Kip Thorne served as a consultant and executive producer on the film. Thorne worked out equations that theorized how light would behave inside a black hole or wormhole, and the CGI renderings based on these equations provided Thorne with insights that resulted in the publication of three scientific papers. The physicist reportedly spent a couple of weeks disabusing the director of the notion that faster-than-light travel was possible. While *Interstellar* is a hard-science departure from the pseudo-science of the vast majority of pop sci-fi cinema, an advanced degree in theoretical physics would assist in the full understanding and appreciation of many of the film's concepts featured.

All this having been said, some of the movie's science seems like a stretch. As previously discussed, wormholes are a theoretical concept that have never been observed in space or anywhere else. Their existence in the film (and in science fiction literature) provides a work-around plot device for space travelers to overcome the relativistic conundrum of being unable to travel faster than the speed of light. Wormholes supposedly enable interstellar travel by "folding space" to eliminate the vast distances between the stars. Some scientists believe that such travel through wormholes would be impossible. In *Contact*, an advanced alien intelligence has constructed a series of wormholes as part of an interstellar transportation system that humans can utilize to travel to other worlds.

Unlike wormholes, black holes have been actually observed by astronomers and have also been used by writers and filmmakers to transport space travelers around the universe. In *Interstellar*, Mann's planet is located in orbit around the super-massive black hole Gargantua, but the enormous gravity generated by the black hole would be so intense that astronauts attempting to land on the planet's surface would be crushed. Additionally, some astronomers believe that a planet located so close to a black hole could not even exist because the immense gravity would generate tidal forces that would tear the planet apart. Other scientists theorize that astronauts attempting to travel through Gargantua would be killed by the radiation generated by material in the accretion disk surrounding the object, or their bodies would be "spaghettified" by the black hole's gravitational forces.

Director Nolan visited NASA and SpaceX facilities as part of his research, and former astronaut Marsha Ivins was on the set to provide input. Production designer Nathan Crowley reportedly based the *Endurance* spacecraft designs on the modular composition of the International Space Station. Four different space vehicles are featured in the film. The launch vehicle that lofts the astronauts into Earth orbit was based on NASA's Space Launch System, although it lacks the pair of solid rocket boosters on the proposed SLS design. The *Endurance* mothership is a ring-shaped assemblage of modules that rotates at 5.6 times per minute to produce artificial gravity. It contains modules of various functions, including four main engine modules that provide interplanetary propulsion, two habitat modules, a command module containing the flight deck, a hibernation bay and four landing pods for use as surface habitat modules.

The individual modules are connected by a system of tunnels that also contain exterior airlocks. There is also a core docking hub in the spacecraft's center where two Ranger landing craft and two heavy lift landers are attached. The Ranger craft are single-stage ships designed for travel to and from planetary surfaces, powered by chemical rockets and plasma jets. They also contain hibernation chambers for long-duration missions. The two landers are heavy cargo shuttles capable of transporting the *Endurance*'s habitat modules to a planet's surface. Like the Rangers, they are propelled by rockets and plasma jets. *Interstellar*'s quadrilateral robots were designed to be non-anthropomorphic and are quite unlike the robotic entities appearing in previous science fiction films. The Cooper Station space colony is composed of two counter-rotating cylinders. It was based on designs proposed by physicist Gerard K. O'Neill in his 1976 book *The High Frontier: Human Colonies in Space*.

Interstellar depicts the beginnings of human colonization of other star systems; in *Passengers* (2016), it has become an established commercial venture. Centuries in the future, the Homestead Corporation transports large groups of colonists to the planet Homestead II in a star system 60 light years from Earth. As the film opens, the massive starship *Avalon* is conveying 5000 colonists and 258 crew members in hibernation pods to their new home; the voyage will take 120 years.

Thirty years into the journey, a meteor swarm causes what seems to be a momentary interruption in the ship's control systems. The glitch results in mechanical engineer Jim Preston (Chris Pratt) being awakened prematurely. Rising from his hibernation pod, he is greeted by the ship's computer, who informs him that they have arrived at their destination and guides him to his cabin where he can recover from the effects of the long nap. The next day he wakes up and goes to the ship's main concourse area, where he is surprised to find himself alone. He is the only person taking a meal in the ship's cafeteria, and later in an orientation about life as a colonist on Homestead. The ugly truth finally dawns on him. He has awakened prematurely and is alone among the

Interstellar colonist Jim Preston (Chris Pratt) tries to figure out how to return to hypersleep in *Passengers* **(2016).**

sleeping colonists and crew onboard the ship. He eventually learns that he is only 30 years into the mission, with 90 years to go.

Jim sends a message back to the company on Earth, but is told by the ship's computer that the message will take 15 years to arrive. He studies the manuals for the hibernation pods, but with all his mechanical expertise he cannot figure out how to put himself back into hypersleep, and lacks the necessary clearance to enter the ship's command area. His only companionship is provided by the vessel's android bartender Arthur (Michael Sheen), who offers a semblance of humanity but can only converse using preprogrammed dialogue. Resigned to his solitude, he has the run of the ship and makes full use of its extensive recreation facilities. One of these is an area where passengers can don a spacesuit and go outside the ship to view the universe. In his lonely despair, he considers committing suicide by going into the airlock without a suit.

While walking through the hibernation bay, Jim comes across the pod that contains Aurora Lane (Jennifer Lawrence), and feels an instant attraction to her. Reading the passenger profile recorded before she went into hibernation, he learns that she is a journalist and reads some of her stories, which further endears him to her. Lost in his isolation and despair, Jim contemplates waking her from hibernation and wrestles with his conscience, knowing it will mean she will be long dead before the *Avalon* reaches its destination. In the end, however, he decides to bring her out of hibernation, but does not reveal himself to her right away.

The next day, after she has fully recovered from the effects of hypersleep, Jim greets her in the main concourse area. He tells her that, like himself, her awakening was due to a malfunction. The couple is drawn together by their mutual isolation and soon become lovers. Taking advantage of the ship's extensive recreation facilities, they achieve a modicum of happiness together. After a year, Arthur inadvertently reveals that Jim awakened her on purpose and she is furious at being deprived of a meaningful future. She becomes Jim's adversary and separates herself from him as much as possible.

While their relationship is on hold, they both begin to notice that various systems on the ship are beginning to malfunction, and one day another hibernation pod prematurely awakens Gus Mancuso (Laurence Fishburne). Gus is a crew chief who has access to the ship's command center, where he runs a series of diagnostic tests that reveal major system failures that can be traced back to the meteor strike that awakened Jim. One of these malfunctions occurs when Aurora is swimming in the ship's pool and the artificial gravity fails, causing the water to rise up into a floating globe in which she is almost drowned. After performing diagnostic tests, Gus realizes that a series of cascading failures will eventually doom the ship.

At this critical juncture, Gus suddenly becomes critically ill, and the ship's automated medical diagnostic scanner reveals that he has suffered massive internal injuries due to the malfunctioning hibernation pod and has only hours to live. Before he expires, he gives Jim his wristband that will enable Jim to access areas of the ship that will need to be repaired. During an inspection of the engineering bay, they discover a hole where the meteor breached the ship's hull and Aurora is nearly sucked out into space before Jim seals the breach. Their next step is to restart the fusion engine, which can only be accomplished from outside. Jim performs a difficult EVA and barely manages to perform the repair before his suit is ripped and he becomes untethered from the hull. Aurora suits up and rescues him. Aurora drags Jim to the medical bay, where he at first declared clinically dead but is eventually revived by the automated system.

Jim tinkers with the medical pod and figures out that he could use the machine to place Aurora back in hypersleep for the remainder of the journey, although it will mean that he will die alone. Rather than allow this to happen, she elects to spend the rest of her existence with him. When the *Aurora* arrives at its destination, the colonists and crew come out of hibernation to find the concourse area has been beautifully decorated by the couple and hear Aurora's voice reading her story about their love and their lives together.

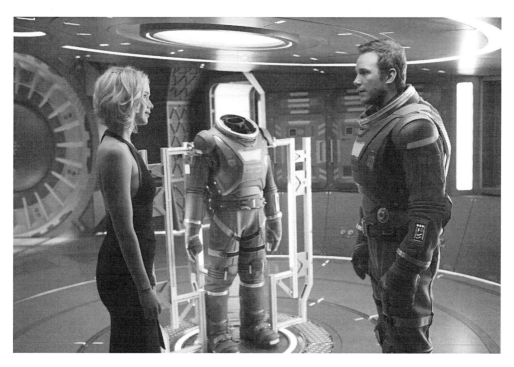

Aurora Lane (Jennifer Lawrence) and Jim Preston (Chris Pratt) suit up to perform an EVA in *Passengers* **(2016).**

An unusual meld of romance and science fiction, *Passengers* succeeds on both levels, buoyed by the intense screen chemistry between Chris Pratt and Jennifer Lawrence. Laurence Fishburne and Michael Sheen do fine jobs in supporting roles. Norwegian director Morten Tyldum is best known for his 2014 biopic of computer legend Alan Turing, *The Imitation Game*. The screenplay by Jon Spaihts is highly original and, like *The Andromeda Nebula* and *Interstellar*, plays upon the poetry and tragedy of the enormous distances and relativistic conundrums of journeys to the stars. Critics have pointed out similarities with the doomed shipboard romance in *Titanic* and the trapped protagonists, immense confined spaces and spectral bartender in *The Shining*. The outer space romance between the principals has also been compared to the relationship between astronauts Sandra Bullock and George Clooney in *Gravity*. Apart from the human element, the film's most memorable achievements are the stunning (and Oscar-nominated) production designs of Guy Hendrix Dyas and Gene Serdena that elevate the palatial starship to the level of one of the film's characters. Initially released in 3-D format, *Passengers* received mixed critical reviews but was a box office success.

The *Avalon* is a sleek-looking starship rivaled in its elegance only by the *Cygnus* in *The Black Hole*. It consists of three long, thin modules that spin around the ship's central core and create artificial gravity. Production designer Dyas revealed that the film's immense vessel was one kilometer in length and was assembled in space over a span of decades from materials mined from nearby asteroids. The ship travels at half the speed of light, but its propulsion system is not specified. Dyas related that his design incorporated elements of cruise ship design and contained lavish entertainment facilities in addition to more functional areas. One of the film's most dramatic visuals consists of Jim and Aurora watching their transit of the star Arcturus on an immense viewing screen. The ship contained over 5000 hibernation chambers for the colonists and crew housed in enormous bays, but keeping humans in hypersleep for 120 years is a highly problematical proposition.

Traveling to the stars has been a dream of science fiction writers from the inception of the genre. These fantasies were later adopted by science fiction filmmakers for popular space opera franchises by resorting to pseudo-scientific means allowing interstellar flight. None of the films cited here, however, allow spacefarers to travel faster than the speed of light as dictated by relativity physics. Some of them, like *Contact* and *Interstellar*, get around this limitation by "folding space" using wormholes conveniently placed by aliens as passageways around the cosmos, a notion that seems just a tad less fantastic than faster-than-light space travel. Others, such as *Spaceflight IC-1*, *The Andromeda Nebula* and *Passengers,* posit long-duration star voyages at a fraction of the speed of light.

In 1950, the Italian physicist Enrico Fermi posited that, given the age of the galaxy and the relative youth of our own solar system, advanced extraterrestrial civilizations should have colonized the Earth millennia ago, a theory that has come to be known as the Fermi Paradox. Some scientists believe that the reason that aliens have not yet arrived on our planet is that interstellar travel is impossible due to the enormous distances between the stars. Perhaps human ingenuity and technology may one day solve the myriad problems posed by interstellar journeys … or perhaps not.

Conclusion:
Dreams of Space

On May 30, 2020, astronauts Doug Hurley and Bob Behnken were launched from Cape Canaveral via a SpaceX rocket on a mission to dock with the International Space Station. Their Dragon capsule successfully docked with the ISS, heralding a new era in American space flight, as Americans had not flown in space since the space shuttle program was retired in 2011. After a stay of several weeks at the station, the astronauts returned to Earth on August 20.

During the televised launch, the astronauts sported sleek pressure suits that were a departure from the bulky garments worn by earlier generations of spacefarers. Instead, they resembled costumes worn by characters in science fiction movies like *Interstellar*. In fact, the so-called "Starman" suits were fashioned by Hollywood designer Jose Fernandez, who had worked on costume designs for the big-budget superhero flicks *Captain America: Civil War* and *Batman vs. Superman: Dawn of Justice*. Once again, science fiction has been overtaken by science fact.

Space has been making news frequently during the last few years. In 2019, the Chinese landed the first lunar rover on the far side of the Moon, where it discovered an unusual gel-like substance. In November 2017, the first object of interstellar origin to enter the solar system was detected. Dubbed Oumuamua, a Hawaiian word that translates as "first distant messenger," the mysterious object zipped past the Sun before heading into the outer solar system. Although the consensus opinion was that Oumuamua was an asteroid, some scientists theorized it might have been a spacecraft from another star system. The second interstellar visitor, a comet designated 21 Borisev, was detected in August 2019. In other space news making international headlines, in September 2020, scientists detected a chemical called phosphine high in the atmosphere of the planet Venus. On Earth, phosphine is usually associated with biological activity, leading to speculation that microbial life might exist in clouds in the otherwise hostile Venusian environment.

These discoveries, along with future ones, will no doubt inspire cinematic voyages to the Moon, Mars and the farthest reaches of our imagination, as the science fiction of today will no doubt once more be eclipsed by the scientific reality of tomorrow.

Filmography

Ad Astra (2019) Director-Producer: James Gray. Producers: Brad Pitt, Dede Gardner, Jeremy Kleiner. Screenplay: James Gray, Ethan Gross. Cast: Brad Pitt, Tommy Lee Jones, Liv Tyler, Ruth Negga, Donald Sutherland. U.S. (20th Century–Fox). Color. 123 minutes.

Aelita (1924) Director-Producer: Yakov Protozanov. Screenplay: Fedor Ozep. Cast: Valentina Kuindzji, Nikolai Tseretelli, Yulia Solnetseva, Pavel Pol, Igor Ilyinsky. U.S.S.R. (Mezhrabpom-Rus). B&W. Silent. 113 minutes.

The Andromeda Nebula (1967) Director-Producer: Yevgeni Sherstobitov. Screenplay: Ivan Yefremov. Cast: Sergei Stolyarov, Vija Artmane, Nikolai Kryukov. U.S.S.R. (Dovzhenko). Color. 77 minutes.

The Andromeda Strain (1971) Director-Producer: Robert Wise. Screenplay: Nelson Gidding. Cast: Arthur Hill, James Olson, Kate Reid, David Wayne, George Mitchell. U.S. (Universal). Color. 130 minutes.

Apollo 13 (1995) Director: Ron Howard. Producer: Brian Grazer. Screenplay: William Broyles Jr., Al Reinert. Cast: Tom Hanks, Kevin Bacon, Bill Paxton, Gary Sinise, Kathleen Quinlan. U.S. (Universal). Color. 140 minutes.

Apollo 18 (2011) Director: Gonzalo Lopez-Gallego. Producers: Timur Bekmambetov, Michelle Wolkoff. Screenplay: Brian Miller. Cast: Warren Christie, Lloyd Owen, Ryan Robbins. U.S.-Canada (Dimension Films). Color. 86 minutes.

Armageddon (1999) Director-Producer: Michael Bay. Producers: Jerry Bruckheimer, Gale Anne Hurd. Screenplay: Jonathan Hensleigh, J.J. Abrams. Cast: Bruce Willis, Liv Tyler, Ben Affleck, Billy Bob Thornton, Will Patton, Peter Stormare. U.S. (Buena Vista). Color. 151 minutes.

Assignment Outer Space (a.k.a. *Space Men*, 1960) Director-Producer: Antonio Margheriti. Screenplay: Antonio Margheriti, Ennio De Concini. Cast: Rik Van Nutter, Gabriella Farinon, David Montressor, Archie Savage. Italy (Titanus). Color. 73 minutes.

The Astronaut Farmer (2006) Director: Michael Polish. Producers: Len Amato, Paula Weinstein. Screenplay: Michael Polish. Cast: Billy Bob Thornton, Virginia Madsen, Bruce Dern, Tim Blake Nelson, Bruce Willis. U.S. (Warner Bros.). Color. 104 minutes.

Astronaut: The Last Push (2012) Director-Screenplay: Eric Hayden. Producers: Kimberly Hayden, A.J. Raitano. Cast: Khary Payton, Lance Henriksen, Brian Baumgartner, Canada (Vision Films). Color. 85 minutes.

The Black Hole (1979) Director: Gary Nelson. Producer: Ron Miller. Screenplay: Gerry Day, Jeb Rosebrook. Cast: Anthony Perkins, Maximilian Schell, Robert Forster, Yvette Mimieux, Ernest Borgnine, Joseph Bottoms. U.S. (Buena Vista). Color. 98 minutes.

Capricorn One (1977) Director-Screenplay: Peter Hyams. Producer: Paul N. Lazarus III. Cast: Elliott Gould, James Brolin, Sam Waterston, O.J. Simpson, Hal Holbrook, Telly Savalas. U.S. (Warner Bros.). Color. 124 minutes.

Conquest of Space (1955) Director: Byron Haskin. Producer: George Pal. Screenplay: James O'Hanlon. Cast: Walter Brooke, Eric Fleming, Mickey Shaughnessy. U.S. (Paramount). Color. 91 minutes.

Contact (1997) Director-Producer: Robert Zemeckis. Producer: Steve Starkey. Screenplay: James V. Hart, Michael Goldenberg. Cast: Jodie Foster, Matthew McConaughey, James Woods, Angela Bassett, John Hurt, Tom Skerritt. U.S. (Warner Bros.). Color. 150 minutes.

Cosmic Voyage (1936) Director: Vasili Zhuravlov. Producer: Boris Shumyatskiy. Screenplay: Aleksandr Filimonov, Konstantin Tsiolkovsky. Cast: Serfei Komarov, Kselniya Moskalenko, Vassili Gaponeko, Nikolai Feoktistov. U.S.S.R. (Mosfilm). B&W. 70 minutes.

Countdown (1968) Director: Robert Altman. Producer: William Conrad. Screenplay: Loring Mandel. Cast: James Caan, Robert Duvall, Joanna Moore, Ted Knight. U.S. (Warner Bros.). Color. 101 minutes.

The Day the Sky Exploded (1958) Directors: Paolo Heusch, Mario Bava. Producer: Guido Giambartolomei. Screenplay: Marcello Coscia, Alessandro Continenza. Cast: Paul Hubschmid, Madeline Fischer, Fiorella Mari, Ivo Garrabi. Italy-France (Lux Film). B&W. 82 minutes.

Deep Impact (1999) Director: Mimi Leder. Producers: David Brown, Richard D. Zanuck. Screenplay: Bruce Joel Rubin, Michael Tolkin. Cast: Tea Leoni, Robert Duvall, Vanessa Redgrave, Maximilian Schell, Morgan Freeman. U.S. (Paramount). Color. 121 minutes.

Destination Moon (1950) Director: Irving Pichel. Producer: George Pal. Screenplay: Rip Van Ronkel, Robert A. Heinlein, James O'Hanlon. Cast: John Archer, Warner Anderson, Tom Powers, Dick Wesson. U.S. (Eagle-Lion). Color. 91 minutes.

Europa Report (2013) Director: Sebastian Cordero. Producer: Ben Browning. Screenplay: Philip Gelatt. Cast: Christian Camargo, Michael Nyqvist, Karolina Wydra, Daniel Wu, Embeth Davidtz. U.S. (Magnet Releasing). Color. 89 minutes.

First Man (2018) Director: Damien Chazelle. Producer: Wyck Godfrey. Screenplay: Josh Singer. Cast: Ryan Gosling, Claire Foy, Jason Clarke, Kyle Chandler. U.S. (Universal). Color. 141 minutes.

First Men in the Moon (1919) Directors: Bruce Gordon, J.L.V. Leigh. Screenplay: R. Byron Webber. Cast: Bruce Gordon, Heather Thatcher, Lionel d'Aragon. U.K. (Gaumont). B&W. Silent.

First Men in the Moon (1964) Director: Nathan Juran. Producer: Charles H. Schneer. Screenplay: Nigel Kneale, Jan Read. Cast: Edward Judd, Martha Hyer, Lionel Jeffries. U.K. (Columbia). Color. 103 minutes.

Forbidden Planet (1956) Director: Fred McLeod Wilcox. Producer: Nicholas Nayfack. Screenplay: Cyril Hume. Cast: Leslie Nielsen, Walter Pidgeon, Anne Francis, Warren Stevens. U.S. (MGM). 98 minutes. Color.

Gagarin: First in Space (2013) Director: Pavel Parkhoromenko. Producers-Screenplay: Andrey Dmitriev, Oleg Kapanets. Cast: Yaroslev Zhalnin, Mikhail Filippov, Olga Ivanova, Vadim Michman. Russia (Central Partnership). Color. 108 minutes.

Gog (1954) Director: Herbert L. Strock. Producer: Ivan Tors. Screenplay: Tom Taggart. Cast: Richard Egan, Constance Dowling, Herbert Marshall, John Wengraf. U.S. (United Artists). Color. 83 minutes.

Gravity (2013) Director: Alfonso Cuaron. Producers: Alfonso Cuaron, David Heyman. Screenplay: Alfonso Cuaron, Jonas Cuaron. Cast: Sandra Bullock, George Clooney. U.S.-U.K. (Warner Bros.). Color. 91 minutes.

Heaven Ship (1918) Director: Holger-Madsen. Producer: Ole Olsen. Screenplay: Sophus Michaelis, Ole Olsen. Cast: Gunnar Tolnaes, Zanny Petersen, Nicolai Neiiendam, Alf Blutecher, Lily Jacobsen. Denmark (Nordisk). B&W. Silent. 81 minutes.

The Heavens Call (*Nebo Zovyot*, 1959) Director: Valery Fokin. Producers: Mikhail Karyukov, Alexandr Kozyr. Screenplay: Aleksei Sazonov, Yevgeni Pomeshcikov. Cast: Ivan Pereverzev, Alexander Shvoryn, Constantine Bartashevich, Gurgwn Tonuts. U.S.S.R. (Dovzhenko). Color. 77 minutes.

Hidden Figures (2016) Director-Screenplay: Theodore Melfi. Producers: Donna Gigliotti, Peter Chernin, Jenno Topping. Screenplay: Allison Schroeder. Cast: Taraji P. Henson, Octavia Spencer, Janelle Monae, Kevin Costner. U.S. (Fox 2000). Color. 127 minutes.

I Aim at the Stars (1960) Director: J. Lee Thompson. Producer: Charles H. Schneer. Screenplay: Jay Dratler. Cast: Curt Jurgens, Victoria Shaw, Herbert Lom, Gia Scala. U.S. (Columbia). B&W. 107 minutes.

Ikarie XB-1 (1963) Director-Screenplay: Jindrich Polak. Producer: Rudolf Wolf. Screenplay: Pavel Juracek. Cast: Zdenek Stepanek, Radovan Lukavsky, Frantisek Smolik, Dana Medricka. Czechoslovakia (Ustredni Pujcovna Barradov). B&W. 86 minutes.

Inquest of Pilot Pirx (1978) Director: Marek Piestrak. Producer: Jerzy Ciemnolonski. Screenplay: Vladimir Valutsky. Cast: Sergei Desnitsky, Boleslaw Abart, Vladimir Ivashov, Aleksandr Kaydanovskiy. Poland–U.S.S.R. (Tallinnfilm). Color, 104 minutes.

Interstellar (2014) Director-Producer: Christopher Nolan. Producers: Emma Thomas, Lynda Obst. Screenplay: Christopher Nolan, Jonathan Nolan. Cast: Matthew McConaughey, Anne Hathaway, Michael Caine, Jessica Chastain, Bill Irwin. U.S. (Paramount). Color. 169 minutes.

Jules Verne's Rocket to the Moon (1967) Director: Don Sharp. Producer: Harry Alan Towers. Screenplay: Dave Freeman. Cast: Troy Donahue, Burl Ives, Terry-Thomas, Gert Frobe, Lionel Jeffries. U.K. (AIP–Warner-Pathe). Color. 117 minutes.

Just Imagine (1930) Director: David Butler. Producer: Buddy G. DeSylva. Screenplay: Buddy G. DeSylva, Lew Brown, Ray Henderson. Cast: El Brendel, Maureen O'Sullivan, John Garrick, Marjorie White. U.S. (Fox Film Corp.). B&W. 109 minutes.

Lucy in the Sky (2019) Director-Producer: Noah Hawley. Producers: Reese Witherspoon, Bruna Papandrea. Screenplay: Noah Hawley, Brian C. Brown, Elliott DiGuiseppi. Cast: Natalie Portman, Jon Hamm, Ellen Burstyn, Zazie Beetz, Dan Stevens. U.S. (Fox Searchlight). Color. 124 minutes.

Marooned (1969) Director: John Sturges. Producer: M.J. Frankovich. Screenplay: Mayo Simon. Cast: Gregory Peck, Richard Crenna, Gene Hackman, James Franciscus, David Janssen. U.S. (Columbia). Color. 134 minutes.

The Martian (2015) Director-Producer: Ridley Scott. Producers: Simon Kinberg, Michael Schaefer. Screenplay: Drew Goddard. Cast: Matt Damon, Jessica Chastain, Kristen Wiig, Jeff Daniels, Sean Bean. U.S. (20th Century–Fox). Color. 141 minutes.

Meteor (1979) Director: Roland Neame. Producer: Run Shaw. Screenplay: Stanley Mann, Edmund H. North. Cast: Sean Connery, Natalie Wood, Karl Malden, Brian Keith, Martin Landau. U.S. (American-International). Color. 107 minutes.

Mission Mars (1968) Director: Nick Webster. Producer: Everett Rosenthal. Screenplay: Mike St. Clair. Cast: Darren McGavin, Nick Adams, George De Vries, Michael DeBeausset. U.S. (Allied Artists). Color. 90 minutes.

Mission to Mars (2000) Director: Brian De Palma. Producer: Tom Jacobson. Screenplay: Jim Thomas, John Thomas, Graham Yost. Cast: Gary Sinise, Tim Robbins, Don Cheadle, Connie Nielsen. U.S. (Buena Vista). Color. 114 minutes.

Moon (2009) Director: Duncan Jones. Producers: Stuart Fenegan, Trudie Styler. Screenplay: Nathan Parker. Cast: Sam Rockwell, Kevin Spacey, Dominique McElligott, Kaya Scodelario. U.K. (Sony Pictures). Color. 97 minutes.

Moon 44 (1990) Director-Producer: Roland Emmerich. Producer: Dean Heyde. Screenplay: Dean Heyde, Oliver Eberle. Cast: Michael Pare, Dean Devlin, Malcolm McDowell. West Germany (Kinowelt). Color. 99 minutes.

Moon Zero Two (1969) Director: Roy Ward Baker. Producer: Michael Carreras. Screenplay: Michael Carreras, Martin Davidson, Gavin Lyall. Cast: James Olson, Catherine Schell, Warren Mitchell, Adrienne Corn. U.K. (Warner Bros.). Color. 100 minutes.

Moonraker (1979) Director: Lewis Gilbert. Producer: Albert R. Broccoli. Screenplay: Christopher Wood. Cast: Roger Moore, Richard Kiel, Michael Lonsdale, Lois Chiles. U.K. (United Artists) Color. 126 minutes.

October Sky (1999) Director: Joe Johnson. Producers: Charles Gordon, Larry J. Franco. Screenplay: Lewis Colick. Cast: Jake Gyllenhaal, Chris Cooper, Chris Owen, Laura Dern. U.S. (Universal). Color. 103 minutes.

Outland (1981) Director-Screenplay: Peter Hyams. Producers: Richard A. Roth, Stanley O'Toole. Cast: Sean Connery, Peter Boyle, Frances Sternhagen, Kika Markham. U.K. (Warner Bros.). Color. 109 minutes.

Passengers (2016) Director: Morten Tyldum. Producer: Neal H. Montz. Screenplay: John Spaihts. Cast: Jennifer Lawrence, Chris Pratt, Michael Sheen, Laurence Fishburne, Andy Garcia. U.S. (Sony Pictures). Color. 116 minutes.

Planeta Bur (1962) Director: Pavel Klushantsev. Producers: L. Presnyakova, Vladimir Yemelyanov. Screenplay: Pavel Klushantsev, Aleksandr Kazantsev. Cast: Vladimir Yemelyanov, Georgiy Zhzhonov, Gennadi Vernov, Yuri Sarantsev, U.S.S.R. (Lennauchfilm). Color. 72 minutes.

Red Planet (2000) Director: Anthony Hoffman. Producers: Bruce Berman, Mark Canton. Screenplay: Chuck Pfarrer, Jonathan Lemkin. Cast: Val Kilmer, Carrie-Anne Moss, Tom Sizemore, Benjamin Bratt. U.S.-Australia (Warner Bros.). Color. 106 minutes.

Return from Orbit (*Vozvrashchenie orbity*, 1984) Director: Aleksandr Surin. Producer: Igor Chalenko. Screenplay: Yevgeni Mesyatsev. Cast: Juozas Budraitis, Vitali Solomin, Aleksandr Porokhovshchikov, Tamara Akulova, Igor Vasilev. U.S.S.R. (Dovzhenko). Color. 89 minutes.

Riders to the Stars (1954) Director: Richard Carlson. Producer: Ivan Tors. Screenplay: Curt Siodmak. Cast: Richard Carlson, William Lundigan, Martha Hyer, Herbert Marshall. U.S. (United Artists). B&W. 81 minutes.

The Right Stuff (1983) Director-Screenplay: Philip Kaufman. Producers: Irwin Winkler, Robert Chartoff. Cast: Scott Glenn, Ed Harris, Dennis Quaid, Sam Shepard, Fred Ward. U.S. (Warner Bros.). Color. 192 minutes.

Road to the Stars (*Doroga K Zvezdam*, 1957) Director-Producer: Pavel Klushantsev. Screenplay: Boris Liapunov, Vasily Solovyov. Cast: Georgi Solovyov, Leonid Khmara, Georgi Kulbush. U.S.S.R. (Lennauchfilm). Color. 50 minutes.

Robinson Crusoe on Mars (1964) Director: Byron Haskin. Producer: Aubrey Schenck. Screenplay: Ib Melchior, John C. Higgins. Cast: Paul Mantee, Victor Lundin, Adam West. U.S. (Paramount). Color. 110 minutes.

Rocketship X-M (1950) Director-Producer: Kurt Neumann. Producer: Robert L. Lippert. Screenplay: Kurt Neumann, Orville H. Hampton, Dalton Trumbo. Cast: Lloyd Bridges, Osa Massen, Noah Beery Jr., Hugh O'Brian, Morris Ankrum. U.S. (Lippert). B&W. 78 minutes.

Salyut 7 (2017) Director: Klim Shipenko. Producers: Bakur Bakuradze, Yulia Mishkinene, Sergey Selyanov. Screenplay: Klim Shipenko, Natalya Merkulova. Cast: Vladimir Vdovichenkov, Pavel Derevyanko, Aleksandr Samoylenko, Vitaly Khaev. Russia (Nashe Kino). Color. 118 minutes.

Silent Running (1972) Director-Producer: Douglas Trumbull. Producers: Michael Gruskoff, Marty Hornstein. Screenplay: Deric Washburn, Michael Cimino, Steve Bochco. Cast: Bruce Dern, Cliff Potts, Ron Rifkin, Jesse Vint. U.S. (Universal). Color. 89 minutes.

Solar Crisis (1990) Director: Richard C. Sarafian. Producers: Richard Edlund, James Nelson. Screenplay: Joe Gannon, Tedi Sarafian. Cast: Tim Matheson, Charlton Heston, Peter Boyle, Corin Nemec, Jack Palance. Japan–U.S. (Trimark). Color. 111 minutes. DVD: Lions Gate.

Solaris (1972) Director: Andrei Tarkovsky. Producer: Viacheslav Tarasov. Screenplay: Andrei Tarkovsky, Fridrikh Gorenshtein. Cast: Donatas Banionis, Natalya Bondarchuk, Juri Jarvet, Vladislav Dvorzhetsky. U.S.S.R. (Mosfilm). Color. 166 minutes.

Space Cowboys (2000) Director-Producer: Clint Eastwood. Producer: Andrew Lazar. Screenplay: Ken Kaufman, Howard Klausner. Cast: Clint Eastwood, Donald Sutherland, Tommy Lee Jones, James Garner, Loren Dean, James Cromwell. U.S. (Warner Bros.). Color. 130 minutes.

Space Monster (1965) Director-Screenplay: Leonard Katzman. Producers: Burt Topper, Leon D. Selznick. Cast: Francine York, James Brown, Baynes Barron, Russ Bender. U.S. (American International). B&W. 81 minutes.

Spaceflight IC-1: An Adventure in Space (1965) Director: Bernard Knowles. Producers: Jack Parsons, Robert Lippert. Screenplay: Henry Cross [Harry Spalding]. Cast: Bill Williams, Norma West, John Cairney. U.K. (20th Century–Fox). B&W. 65 minutes.

The Spacewalker (2017) Director: Dmitriy Kiselev. Producers: Yevgeny Mironov, Sergei Ageyev, Timur Bekmambetov. Screenplay: Yury Korotkov, Sergey Kaluzhanov, Irina Pivovarona. Cast: Yevgeny Mironov, Konstantin Khabensky, Vladimir Ilyin, Anatoly Kotenyov. Russia (Bazelevs). Color. 140 minutes.

Things to Come (1936) Director: William Cameron Menzies. Producer: Alexander Korda. Screenplay: H.G. Wells. Cast: Raymond Massey, Ralph Richardson, Cedric Hardwicke, Edward Chapman, Margarita Scott. U.K. (United Artists). B&W. 109 minutes.

A Trip to Mars (1910) Director: Ashley Miller. U.S. (Edison). B&W. Silent. 5 minutes.

A Trip to the Moon (1902) Director-Producer-Screenplay: Georges Méliès. Cast: Victor Andrè, Jehanne D'Alcy, Jules-Eugene Legris, Francois Lallement. France (Star Film Company). B&W. Silent. 16 minutes.

2001: A Space Odyssey (1968) Director-Producer: Stanley Kubrick. Screenplay: Arthur C. Clarke, Stanley Kubrick. Cast: Keir Dullea, Gary Lockwood, William Sylvester. U.K.-U.S. (MGM). Color. 142 minutes.

2010: The Year We Make Contact (1984) Director-Producer- Screenplay: Peter Hyams. Cast: Roy Scheider, John Lithgow, Helen Mirren, Bob Balaban, Keir Dullea. U.S. (MGM). Color. 116 minutes.

The Wandering Earth (2019) Director: Frant Gwo. Producer: Gong Ge'er. Screenplay: Yan Dongxu, Ye Junce, Yang Zhixue, Wu Yi. Cast: Qu Chuxiao, Li Guangje, Ng Man-Tat, Wu Jing. China (China Film Group). Color. 125 minutes.

When Worlds Collide (1951) Director: Rudolph Maté. Producer: George Pal. Screenplay: Sydney Boehm. Cast: Richard Derr, Barbara Rush, Peter Hansen, John Hoyt. U.S. (Paramount). Color. 83 minutes.

Woman in the Moon (1929) Director-Producer: Fritz Lang. Screenplay: Thea von Harbou. Cast: Willy Fritsch, Gerda Marcus, Klaus Pohl, Fritz Rasp. Germany (UFA). B&W. Silent. 156 minutes.

X-15 (1961) Director: Richard Donner. Producers: Henry Sanicola, Tony Lazzarino. Screenplay: Tony Lazzarino, James Warren Bellah. Cast: David McLean, Charles Bronson, Mary Tyler Moore, Kenneth Tobey. U.S. (United Artists–MGM). Color. 107 minutes.

Chapter Notes

Chapter One

1. Roger D. Launius, *The Smithsonian History of Space Exploration from the Ancient World to the Extraterrestrial Future* (Washington, D.C.: Smithsonian Books, 2018), 249.
2. Tim Fernholz, *Rocket Billionaires: Elon Musk, Jeff Bezos and the New Space Race* (Boston: Houghton Mifflin Harcourt, 2018), 49.

Chapter Two

1. John Baxter, *Science Fiction in the Cinema* (New York: Paperback Library, 1970), 15–16.

Chapter Three

1. Stephen King, *Danse Macabre* (New York: Berkley Books, 1983), 1.
2. *Ibid.*, 7.
3. *Ibid.*, 8.

Chapter Six

1. Andrew Chaikin, *A Man on the Moon: The Voyages of the Apollo Astronauts* (New York: Penguin Books, 1994), 221.
2. *Ibid.*, 360.
3. *Ibid.*, 512.

Bibliography

Aderin-Popcock, Maggie. *The Book of the Moon: A Guide to Our Closest Celestial Neighbor*. New York: Abrams Image, 2018

Baxter, John. *Science Fiction in the Cinema*. New York: Paperback Library, 1970.

Chaikin, Andrew. *A Man on the Moon: The Voyages of the Apollo Astronauts*. New York: Penguin, 1994.

Clarke, Arthur C. *2001: A Space Odyssey*. New York: Signet, 1968.

Clute, John. *Science Fiction: The Illustrated Encyclopedia*. London: Dorling Kindersley, 1995.

Donovan, James. *Shoot for the Moon: The Space Race and the Extraordinary Voyage of Apollo 11*. New York: Little Brown, 2019.

Fernholz, Tim. *Rocket Billionaires: Elon Musk, Jeff Bezos and the New Space Race*. Boston: Houghton Mifflin Harcourt, 2018.

Gifford, Denis. *Science Fiction Film*. London: Studio Vista/Dutton, 1971.

Hunter, I. Q. *British Science Fiction Cinema*. London: Taylor & Francis, 1999.

King, Stephen. *Danse Macabre*. New York: Berkley, 1983.

Launius, Roger D. *Apollo's Legacy: Perspectives on the Moon Landing*. Washington, D.C.: Smithsonian, 2019.

Launius, Roger D. *The Smithsonian History of Space Exploration from the Ancient World to the Extraterrestrial Future*. Washington, D.C.: Smithsonian, 2018.

Melville, Douglas, and Robert Reginald. *Things to Come: An Illustrated History of the Science Fiction Film*. New York: New York Times Books, 1978.

Morton, Oliver. *The Moon: A History for the Future*. New York: The Economist Books, 2019.

Naha, Ed. *The Science Fictionary*. New York: Wideview Books, 1980.

Oberg, James. *UFOs and Outer Space Mysteries: A Sympathetic Skeptic's Report*. Norfolk: Donning Company, 1982.

Rickman, Gregg, ed. *The Science Fiction Film Reader*. New York: Limelight Editions, 2004.

Schwam, Stephanie. *The Making of 2001: A Space Odyssey*. New York: Random House, 2000.

Shetterly, Margot Lee. *Hidden Figures*. New York: William Morrow, 2016.

Sparrow, Giles. *Spaceflight: The Complete Story from Sputnik to Shuttle and Beyond*. New York: DK, 2007.

Strick, Philip. *Science Fiction Movies*. London: Octopus Books, 1976.

Stuart, Colin. *How to Live in Space: Everything You Need to Know About the Not So Distant Future*. London: Carlton, 2018.

Von Gunden, Kenneth. *20 All Time Great Science Fiction Films*. New York: Random House, 1988.

Weir, Andy. *The Martian*. New York: Crown, 2014.

Wolfe, Tom. *The Right Stuff*. New York: Farrar, Strauss & Giroux, 1979.

Index